WITHDRAWN
UTSA LIBRARIES

The Sociology of Agriculture

This volume is one of a series of six studies to be published by Greenwood Press under the auspices of the Rural Sociological Society. Professor James J. Zuiches, of Washington State University, is the series editor. The topics covered by this series include community, natural resources, structure of agriculture, diffusion of innovations, population, and the history and social context of rural sociological research.

Published Titles

Rural Sociology and the Environment
Donald R. Field and William R. Burch, Jr.

Population and Community in Rural America
Lorraine Garkovich

THE SOCIOLOGY OF AGRICULTURE

FREDERICK H. BUTTEL,
OLAF F. LARSON,
&
GILBERT W. GILLESPIE JR.

UNDER THE AUSPICES OF THE
RURAL SOCIOLOGICAL SOCIETY

Contributions in Sociology, Number 88

Greenwood Press
New York • Westport, Connecticut • London

Library of Congress Cataloging-in-Publication Data

Buttel, Frederick H.
    The sociology of agriculture / Frederick H. Buttel, Olaf F.
Larson, and Gilbert W. Gillespie Jr. : under the auspices of the
Rural Sociological Society.
        p. cm. — (Contributions in sociology, ISSN 0084–9278 ; no.
88)
    Includes bibliographical references.
    ISBN 0–313–26444–9 (lib. bdg. : alk. paper)
    1. Agriculture—Social aspects. 2. Sociology, Rural. I. Larson,
Olaf F. II. Gillespie, Gilbert W. III. Rural Sociological Society.
IV. Title. V. Series.
HD1501.B88 1990
306.3'49—dc20   89–17099

British Library Cataloguing in Publication Data is available.

Copyright ©1990 by the Rural Sociological Society

All rights reserved. No portion of this book may be
reproduced, by any process or technique, without the
express written consent of the publisher.

Library of Congress Catalog Card Number: 89–17099
ISBN: 0–313–26444–9
ISSN: 0084–9278

First Published in 1990

Greenwood Press, Inc.
88 Post Road West, Westport, Connecticut 06881

Printed in the United States of America

The paper used in this book complies with the
Permanent Paper Standard issued by the National
Information Standards Organization (Z39.48–1984).

10 9 8 7 6 5 4 3 2 1

Copyright Acknowledgments

The publisher and authors are grateful to the following for granting use of their material:

Table 1 is reproduced by permission from Richard D. Rodefeld et al. (eds.), *Change in Rural America*, St. Louis, 1978, The C. V. Mosby Co.

Figure 1 is redrawn from a figure by Patrick H. Mooney, "Toward a classs analysis of midwestern agriculture," *Rural Sociology* 48, no. 4 (Winter 1983). By permission of *Rural Sociology*.

Frederick H. Buttel, "The sociology of agriculture: current conceptual status," *The Rural Sociologist* 9 (1989). By permission of *The Rural Sociologist*.

Frederick H. Buttel and David Goodman, "Class, state, technology, and international food regimes," *Sociologia Ruralis* 29, no. 2 (1989). By permission of *Sociologia Ruralis*.

Frederick H. Buttel, Steve H. Murdock, F. Larry Leistritz, and Rita R. Hamm, "Rural environments," in *Advances in Environment, Behavior, and Design*, ed. E. H. Sube and G. T. Moore (New York: Plenum, 1987). By permission of authors and Plenum Publishing.

Contents

Preface ... xi

Introduction: Three Eras of Rural Sociological Research on Agriculture ... xv

1. **Rural Sociological Research on the Structure of Agriculture, 1900 to the Early 1950s** ... 1

    Introduction ... 1
    Research Prior to the 1930s ... 2
    Studies with the Type of Agricultural System
       as the Organizing Theme ... 22
    Specialized Studies: Tenure, Part-Time Farming,
       Low-Income Farmers, and Other Structural
       Components of Agriculture ... 33
    Conclusion ... 42

2. **Rural Sociological Research on the Structure of Agriculture, the Early 1950s to the Early 1970s: Behaviorism and the Social Psychology of Agricultural Activities** ... 43

    Introduction ... 43
    The Diffusion and Adoption
       of Agricultural Innovations ... 46

	The Value Orientations of Farmers	63
	Educational and Occupational Aspirations and Achievements Among Farm-Reared People	67
	Conclusion	72
3.	**The New Sociology of Agriculture, I: The Political Economy and Social Structure of Farms, Farm Households, and Farm Labor**	**73**
	Introduction	73
	Political Economy and the New Sociology of Agriculture	78
	Subculture and Agricultural Structure	94
	Industrial Agriculture	95
	The Agricultural Wage Labor Force	101
	Small Farms and Part-Time Farming	106
	Gender and Agriculture	115
	Conclusion	125
4.	**The New Sociology of Agriculture, II: The Environment of Agriculture**	**127**
	The Impact of Technological Change on Agriculture	128
	The Sociology of Agricultural Science	135
	Agriculture and the Rural Community	145
	The Farm Crisis of the 1980s	151
	Impacts of Agriculture on the Environment: The Case of Soil Erosion and Conservation	155
	The "New Environmental Debates"	163
	Conclusion	169
5.	**The New Political Economy of Agriculture: An Evaluation**	**171**
	Introduction	171

	Major Theoretical Trends in the Sociology of Agriculture	171
	Major Gaps in the Sociology of Agriculture	181
	Conclusion	186
	Notes	186
6.	**Rural Sociological Research on Agriculture: A Backward Glance Toward the Future**	**187**

References 197

Name Index 243

Subject Index 253

Preface

The 50th anniversary of the Rural Sociological Society has come at a propitious time for the sociology of agriculture. The sociology of agriculture has been a recognized—and growing—field in rural sociology for nearly 15 years, which represents a sufficient span of time over which to take stock of the field in a 50th anniversary monograph.

As we emphasize several times, the "sociology of agriculture" is, in a sense, rural sociology's oldest specialty area at the same time that, to the best of our knowledge, the expression was never employed prior to the mid-1970s. There are a good number of continuities between early-twentieth-century rural sociology and what is now called the sociology of agriculture, perhaps to a far greater degree than most contemporary sociologists of agriculture have recognized. By the same token, there are very substantial differences between contemporary sociology of agriculture scholarship and that which preceded it. Our aim is to convey both continuities and discontinuities in theory, method, and approach.

Those who reviewed the initial drafts of the manuscript will note that it has shrunk, and then expanded, since it was presented in first draft at the annual meeting of the Rural Sociological Society in 1986 at Salt Lake City. Shifting exigencies of publication arrangements largely accounted for this unusual metamorphosis. We are nonetheless pleased to be able to publish an extended version of this monograph, since we feel its comprehensiveness will make it a more useful research and teaching resource.

We are grateful to the 50th anniversary committee for their confidence in our ability to inventory and assess the nearly 90 years of rural sociological literature on the social structure and social relations of agriculture. We have benefited greatly from this assignment, since we all found ourselves delving into literature that we might never have encountered during the course of our careers.

In assembling and selecting among this vast potential literature, we have made use of several bibliographic sources. First and foremost, Douglas Smith, formerly an undergraduate student at Cornell University and currently a graduate student at the University of Wisconsin, devoted a great deal of effort to annotating sociological studies on agriculture published in *Rural Sociology*, *Sociologia Ruralis*, and *The Rural Sociologist* over the past 30 years. Smith's excellent annotated bibliography was an indispensable resource for preparation of this book. Second, we benefited greatly from the Campbell and Campbell (1986) bibliography prepared for the Sociology of Agriculture Research Group of the Rural Sociological Society and from Newby's (1980) "trend report" on rural sociology. Finally, Garkovich's (1985) index to the first 50 volumes of *Rural Sociology* proved to be tremendously valuable as a research resource.

We have received invaluable assistance from several persons in the preparation of this monograph, especially from Lillian Kirk who typed the original version of the manuscript and its many subsequent revisions. We also appreciate the detailed comments on previous drafts of the manuscript by, first and foremost, C. Milton Coughenour and Jess Gilbert, and also by James Zuiches, Louis Swanson, and Patrick Mooney. Also, many RSS members generously provided us with reprints, copies of manuscripts, bibliographic assistance, and so on. Finally, Stacy Stephans gave us valuable last-minute help in organizing the bibliography.

We have dedicated this book to the memory of Frederick C. Fliegel, who was a professor of rural sociology at the University of Illinois and a fellow author of a 50th anniversary monograph when he died on September 11, 1987, in Islamabad, Pakistan. The frequency with which his publications appear in the bibliography of this book testifies to the important role he has played in sociological research on agriculture (among other topics). Fritz was an extraordinary scholar in his breadth of interests and his active, productive scholarship during the three decades of his career. He was also exemplary in his colleagueship, citizenship, sense of social justice, and good humor. We shall all miss him.

Introduction: Three Eras of Rural Sociological Research on Agriculture

If there had been a celebration of the 40th anniversary of the Rural Sociological Society in 1979 with a series of books to commemorate the occasion, it is unlikely that one would have been written on the "sociology of agriculture," or even that one could have imagined such a volume 10 years hence. The past decade, however, has witnessed some vast shifts in rural sociological scholarship, among the most important of which have been the increased emphasis on research on agriculture and the innovative theoretical orientations nurtured in that process. It now seems equally inconceivable, given the immense outpouring of research in the sociology of agriculture since the mid-1970s, that a 50th anniversary monograph series could fail to include a volume on agriculture.

The purpose of this book is to take stock of the 50-plus years of rural sociological research on agriculture and to provide an overview of changing research foci and theoretical approaches. Indeed, as is implied in this statement of purpose, it is important to recognize that there has been a long tradition of rural sociological inquiry into agriculture. To be sure, we do see that contemporary research on agriculture is far different in character from what preceded it from the turn of the century to the early 1970s. We nonetheless feel that much can be gained by identifying both continuities as well as watersheds in the development of rural sociological scholarship on agriculture, its structure, and its natural and socioeconomic environments.

The book is largely organized in terms of what we feel are three major eras of rural sociological conceptualization of agriculture that effectively capture major differences in theory, method, and approach. The first era, which we examine in Chapter 1, is from the founding of U.S. rural sociology shortly after the turn of the century until the early 1950s. During this initial era of U.S. rural sociology we have observed that the study of agriculture was largely construed as one of many elements necessary for understanding the social fabric of rural community life.

The second major era of rural sociological research on agriculture is referred to below as the era of social psychological-behaviorist approaches, following Fliegel and van Es' (1983) treatment of the diffusion-adoption of innovations and related perspectives during the 1950s and 1960s. We note that during this period, which lasted roughly from the early 1950s to the early 1970s, rural sociological inquiry into agriculture was dominated by a social psychological perspective that conceptualized farmers and other agricultural persons as actors responding to stimuli such as new technologies, educational and occupational opportunities, and so on. Chapter 2 is devoted to an overview of the research conducted within the social psychological-behaviorist tradition. A much more comprehensive treatment of this topic can be found in Fliegel's *Diffusion Processes*, a companion monograph in this 50th anniversary series.

The third era of concern in this book is referred to as that of the "new sociology of agriculture." We do so following Newby (1983a), who has argued that the innovative work on agriculture since the mid-1970s has constituted a "new rural sociology." The most distinctive aspect of rural sociological research on agriculture from the mid-1970s to the present has been an overriding concern with the "structure of agriculture"—a concept that received virtually no mention, let alone systematic research, prior to the 1970s.

Chapters 3, 4, and 5 are devoted to the past 12 or so years of research in the emerging tradition of the "new rural sociology" or the "new sociology of agriculture." Chapter 3 includes material relating to several topics concerning the political economy and the internal structure and dynamics of agriculture. The topics treated

Introduction xvii

in Chapter 3 are neo-Marxist and neo-Weberian theories of agricultural structure, forms of agricultural production, and agrarian change; the role of ethnicity in the persistence of family farming; industrial agriculture; the agricultural wage labor force; small farms and part-time farming; and gender and agriculture. Chapter 4 is devoted to the "environment of agriculture," which we construe both literally and metaphorically. In the literal sense of the environment of agriculture, we explore several themes relating to the role of natural-ecological factors as antecedents of agricultural structure and to the impacts of agriculture on the natural environment. In Chapter 4 we also examine several themes relating to the socioeconomic environment of agriculture: technological change in agriculture, the sociology of agricultural science, the impacts of farm structure on rural communities, and the farm crisis (particularly its origins in the public policy "environment").

Chapter 5 is also devoted to the "new rural sociology," particularly its political economy variant. But instead of providing an overview of particular substantive areas of theory and research as in Chapters 1 through 4, Chapter 5 is more evaluative in nature. Here we identify what we feel are both positive trends and major gaps in theory and research on the political economy of agriculture in the advanced countries.

In our concluding chapter, Chapter 6, we make some additional observations about the three eras of sociological research on agriculture. We also identify what we feel is a central dilemma in the sociology of agriculture as it moves into the 1990s: the integrative as well as fractionalizing tendencies that may result from the hyperpluralism in contemporary American rural sociology.

As we stress throughout, this demarcation of eras of sociological research on agriculture is somewhat arbitrary. We find, for example, that the community studies orientation toward agriculture that predominated until the Korean War continued to result in significant publications well into the 1960s and 1970s and, in fact, persists to this day. Also, diffusion-adoption and other social psychological research that was at its heyday from the early 1950s to the early 1970s has continued up to the present with a fair amount of vitality. The era of the "new" sociology and political agriculture differs from previous ones in that this era lacks a hegemonic or overriding theoretical and methodological posture. As we note in Chapter 6, the current era of the sociology of agriculture is better characterized in terms of theoretical and methodological pluralism than by the dominance of particular perspectives such as the political economy of agriculture. Put somewhat differently, much of the current era of the sociology of agriculture is not "new," but rather involves a coexistence of "old" and "new" perspectives that have been brought to bear on old and new empirical problems. Given the inevitable overlapping of eras, we have elected to discuss virtually all relevant studies in the community studies and behaviorist traditions in Chapters 1 and 2, respectively, even if their dates of publication fail to correspond with our temporal demarcation of eras. By contrast, Chapters 3 through 5 are almost entirely devoted to theory and research since the mid-1970s.

We have also attempted to approach the subject matter of this book with both open and questioning minds. On one hand, each of the authors has certain biases and preferences in rural sociological inquiry and opinions on how future scholarship can lead to major advances in our knowledge. On the other hand, we feel an obligation to prepare this book in such a way that readers from a variety of theoretical persuasions will find the material useful. We have tried to combine the best of both strategies. The book is primarily intended to be a straightforward exposition of major scholarly themes and of studies that are representative of these themes. Where it was considered appropriate, however, we have taken the opportunity to make our opinions known, particularly about weaknesses in theoretical or methodological approach that should be addressed in future research. We have done so particularly in Chapter 5 in our comments on positive trends and major gaps in scholarship in the political economy of agriculture.

We have intended this book to be an interpretive overview of the literature in the sociology of agriculture, and accordingly we hope that the extensive bibliography that has resulted from this

Introduction   xix

effort will be useful to current and to future generations of scholars. Even so, those closely familiar with the sociology of agriculture will see that we have had to be highly selective in our coverage of the relevant literature. A comprehensive bibliography in the sociology of American agriculture since the turn of the century would have involved several thousand bibliographic entries. Accordingly, we have strived to identify the most important literature and to discuss representative studies, consistent with the interpretive objective of this book.

In this book we have attempted to approach agriculture in a fairly broad way. For example, we see the scope of the book as being more than a summary of research on the "structure of agriculture," an expression that became prevalent in the 1970s, and the study of which is seen by many to be synonymous with the sociology of agriculture. We have construed our subject matter to extend beyond the structure of agriculture and to include, among other things, the social psychology, motivations, and behaviors of farm operators, farm family members, and other actors related to agriculture. However, we do not intend this book to be a primary source on or overview of structural trends in agriculture since the founding of the Rural Sociological Society. To be sure, we hope that many readers will learn a great deal about the evolution of U.S. farm structure by reading our overviews of the three eras of rural sociological scholarship. By the same token, however, we have felt it unwise to attempt to present comprehensive data on farm structural change, given the large number of overviews (e.g., Rodefeld, 1978, 1980; Tweeten and Huffman, 1980; USDA, 1981) that are already available and the scarce space that would be consumed in the process. Further, as implied above, we have elected to place major emphasis on rural sociological research pertaining to U.S. agriculture. At several junctures we have included studies by Canadian rural sociologists when they enable us to make points germane to a particular substantive topic. Nonetheless, we recognize that our coverage of the Canadian rural sociology literature—and especially of Canadian farm structure—is scanty. We have also given little attention to rural sociological research on industrial country agricultures outside of North America (excellent coverage of which can be found in Wilkening and Galeski, 1987) or to international agricultural development.

The Sociology of Agriculture

Rural Sociological Research on the Structure of Agriculture, 1900 to the Early 1950s

INTRODUCTION

As compared with community and population, which are among the topics for other books in this 50th anniversary series, the "structure of agriculture" was late to emerge as a major subject matter area for rural sociological research. In fact, as noted earlier, a case may be made that it did not attain such status until the decade of the 1970s and that the "sociology of agriculture" until the 1950s overlapped considerably with sociological research on rural communities. Thus, although there is a chapter on "Sociological Aspects of Economic Problems" in Brunner's *The Growth of a Science: A Half-Century of Rural Sociological Research in the United States* (1957), which identifies research on such topics as farm tenancy and farm labor, the term "structure" does not appear. Similarly, in other comprehensive classifications or reviews contemporary with Brunner's, i.e., Anderson's *Bibliography of Researches in Rural Sociology* (1957), Smith's (1957) "trend report" on rural sociology in Canada and the United States, and classifications by the USDA Agricultural Research Service (1958) of federal grant research at the state agricultural experiment stations, we do not find the concept "structure of agriculture," although some components are mentioned.

Nevertheless, some aspects of the structure of agriculture, especially tenure and type of farming enterprises, received attention from virtually the beginning of rural life studies. Until about 1930, however, the attention was typically descriptive and partial, limited to some aspects of the food and fiber production system. The topic was generally included as part of a general survey approach —subordinate to the emphasis given other areas, especially community and rural social organization, or inserted to provide background information. The depression period of the 1930s, with its accompanying agricultural crisis and widespread distress throughout rural America and the resultant active federal interventionist policies and programs, set forth a number of changes in rural sociological research. One result was a rapid expansion of resources and effort devoted to fact-finding, which could be broadly characterized as public-problem-oriented and public-policy-oriented in purpose. Research on important segments of the structure of agriculture such as low-income farmers, hired agricultural workers, farm tenancy, and plantation agriculture was stimulated. As this orientation continued, the 1940s also saw research in which the structure of agriculture was used, in some sense, as an independent variable—whether as an organizing theme for investigating the culture and social organization of rural life or for a comprehensive comparative study of small communities. Even during the 1950s and 1960s, despite the growing national concern with a broad range of post-World War II agricultural adjustment issues (see Smith and Christian, 1961), sociological work on structural aspects of agriculture remained segmented and partial, subordinate in emphasis to the areas receiving major attention such as demography and the adoption and diffusion of agricultural innovations.

RESEARCH PRIOR TO THE 1930s

Agriculture and the Early Studies of Rural Life and Small Communities

Field investigation of rural life was initiated by the black sociologist W.E.B. DuBois (1898) when, in 1897, as a staff member of the U.S. Department of Labor in Washington, D.C., he selected Farmville, Virginia, for the first in a series of studies made for the purpose of understanding the economic conditions of small, well-defined groups of blacks in the United States. As part of the context for his study, DuBois described the agriculture of Prince Edward County, a major tobacco-growing area, including census data on the distribution of farms by size, 1880–1890, and by tenure, 1880–1890. He presented data on the principal agricultural products of the county from 1850 to 1890 and used local records to identify the acreage of black-owned land and its assessed value from 1891 to 1895. In addition, he gave an account, including information on tenure, for the 25 black families who lived in the nearby farming locality group of Israel Hill.

Shortly thereafter, still under Department of Labor auspices, DuBois published a comprehensive study of "The Negro Landholder of Georgia"(1901). The study, focused on the acquisition of land by Freedmen after their emancipation, dealt with the process of land acquisition by blacks, including the role of public policy actions such as the Freedmen's Bureau Law of 1866 and the several communal and cooperative land purchase and farm operation experiments conducted by freed blacks. Data were obtained from assessment records for 1899 for 56 of Georgia's 137 counties on the distribution of size of holdings owned by blacks. The crop-lien credit system was described with the assertion that, especially when applied to a nonperishable crop like cotton, the system had the effect of checking and, often, absolutely forbidding diversity in agriculture on the part of those dependent on the system.

The first comprehensive information about the status of black farmers was provided by DuBois' (1904) analysis of data from the U.S. Census of 1900. Here DuBois gave information on the distribution of black-operated farms by size, tenure, gross income, and principal source of farm income along with data on the value of farm property by tenure. A special analysis was also made for what was defined as the "Farming Black Belt"—those counties in which black farmers constituted one-half or more of all farmers.

Some aspects of agriculture, although in widely varying degrees, were considered in each of the pioneering American rural community studies made by doctoral students under the direction of Franklin Hiram Giddings, sociologist at Columbia University, although Giddings himself had no special interest in or knowledge of country life and little sympathy for farmers' problems (Nelson, 1969:28–29). Giddings was trying to develop a quantitative "inductive sociology" instead of a strictly qualitative sociology. The small community offered an opportunity for the student to gain the desired training in the collection and interpretation of data. Thus James M. Williams returned to "Blanktown" (actually the village-country community of Waterville in Oneida County, New York, where he had been born and reared) for the study that resulted in *An American Town: A Sociological Study* (1906). Warren H. Wilson used the open-country, neighborhood-type locality in Dutchess County, New York, where he had been an active pastor, for his study of *Quaker Hill: A Sociological Study* (1907). And Newell L. Sims chose "Aton," an agricultural village-centered community in northeastern Indiana, where he had been born and reared on a farm, for his *A Hoosier Village: A Sociological Study with Special Reference to Social Causation* (1912). All three took a long-term perspective of the development of the locality studied, making their analysis by time periods related to agricultural and other economic phases of change.

Williams (1906:3) sought to determine and analyze "the social forces involved in the several phases of a remarkable social development." He used a variety of written records such as census returns, assessment rolls, town meeting and school district meeting records, church records, and newspaper files. He also took his own local census. He relied much, however, on informal, open-ended interviews and observation, a method that Lowry Nelson (1969:169) noted was akin to the participant observer method of the cultural anthropologist.

Williams concluded that agriculture was the most important economic activity in the entire history of Blanktown up to the ending period of the study, 1900. He described effects of the major agricultural enterprise, hop-raising, on the community and on the behavior of farmers. This was a high-value commercial crop whose selling price fluctuated enormously, not only year to year but even day to day—a characteristic that shifted the relative importance for the farmer from the raising of the crop to speculative selling in an uncertain market. One consequence was increased differentiation of farmers into two classes: (1) the "reckless" who were profit-oriented, who turned all available acreage into hops, and in some cases went into debt to purchase more land at extravagant prices, and (2) the "conservative" whose goal was independence, not to make money but to "make a living," and who maintained customary enterprises from year to year. From 1875 to 1895 hop-raising was the chief enterprise of at least 92 percent of the farmers and provided about four-fifths of the gross income from farming. During these years, the price of hops furnished a convenient index of the economic prosperity of the community.

Williams generalized that the hop-generated prosperity "started certain entirely new phases of social activity, which, once started, went on through their own inherent forces" (p. 115). For instance, several farmers bought fast horses, leading to the building of a driving park and horse racing during the following years. Purchases of goods for personal use and conspicuous consumption increased. Among farmers this first took the form of goods such as the harnesses, carriages, and fast horses which could be displayed in the village. It also took the form of apparel and house furnishings, the painting and enlargement of farm houses, and the upgrading of lawn care—even the use of a lawn mower—around the house in imitation of village homes. Travel outside the community increased. Theater-going and other forms of both organized and informal "pleasure" showed a response to prosperity. Churches bought new organs but the controlling power of the churches over members diminished. Williams also associated the hops-brought prosperity with ebbing farmer interest in the Grange and a shift in its membership toward a predominance of village residents and with a waning interest in the annual local fair. The local autonomous Farmers' Club, which had met weekly, waned and finally disappeared as hop-raising became all-important, giving way to an intertown farmers' educational group of short duration and with a state-level linkage. The village changed its primary function from being a distribution and industrial center to being a commercial center as the farmers' change from an economy of independence to an economy of dependence meant a change in their economic relations with the center.

The farmers' shift from old-time frugality and "pay-as-you-go" brought a growth of the credit business by village merchants (and villagers). Williams concluded that "the reckless purchase of goods on credit tends to increase and decrease with the fluctuation in the condition of the hop industry" (p. 212). The community possessed greater total wealth in 1900 than a quarter-century earlier as measured by the assessed value of property, but the inequality of distribution had increased. Smallholders gradually disappeared as the farming land passed into the possession of larger holders; in 1950s adoption and diffusion terms, the "laggards" and "late adopters" dropped out or were squeezed out by "managers" who adopted intensive cultivation methods. The collapse in the price of hops replaced prosperity with depression around 1894–97, reducing the hop acreage by at least half in 1898. This was followed by a great increase in the importance of dairy production with associated efforts, unsuccessful at the time, to organize milk producers to sell their milk cooperatively.

After further research, he expanded his work into *Our Rural Heritage: The Social Psychology of Rural Development* (1925) and *The Expansion of Rural Life: The Social Psychology of Rural Development* (1926). In the second volume, Williams touched on the shift to dairy and vegetable farming in the post-hop period of Blankville. He also characterized the psychological effects of different major types of farming enterprises found in New York, i.e., fruit growing, dairy farming, vegetable farming (with the separate categories of truck farming, market gardening, and canning crops), and grain farming. He identified the post-hop era as one in which there was a transition from the earlier individualism among farmers to cooperation, and he dealt at some length with the rise of the Dairymen's League (a milk marketing cooperative), with other farmer cooperative societies, and with other farmers' organizations. Further studies of the development of Blanktown (now identified by its real name of Waterville) by rural sociologists at Cornell, published in 1934 (Mather, Townsend, and Sanderson) and in 1954 (W. A. Anderson), found that traces of the hop era lingered long. Thus between 1934 and 1951 there were attempts—albeit unsuccessful—with outside promotion and the latest scientific and machine technology to rejuvenate the hops industry. The Cornell restudies verified Williams' observation that dairying had continued to replace hops as the main agricultural industry and that cash crops—such as potatoes, cabbage, string beans, and green peas—had also become important. The shift in the type of agricultural production was seen to have reversed the hops-generated pattern of increased social prestige and status differentiation and fostered a general leveling of social classes in the farming area. One exception to this leveling was the large cash-crop operators, seen potentially as becoming a small but powerful upperclass group. The depression of the 1930s, when many farms were put up for sale, was seen as setting the stage for the large cash-crop operators as land was bought or leased and merged into large units. The readjustment of agriculture to dairying was accompanied by Welsh, Swiss and others, locally described as "solid citizens" and hard workers, taking over the land. Hops had required seasonal labor, obtained from nearby city places and temporarily resident in the community, to pick the blossoms. But the new large-scale cash crop operations required large numbers of seasonal workers, no longer available nearby. The new workers were seasonal migrants, particularly blacks from the South, leading to problems for the community such as child care, school facilities for the children of migrants, and to the larger problem of acceptance of the migrants in the community. Throughout the changes, the economy of Waterville continued to be—as of 1954—firmly rooted in agriculture.

Warren Wilson's *Quaker Hill* study had a general similarity in purpose and method to Williams' work in Blanktown. He aimed at studying each factor that had played a part in the life of Quaker Hill, using as sources the reminiscences of older residents, church and general store records, tax lists, local histories and related documents, and participant observation. Farming was primarily milk production for the city market, although some farm families kept summer boarders from the city. Wilson generalized as to the close fit of the Quaker tradition and dairying, stating:

> Nearness to the soil has, under the influences of Quaker ethics and economic ambition, cultivated in this population a patient and steadfast industry, which expresses itself in the milk dairy, a form of farming by its nature requiring early hours and late, with all the day between filled by various duties. (P. 108)

Sims' methods for his *A Hoosier Village* study were akin to those used in the two previous doctoral studies under Giddings. The first part of his work was an historical and descriptive treatment of the social development of the community with some analysis of the forces producing the development. In the second part he tried to discover the local and particular forces that were the proximate causes of certain phenomena unique to this Indiana community such as in the areas of religion and politics. Sims saw agriculture as the dominant force in the economic development of the village center until 1869, when the village provided only the services "necessary to meet the simple demands of a new agricultural region under the process of being reclaimed from the wilderness" (p. 27). As types of agricultural production shifted over time, by 1908 freight shipments out of the community showed a preponderance of poultry products, livestock, hay, and straw. The growth of poultry raising was the basis for a poultry-packing industry which provided employment for women and children for three months in the fall. The production of sheep and wool was important from the early days up to the time of field study, especially in the rougher sections of the area. Sims observed that the Republican policy of a protective tariff on wool had been the vital issue with most growers and concluded that, in consequence, wool growers generally gave their support to the Republican party rather than to the "free wool" Democratic ticket. All three pioneering community studies by Giddings' students, and especially the one by Williams, offered provocative leads for further research on agriculture, its changes, and its interrelationships. As Brunner noted (1957:4–5), few of these leads were ever followed up by later investigators.

The Country Life Commission's *Report* and Its Unpublished Survey

President Theodore Roosevelt appointed a Commission on Country Life in 1908 to give a summary of what was already known about the present condition of country life and to recommend measures to ameliorate deficiencies found to exist. The terms "farmer," "country," and "rural" were used loosely in the president's appointment letter and in the Commission's *Report* (U.S. Congress, 1909), but in a letter to Liberty Hyde Bailey, the chairman of the Commission, Roosevelt indicated that by the word "farmers" he meant to include all those living in the open country and intimately connected with those who do the farm work (Larson and Jones, 1976). The Commission's *Report* proved to be a document of lasting significance for students of rural life in the United States.

The Commission took as its field of inquiry the general social, economic, sanitary, educational, and labor conditions of the open country, with the condition of farmers and farming clearly at the heart of its inquiries and recommendations. Among other fact-gathering activities, the Commission had circulated nationwide about 550,000 copies of what we would today describe as a mail questionnaire. Each of the 12 opinion questions—which included, among others, topics such as the organization of farmers for buying and selling and satisfaction with credit and other services—were tabulated by the Census Bureau for preliminary typed reports.

Although the data from what was very likely the first nationwide survey of country life in the United States (aside from the periodic Census Bureau counts) were essentially unused by the Commission in preparing its final *Report*, the 12 typed summaries were preserved in the archives at Cornell University to be the basis, many years later, for an analysis by Larson and Jones (1976). They found, for instance, wide regional differences in farmer opinion about the local farm economy. Most positive were farmers in the North Central states. Most negative were the farmers in the South Central states. They found, to give another example, that the majority of farmers were unqualifiedly dissatisfied with their organization locally to promote their mutual buying and selling interest.

Among the several special deficiencies discussed in the Commission's *Report* was the speculative holding of land (pp. 62–64). The procurement of large areas of agricultural land for speculative purposes, it was asserted, in many cases prevented the development of an agricultural community, isolated small landowners, and tended to develop a system of tenantry and absentee farming. The *Report* called attention to the loss of soil fertility and the adverse social consequences associated with a one-crop system of agriculture (pp. 83–91), especially marked in the cotton-growing states but beginning to appear in all regions. Among the other farm-specific issues discussed were the control of streams and waterways (for irrigation water, transportation, and power), marketing, trade, transportation, and agricultural credit.

The Commission *Report* itself should be consulted for its numerous and far-reaching recommendations for federal and state action and for the public at large. For present purposes we take particular note of the recommendation that among two or three great movements that should be set underway at the earliest possible time was "taking stock of country life" (pp. 20–21, 28–29, 118–121). A system of thorough-going surveys of all agricultural regions should be encouraged, it was proposed, with the cooperation of federal and state governments, agricultural colleges and other educational agencies, and organizations of various types (see

Danbom, 1979, for further detail and critical reflections on the *Report*).

Agriculture, the Social Survey Movement, and the Subsequent Village-Centered Community Studies

The Country Life Commission's *Report* did, indeed, lead to a large number of social surveys of rural conditions during the following 15 years or so (see Eaton and Harrison, 1930). These surveys, usually of a county or a community, commonly had some agricultural content, although farming as such was rarely, if ever, the central focus. For more than a decade much of the leadership in the rural social survey movement rested with Protestant denominational or church-related organizations concerned with the country church. Also prominent in such work was the Georgia State Normal School at Athens where social and economic surveys of 6 counties were published between 1912 and 1917; the Department of Rural Social Science at the University of North Carolina, which issued reports on 8 counties during 1917–1924, reflecting the initiative of E. C. Branson; the Department of Rural Science, University of South Carolina, which conducted 14 county studies from 1921–24; and the University of Virginia, under the leadership of Wilson Gee in the Department of Rural Social Economics, which issued 7 county survey reports during 1922–25 (Eaton and Harrison, 1930:10–15; Nelson, 1969:66–67, 75–76). Among the land-grant institutions, economists at the University of Minnesota were the pioneers in such rural community surveys (Nelson, 1966, 1969:31). The 3 surveys published between 1913 and 1915 under the auspices of the University's Bureau of Research in Agricultural Economics were as much social as economic. Land-grant rural sociologists had but a minor role in the rural social survey movement prior to the 1920s. They were few in number and lacked an institutional support structure. Recall that there would be no Farm Life Studies unit in the U.S. Department of Agriculture until 1919 when Charles J. Galpin went from Wisconsin to Washington to develop such a unit and to instigate, with the meager funds available to him, cooperative research with college and university staff. There would be no systematic provision for funds to the agricultural experiment stations that could be used for rural sociological research until passage of the Purnell Act in 1925.

Especially prominent in the church-related social survey activity was the Board of Home Missions of the Presbyterian Church, which in 1910 established a Department of Church and Country Life under Warren H. Wilson, the author of *Quaker Hill* (Nelson, 1969:46; Morse, 1924:93–94). Wilson's department conducted or guided county and community surveys in 15 states between 1910 and 1916—surveys that provided data about country life, including farming, as well as about the country church in particular (Morse, 1924:93). The survey methods evolved from relying rather heavily at first on more-or-less unstructured individual and group interviews for the general community information. Over time, a schedule was developed to record information for the unit under investigation; the schedule form included a few questions on agriculture such as the major sources of farm income and the marketing arrangements. The main steps for the field work in Gibson County, Tennessee, in 1911 were especially clearly specified, as follows: (1) interviews with well-informed men in each neighborhood, (2) visits with 20 or 30 families in each community, and (3) intensive study of 21 carefully distributed neighborhoods in "sample plots" containing 607 families, a sampling procedure strikingly similar to the "sample segment" technique developed much later for survey purposes.

Space permits only a small selection of the conclusions and observations about agriculture one can draw from the published reports issued by the Presbyterian Department of Church and Country Life. On the interrelationships of farming and the community: In the wine grape and hop-growing sections in Sonoma County, California, these enterprises were a source of conflict, partly because of the moral issues raised for some churches and partly because the enterprises used foreign workers. On trends: In 44 Illinois communities surveyed, farms were increasing in size and tenancy was increasing, whereas in Tulare County, California, the trend was strongly toward smaller farms (i.e., 20- to 40-acre tracts) and decreasing tenancy. On tenure correlates: In Lane County, Oregon, tenancy was associated with range lands and grain farms rather than with dairy and fruit operations, and in Marin County, California, owners operated smaller farms than tenants. On ethnicity: In Tulare County, California, ethnic background was related to type of farming and tenure. As an example, a high percentage of dairy farm renters were Portuguese.

Ohio was especially conspicuous for the number of its counties surveyed. In 1912 an advisory council was formed, with representation from 12 religious denominations and 18 educational institutions in the state, for the purpose of making an "Ohio Rural Life Survey." The council arranged to have Warren Wilson direct the survey work. Fieldwork, done during 1912 and 1913, resulted in 6 publications issued for the Ohio Rural Life Survey by Wilson's organization. Samples of the conclusions related to the agricultural data and observations follow. Based on the 21 counties surveyed, "Throughout the State the health of the country churches varies quite uniformly according to the degree of agricultural prosperity," and "the proportion of tenants to owners in the church membership is seldom as high as the proportion in the total farming population." In 6 southeastern Ohio counties, half of the farmland was concentrated in the hands of one-eighth of the farmers. And in Claremont County, the report author, Paul L. Vogt, then a sociologist at Miami University, noted some relationships of type of farming to ethnic and religious origin (in this case, Jews and Hungarians doing truck-crop farming) and, in turn, the correlation of these origins with conflict in the local community. The Moravian Country Church Commission also participated in the social survey movement on a limited scale (Eaton and Harrison, 1930:268–270).

Agriculture, understandably, was one aspect of social and economic life covered in the first of the general rural social surveys conducted by land-grant college rural sociologists. Here, von Tungeln (1918) pioneered with his fact-finding survey of Orange township, Blackhawk County, Iowa, in 1915 for the purpose of gaining insight that could aid in directing "thot and activity" in other communities. Every family in the rural township was interviewed, evidently with a uniform set of questions. Descriptions were also obtained for each of the major farmers' organizations within the township such as the cooperative egg-selling association, the cooperative creamery, and the cooperative threshing and silo-filling outfits. A second township was similarly surveyed in 1916 (von Tungeln, 1920), and a third survey of 3 consolidated school districts (von Tungeln and Eells, 1924) incorporated a restudy, after 5 years, of farmers in Orange Township. Among the findings from these studies was evidence on what we have come to refer to as the "agricultural ladder." In the third study, owner-operators were found to average eight and one-half years older than tenants, while landlords (mostly retired farmers) averaged seven and one-half years older than owner-operators. On kinship ties, in the Blackhawk County area half of the tenants were related to their landlord, whereas in the Clay County area, where land values and the tenancy rate were reputed to be increasing, one-fourth of the tenants were so related. The Orange Township restudy showed that after 5 years, half of the 132 farms had not changed in ownership or in the operator's tenure, but 28 percent had changed ownership, 7 percent had changed tenants, and the shifts from owner to tenant operation slightly surpassed those from tenant to owner operation.

In the period immediately following World War I there was an extraordinary amount of rural social survey activity across the nation, which, although undertaken to serve Protestant Church purposes, provided the most comprehensive information yet available on some of the social aspects of agriculture and the regional and local variations. The surveys were designed with due recognition that social and economic conditions affected church life and that in rural communities agriculture was a major factor in the economy (Morse and Brunner, 1923:17). This activity was initiated by the Interchurch World Movement, formed in 1919 by Protestant groups, which had as one of its purposes the conduct of a survey in every rural county of the United States. Before the collapse, in 1920, of this short-lived organization, surveys had been organized in more than 2,400 counties, and 662 counties had completed surveys forwarded to the Town and Country Life Department directed by sociologist Edmund deS. Brunner. To salvage as much as possible of this work, a permanent religious research and survey organization known as the Institute for Social and Religious Research (at first the Committee on Social and Religious Surveys) was established with financial backing from John D. Rockefeller, Jr. From the counties with completed surveys, 25 were selected for intensive field survey and follow-up. An additional 154, yielding a total of 179 from 44 states, were selected for additional analysis of the survey data already collected. The aim was to select counties, each of which would be a "fair specimen" (i.e., representative) of its region. Although the county was one unit of analysis, a departure in these surveys was to make each social community within a county a second study unit. Each town or village-centered community had its boundaries determined using the service area concept. A "community schedule," representing a refinement and much testing of forms first developed by Warren H. Wilson in his work with the Presbyterian Church, included questions on agriculture (e.g., type of farming, tenure, rental arrangements, and farmers' cooperatives). One of these community schedules is reproduced in Brunner's *Surveying Your Community* (1925:35–44).

The results of the work directed by Brunner resulted in a 12-volume Town and Country series, including a summary volume (Morse and Brunner, 1923); a statistical and methodological volume (Morse, 1924); regional reports on the South (Brunner, 1923), the Middle West (Landis, 1922), and the Colonial States (Patten, 1922); 4 books on distinctive situations, i.e., irrigation communities (Brunner and Brunner, 1922), homesteader situations (Belknap, 1922), immigrant communities (Fry, 1922), and areas affected by industrial development (Morse, 1922); and, to illustrate the application of the method in rural units, 3 reports on individual counties.

Some generalizing conclusions from the summary volume are as follows:

> Until the number of tenant farmers exceeds 20 percent of the total number of operating farmers, the Church seems to reach both economic groups with equal facility. This is true apparently without exception. When, however, the percentage of tenancy is above this figure and particularly when it exceeds 33 percent, there is a change in conditions. (P.157)
>
> The Church does not reach the farm tenants as well as it reaches the farm owners. The higher the percentage of tenantry the greater the discrepancy between the two groups in respect to church membership. (P. 74)
>
> [I]n only three regions (of eight) . . . does the Church have approximately the same degree of success in reaching the farm tenants as in reaching farm owners. All of these are regions in which the percentage of tenantry on the farms is comparatively low . (P. 66)

In the Northwest (defined as Minnesota, the two Dakotas, and eastern Montana), "Both wheat and livestock are phases of farming which lend themselves readily to cooperative organizations . . . ." Further, "the size of the farms and the wide dispersion of population have made social life much less cohesive than in the Middle West (pp. 28–29). California agriculture was distinguished by its remarkable development of cooperative organization. "Each crop, particularly each kind of fruit, has its own highly developed cooperative sales organization . . ." (p. 34). In the South, "the type of agriculture and the type of social life have combined to make for a multiplicity of small, open country social units" (p. 40).

In 1923 Brunner and his associates in the Institute of Social and Religious Research, with the cooperation and advice of Charles J. Galpin of the Department of Agriculture's Farm Life Studies unit and of a number of land-grant college rural sociologists and others, initiated a study of 140 agriculturally related villages widely distributed nationwide. The identical communities were restudied in 1930 and again in 1936, thereby providing comprehensive information about rural communities, including some aspects of their agriculture, and about social change in American rural society which has not been equaled since. The very fact that such a large-scale investigation could be launched represented a great stride in the development of an organized continuing support structure for research. The first study likewise clearly represented the application of cumulative, tested knowledge about survey methods and advances in sampling procedures and data analysis.

The unit of analysis was the community. Although the study was referred to as one of agricultural villages, the survey unit was the village center and its contiguous rural territory, with the community boundary determined by the area within which the majority of the people were served by the social, economic, and religious institutions or organizations of the village (Brunner et al., 1927:51–53, 281–289). The study was restricted to incorporated villages between 250 and 2,500 population located in a strictly agricultural area and that was a "service station" for farmers in the surrounding countryside. All villages within commuting distance of cities of more than 100,000 population were rejected from consideration, as were those in predominantly industrial counties. Informed persons within states, such as rural sociologists and extension directors, were asked to suggest incorporated villages that they considered representative of the agricultural areas of these states. A few states were excluded in selecting the sample—namely, the New England states (because of their usual practice of not incorporating centers until they were quite large), Ohio (because so many rural surveys had already been conducted there), and West Virginia, Florida, Louisiana, New Mexico, Arizona, Utah, Wyoming and Nevada (each for special reasons). The outcome of an elaborate effort to seek a sample "which would furnish a fair cross-sectional picture of conditions throughout the nation" was a list of 177 communities, later reduced to 140 in the course of the fieldwork. Field investigations were made between May 1923 and May 1925, by trained interviewers, with each team of 2 or 3 persons spending from 10 days to 3 weeks in each community. The community schedule used, which included questions on agricultural conditions, incorporated the extensive prior survey experience of the Institute staff.

One distinctive feature of the data analysis was the use of crop areas as an independent or control variable. More than a decade earlier, John M. Gillette in the first rural sociology textbook (1913:21–31) had set forth from observation some probable community characteristics associated with specific "pure agricultural" types—namely, small-grain-raising, corn-raising, and cotton-raising communities. Warren Wilson, in the *Evolution of the Country Community* (2nd ed., 1923), had contended that among the four major groups of social forces that mold country people are the kinds of industry; in this he included such types of farming of national significance as cotton, dairying, irrigation, and others (pp. 91–105). Brunner and his associates used four major geographic regions for much of their analysis, finding that "the agricultural environment of a village did not greatly affect its social institutions" (Brunner et al., 1927:283), but this did not hold when it came to the economic life of a village. Therefore, for part of their analysis, they classified villages by nine crop areas in which they were located, following Wilson's general idea but using crop areas developed by O. E. Baker in the USDA. The type of crop area was found to have a major influence on population density in the open-country part of the community and on the average area of the community in square miles. For example, the dry-farming Great Plains communities had the fewest people per square mile (4.98) and the largest community area (426.5 square miles), whereas the cotton areas averaged the most persons per square mile (30.13) and the hay and pasture areas, also densely settled, and characterized by dairying, averaged the smallest community size in square miles (69.1) (Brunner et al., 1927:56, 292). The percentage of farms in the community sold during the past five years and trends in the percentage of farm tenancy were among other agricultural variables analyzed by type of crop area (Brunner et al., 1927:36–47, 114–119). The investigators were highly sensitive to the fact that the research was being done "at a time when conditions in agricultural areas were disturbed by the readjustment following the World War" (p. 27). The conclusion that the depression in agriculture had influenced certain aspects of village life was taken as support for the basic assumption underlying the Institute's field work—namely, the close interrelationship between "the economic conditions of the village and the economic conditions of the surrounding countryside" (p. 50). As stated in the overall summary report on the study, in the village,

> except for certain restricted social organizations, and for those few industries which import their raw material, no one service agency could continue at its present level, and many of them could not survive, without the country populations. (Brunner, 1927:34)

This study marked the use of simple correlation analysis on a modest basis. Thus, the Pearsonian coefficient between farm value per acre and bank deposits per household, with the community the unit of analysis, was 0.85. The coefficient for the average assessed value per farm and per village household was 0.75. An earlier Institute study had discovered a correlation of 0.51 between average value per acre and per capita contributions to village churches and a coefficient of 0.40 when average farm income was substituted for the acreage value (Brunner, 1927:36).

A restudy of the same 140 agricultural communities was conducted in 1930 using field methods and community schedules essentially identical to those employed in the first study. In view of the continued agricultural depression during the 1920s and the approach of the 1930 census, the Institute had planned the resurvey to measure changes since the first study. However, when President Hoover announced, in the fall of 1929, the appointment of a committee to study social change, the Institute's project was combined with the rural part of the President's Research Committee on Social Trends. The work proceeded under the joint direction of Brunner of the Institute (and also of the Columbia University faculty) and J. H. Kolb, professor of rural sociology at the University of Wisconsin. Within the general purpose of the overall trends project—to report upon social trends in the United States, thereby throwing light on emerging problems and providing "a basis for the formulation of large national policies looking to the next phase in the nation's development"—the purpose of the rural phase was to study "changes in rural social life in the first three decades of the present century, and especially in the decade 1920 to 1930." In addition to the 140 communities, restudies were made of 21 counties studied by the Institute of Social and Religious Research in 1921. Intensive restudies were also made of counties in 4 states where neighborhood studies had been previously conducted by sociologists in land-grant colleges.

The basic report on the rural trends study (Brunner and Kolb, 1933; see also the summary chapter "Rural Life" by Kolb and Brunner in the President's Committee final report [1933:497–552]) used little of the information on agriculture from the community and county restudies. The exception was a section on farmer cooperatives that included a portrayal of trends by crop areas from 1924 to 1930 in buying and selling cooperatives (Brunner and Kolb, 1933:55–58). A special feature of the rural social trends report was an analysis to determine the effect of distance from the city on agricultural relationships. For this purpose, 18 medium-size city centers (with populations ranging from 20,760 to 634,394 in 1930) were selected as representative of rural-urban complexes. The counties surrounding these centers were classified into tiers to constitute concentric circles of rurality. Some 18 sets of agricultural census data for 1910, 1920, and 1930 were then used to determine whether a gradient pattern of relationship prevailed by tiers around the center and whether the relationship changed over time. For example, in the Des Moines, Iowa, area the value of field crops per acre was highest in the city county and decreased with distance in the first 3 tiers for each of the 3 census periods. The distance relationships were also presented for the distribution of farms by major type of enterprise, proportion of land in farms, acreage of improved land per farm, proportion of farms operated by owners, and other agricultural variables (see Brunner and Kolb, 1933:111–116, 124–126, 133–143, and 333–348).

The 140 communities were again investigated in 1936, a unique event in the history of rural sociological research in that it was the only time a nationwide sample of communities had been thrice studied. There was also a distinctive aspect in the continuity provided by Brunner again being principal investigator. This time the sponsors were the Council for Research in the Social Sciences at Columbia University, where Brunner was located, in cooperation with the Division of Farm Population and Rural Life, now headed by Carl C. Taylor, in USDA. The field surveys in 69 communities were conducted or supervised by rural sociologists in land-grant colleges by arrangement with the Rural Research Unit of the Division of Social Research, Works Progress Administration (Brunner and Lorge, 1937:v–viii, 373-376).

The purpose of the third study was to discover the changes wrought in these communities by the Great Depression that had been underway since 1930. The method of study was similar to that in the 2 previous researches, with the community schedule questionnaire, which included the few items on agricultural change, modified to fit the study purpose. The data collection in each community, which included about 100 interviews, the use of local weekly newspapers, and examination of other public records, averaged a week of fieldwork time. The chapter on agricultural adjustments dealt with farmer strikes, the reaction to the original Agricultural Adjustment Act passed in 1933 (the major provisions of which were invalidated by the U.S. Supreme Court in 1936), reaction to the reorganized Farm Credit Administration, and—as in the previous studies—with local farmer cooperatives for purchasing and marketing.

The tier analysis technique devised for the second study was again used for the same 18 urban centers for selected agricultural variables (Brunner and Lorge, 1937:12–30) with the finding that certain generalizations from the second study still held true for the 1930–1935 period, whereas some others did not. Except for a chapter on agricultural adjustments, the findings about the agricultural changes during the depression were interwoven with the treatment of community institutions, organizations, and agencies to demonstrate the interrelationships.

Certain of the 140 communities are known to have been restudied with the benefit of the original completed schedules. In 1970 Smith (1974) conducted field investigations of 12 communities in the corn, hay and pasture, and spring wheat areas in Indiana, Minnesota, and North Dakota. Thirteen communities in New York were restudied by Ali (1973), who used Census of Agriculture data for 1919 to 1969, and by Richardson and Larson (1976) who conducted field studies and also used secondary sources.

STUDIES WITH THE TYPE OF AGRICULTURAL SYSTEM AS THE ORGANIZING THEME

We have observed that in the early community studies and in the county and community general social surveys, it was not uncommon to discover that some aspect of the area's agriculture, especially the type of farming enterprise, emerged as of great significance as a factor in shaping the characteristics and development of the area's social organization and social behavior. We noted that the Institute of Social and Religious Research took some steps toward the use of crop areas as an independent variable in analyzing communities. Subsequently, a number of studies were conducted with a sample purposely designed so that the type of agricultural system, be it type of enterprise or scale, was the frame of reference, the organizing theme, or the control or independent variable for comparative analysis. There were other studies in which the type of agricultural system established the domain for the investigation but in which the design did not purposely provide for comparative analysis.

In the present review, we give particular attention to the research in which comparative analysis was incorporated into the design. C. E. Lively (1928) should be credited with the first such study. Lively selected for comparison a dairy-farming community (Prairie Farm in Barron County, Wisconsin) and a grain-farming community (Fisher, Polk County, Minnesota), each considered as "pure" a representative of the type as readily available. Field observations were supplemented by analysis of selected census data on agriculture and population for 10 typical dairy counties (in Wisconsin, Minnesota, and Ohio) and 10 typical grain counties (in North Dakota, Minnesota, South Dakota, and Ohio). The study concluded that type of agriculture conditions community life in such important ways as density and mobility of the population, seasonal and yearly fluctuation in income, variation in seasonal distribution of labor demands, and seasonal variations in the activity of organizations and certain institutions. Further, certain attitudes appeared to be correlated with type of agriculture; for example, grain-farming society appeared to be more dynamic but less stable than dairy-farming society, and more favorable to innovation but less likely to make it succeed. Lively cautioned that he was portraying agriculture as a conditioning factor—not the major controlling element—in the organization of rural community life. He stressed the influence of the social heritage of the past on the institutions, organizations, and behavior patterns in a rural community as independent of the contemporary influence of type of farming. But in his qualifier he also, in effect, set forth a hypothesis in the statement that it was inconceivable that, as the age of the community increased, the stream of social heritage would not gradually yield in some measure to the constant influence of the biophysical and economic complex called type of agriculture.

During 1939 and 1940 the USDA's Division of Farm Population and Rural Welfare studied six communities for the purposes of investigating the cultural, community, and social psychological factors in land use and rural life, with special reference to those factors that facilitate or offer resistance to change, contribute to adjustments and maladjustments, and to stability and instability in individual and community life. The six were selected on the basis of certain criteria as to the stability and instability of community life and farming to be a sampling along a continuum from high community stability to great instability. Selected as most unstable was what was then a Dust Bowl community, Sublette, in Haskell County, Kansas, where farming was based on winter wheat produced under conditions of highly variable rainfall (Bell, 1942). At the other extreme, the Old Order Amish Community of Lancaster

County, Pennsylvania, was selected for its stability. In the latter case, farming was one of the tenets of the Amish religion. The religion-related goals and values were a stimulus to good farming (Kollmorgen, 1942). The Spanish-speaking community of El Cerrito, in New Mexico, was considered stable culturally, but had lost much of the land resources needed for its livestock and was poorly equipped with competitive agriculture technologies (Leonard and Loomis, 1941). The Corn Belt community of Irwin, Iowa (Moe and Taylor, 1942), the bi-racial Harmony, Georgia, which had shifted from cotton to dairying (Wynne, 1943), and the long-established farming community of Landaff, New Hampshire (MacLeish and Young, 1942), now disturbed by external market forces, ranged between the stability-instability extremes. Agriculture was an important component in each of these six "Rural Life Studies."

By far the most ambitious rural sociological research effort to use type of farming as the primary frame of reference or control variable was that undertaken in 1944 by Carl C. Taylor and his associates in what was then the Division of Farm Population and Rural Welfare in the Bureau of Agricultural Economics, USDA. Taylor acknowledged the earlier important sociological contribution to the delineation of the United States into meaningful rural areas done at the University of North Carolina by Howard W. Odum (1936) and Odum and Moore (1938:136–167). Odum and his associates had divided the country into six broad geographic regions along state lines, seeking maximum within-region homogeneity through various indices. Taylor's work also acknowledged that done by A. R. Mangus (1940) who used county units in his delineation of regions. The study conceived of the major-type-of-farming areas in the United States as modal cultural regions (Raper and Taylor, 1949:331). The working hypothesis that guided the decision to use type of farming as the basis for selecting a sample of counties in which comprehensive field research would be done over time ran something as follows: Making a living is one of the major components of the culture of people in any given rural locality, making a living is related to many other traits of the culture, and, for farm people, type of farming is an index of their way of making a living. Or, in Raper and Taylor's words (pp. 331–332), within a major-type-of-farming area,

> first of all, the ways in which most of the farm people make a living are generally similar; second, the material technologies and the non-material techniques of production and marketing are also generally similar; and third, out of these two aspects of rural life arise many common ideologies, opinions, attitudes, and values.

The first step in sampling was to place all U.S. counties, except for 14 with no rural-farm population, into one of 7 major types of farming areas plus a residual "all other" grouping. This utilized the revised delineation in 1943 of such farming areas, on a county boundary basis, by the Division of Farm Management and Costs, Bureau of Agricultural Economics (Hagood and Bernert, 1945; letter, Margaret J. Hagood to Olaf F. Larson, February 7, 1947). This placed 469 counties in the Corn Belt, 690 in the Cotton Belt, 268 in the dairy areas, 552 in the general and self-sufficing areas, 250 in the wheat areas, 333 in the range livestock areas, and 88 in the Western specialty crop areas (Raper and Taylor, p. 330). The remaining 406 counties, placed in the "all other" grouping, included a variety of small-type-of-farming areas such as the intensive tobacco-growing sections of Virginia, North Carolina, and Kentucky and the citrus and winter vegetable farming areas of Florida. These 7 major areas were seen as constituting "meaningful rural universes."

There was, however, a second step in the sampling process. This second step in sampling was to delineate within each of the areas, through the use of component indexes involving some 12 to 14 variables chosen from the 1940 Censuses of Agriculture and Population and related data, strata of relatively homogeneous counties. Each stratum was to include approximately the same number of farm people. It had been administratively determined that the first phase of the research should be conducted in about 70 counties. One sample county was to be selected from each stratum, thereby determining the approximate number of strata to be arrived at. The decision to stratify within farming areas, for sampling purposes, rested on the assumption that the social and economic characteristics of farm people were influenced not only by the type of farming but by other factors as well and that building these factors into a stratification procedure would assume satisfactory representation of their variations. The number of strata within farming areas varied from 6 to 12. Some of the variables used in the correlation analysis out of which came the component indexes were identical across farming areas, while others were specific to an area. The end result was 71 strata, of which one sample county was selected from each. The only published source on the stratification procedures is the paper by Hagood and Bernert (1945). Although random numbers were used in an experimental phase of selecting a county from within each stratum, the available documentation suggests that the final selection took nonquantitative factors into consideration, particularly the judgment of informed persons, in seeking the best possible regional representation (Memorandum, Carl C. Taylor to Division of Farm Population and Rural Welfare regional leaders, May 3, 1944).

The first fieldwork in the 71 counties was the conduct of "cultural reconnaissance surveys" during 1944–46 to provide an overall view of each county. Fieldworkers were provided a detailed outline of the information to be collected from local key informants, who were to be broadly representative of significant categories of rural people within the county, and from other local sources. Selection criteria included tenure, scale of farming, and so on. Fieldwork required from 3 to 4 weeks in each county. A narrative report was prepared for each county, following a suggested outline for the analysis. (None of these outlines or other instructions to the field staff was published; Larson, who was a member of the division staff at that time, has copies in his personal files.) Many of the questions in the reconnaissance survey outline were specific to agriculture. For example, do any significant variations obtain within the community (in agricultural products produced) as between hill and valley farmers, subsistence and commercial farmers, etc? Are there any significant differences in social relationships, mutual aid, cooperative activity, and so forth, as between the communities in the county or between ethnic, religious, or other local groupings? What are the major determinants of such status groups as there are (watch out for such matters as family income, national background, racial identity, religious beliefs, tenure, type of farming, educational attainment, length of local residence, etc.)? Under the heading "Value Systems, Attitudes, Ideas and Ideals," there were questions such as: What sentimental attachment do the people have for the land itself (note any significant differences by local status and ethnic groups)? In what ways do the people show their sentimental attachment for the land? Their lack of it? Do farmers value most security, or the opportunity to make big money? How do the values that farmers place on security express themselves?

The county reconnaissance reports provided the basis for an overall report for each type of farming area. The research program called for the overall reconnaissance surveys to be followed by more intensive surveys of the rural social organizations in each county and type-of-farming area. Before the organization studies could be initiated, however, the whole research program was aborted due to strong opposition to this line of work that had developed among certain members of Congress. Neither the county nor regional reports were published. Members of the Farm Population Division staff did, however, draw upon these reports for 8 of the chapters on rural regions included as a part of their book, *Rural Life in the United States* (Taylor et al., 1949). In response to the political climate, the research program was greatly curtailed and redirected to studies, in cooperation with state agricultural experiment stations, of rural organizations within a few of the counties. Each of the some 14 reports that resulted included a brief section on the influence of type of farming on the types and patterns of organizations, but it is not possible to assert that these few studies represent the major type-of-farming areas of the United States.

Agricultural characteristics accounted for 2 of the 3 classification categories for counties used by Charles S. Johnson and his associates at Fiske University in a compilation of nearly 50 agricultural, demographic, educational, and economic variables for each of 1,104 southern counties (Johnson et al., 1941). Most of the data were from the Census for 1930. One agricultural classification was based on the source of farm income, resulting in 5 major crop-types of counties plus 2 residual groupings. The second agricultural classification was intended to represent a measure of complexity; it was based on harvested crop acreage and resulted in 4 categories of crop diversity, i.e., 1 crop dominant, and so on. Analysis of the data was limited to some illustrative uses. Thus the 551 cotton counties were compared with the 438 noncotton farm counties on selected characteristics. This demonstrated, for example, that the cotton counties had smaller farm operating units, a higher percentage of tenants, a larger percentage of mortgaged farms, and relatively small rural nonfarm populations.

In the quest to delineate relatively small rural regions within which social and economic conditions were relatively uniform and among which significant differences occurred, agricultural variables—especially type of farming—were included in elaborate statistical procedures used to delineate homogeneous areas on a county unit basis. The preeminent example of such work at the national level was that by Mangus (1940), which was conducted when he was a staff member of the rural research unit of the Work Projects Administration. Mangus took 20 recognized type-of-farming areas, already delineated as of 1933 by the U.S. Department of Agriculture, as rough first approximations to rural cultural regions. Through successive approximations, using 83 demographic, plane-of-living, agricultural, and related variables, 218 rural-farm subregions were differentiated. These were collapsed into 32 rural-farm cultural regions covering the United States. Variants of this procedure were used to delineate rural social areas within states, most notably for Louisiana (Bertrand, 1955), Ohio (Lively and Almack, 1938), and Missouri (Lively and Gregory, 1939, 1948; Gregory, 1958).

The Mangus nationwide delineation was prompted by an effort to better understand the rural relief problems that had arisen during the Great Depression, it having been observed that the need for public assistance in the open country, villages, and small towns followed definite geographic patterns (Mangus, 1940:1). There was an anticipation that delineating homogeneous rural areas would have utility for program planning and other administrative purposes. Within states, one important use of the areas was for sampling for specific purposes (Gregory, 1958:48).

Of all the studies for which the type of agricultural system provided the organizing theme, Walter Goldschmidt's study *As You Sow* (1947, 1978a) in the 1940s of a small-farm community and a large-farm community in California's upper San Joaquin Valley has very likely received the most widespread recognition (see Chapter 4). The 2 communities were selected to be similar in soil, climate, and size of the community center. Both produced high-value crops under intensive irrigation. The small-farm community farms averaged 57 acres and the large community's averaged 497 acres; when converted to "standard acres" to account for differences in income-producing capacity, the averages were 84 and 247 acres, respectively. There were also tenure differences in the 2 communities; 78 percent of the small-community farm operators were full owners as against 35 percent in the large-farm community. One correlate of the scale of farming operations was the occupational composition of the community; for example, in the small-farm community, 32 percent of the family heads were unskilled laborers whereas this percentage was 68 in the large-farm situation. A second major concomitant was the difference in a number of indicators of the economic and social life of the 2 communities, with the comparative advantage resting with the small-farm locality. A limited follow-up comparison of the 2 communities 25 years after the first study concluded that the differences in educational, social, and other facilities had persisted (LaRose, 1973:4076–83). One critic (LeVeen, 1979) cautions, however, that even if Goldschmidt's hypothesis was correct at the time of his study, the conclusions of the follow-up study cannot be accepted uncritically, suggesting that there are equally plausible alternative hypotheses to account for the differences observed at the time of the second study.

In contrast with the county or other geographic area as the analytical unit, Wayland (1951) and associates at the Columbia University Seminar for Rural Life used the individual farm and its operator as the unit of analysis in a classification system based on constructed ideal types. The system was proposed as an improvement over the tentative and nonsystematic existing formulations, usually lacking precise definition, represented by reference to family farms, subsistence farms, factory farms, etc. The basic thesis of the study was that social patterns of farming (with the individual as the analytical unit), having distinctive socioeconomic and demographic characteristics, could be delineated. Further, such classification would facilitate the location and refinement of significant relationships. The aim was to achieve homogeneous groupings of farms to raise the level of precision in analyzing relationships in farming. The 3 component factors used in constructing the typologies were: (1) the social unit involved in operating the farm enterprise, with 2 subcategories based on the extent of family and hired labor used, (2) the functions served for the family unit by the farming enterprise such as primarily subsistence, as a retirement residence, or as full-time production for market, and (3) scale of the farm operation, with 4 subcategories based on value of products sold and value of land and buildings. The end product was 10 social patterns of farming, each with precise criteria labeled as follows: (1) employer farms, (2) large commercial family farms, (3) medial commercial family farms, (4) residential-commercial family farms, (5) part-time farms, (6) elder's farms, (7) subsistence farms, (8) small commercial family farms, (9) residential farms, and (10) nominal farms.

To test whether the 10 ideal types in fact differed significantly from each other in their social patterns, 18 basic variables for a sample of 3,000 farms were tabulated for each type from the original schedules collected by the 1945 Census of Agriculture. Tabulations were made separately for the North and South and, within the South, the variable race was also used for certain tabulations. From the number of statistically significant differences observed for each pair of ideal types, it was concluded that the social patterns of farming as delineated were distinctive (p. 76). The fewest significant differences were found, in both the North and the South, between types 3 and 4, and between 9 and 10.

Another example in which the predominant type of agriculture established the sampling frame for comparative analysis is a study of Protestant churches in Montana (Samson, 1958). Sample counties, within which data on all Protestant churches were systematically gathered, were chosen from each of four types of agriculture (dryland wheat farming, livestock ranching, irrigated agriculture, and mountain-diversified agriculture).

In some instances a specific form of agricultural organization or a general system of agriculture with some distinctive characteristic established the domain for studies that were essentially noncomparative in nature with regard to agriculture. One prime example of this is the cotton plantation studies. Rupert B. Vance, University of North Carolina, examined the plantation in the context of the cotton system and cotton culture in his broad-ranging *Human Factors in Cotton Culture* (1929) and also, less comprehensively, in his *Human Geography of the South* (1935). During the 1930s depression situation, a comprehensive field study of landlord-tenant relations was conducted on 646 medium-size and large cotton plantations in 11 large-scale cotton growing areas within 7 southeastern states (Woofter, 1936). In view of the rapid change underway in plantation organization and operation in the Southeast and the characterization of the South as the nation's number one economic problem, a policy-oriented restudy, after 3 years, was made of 246 of the same plantations in 9 areas (Holley et al., 1940). The plantation was also the unit of analysis for a comparative study of mechanized and unmechanized cotton plantation operations in Mississippi (Pedersen and Raper, 1954).

An irrigation project in Oregon, settled between 1931 and 1941, provided the setting for a study of farm owner and farm operator turnover (McKain and Dahlke, 1946). Similarly, a new irrigation project in Washington's Columbia Basin, the nation's largest single irrigation project in the history of reclamation, was the setting for a study of farm families in 1954–55 and 1956–57 to ascertain their social and economic resources for transforming desert land into farms, to determine progress made, and to determine factors in success and failure (Straus, 1958; Straus and Parrish, 1956).

The semiarid Great Plains was the setting for Carl F. Kraenzel's (1955) long-term study of cultural adaptation—or the lack of it—to a frontier environment, a study that included attention to agricultural adaptations in the area and to the minorities he identified in the rural areas of the plains, namely, stockmen, dry-land farmers, dry-land cotton growers, and irrigation farmers.

There were also a few studies in which some nonagricultural criterion was used to provide the overall frame of reference but in which the goal was to study a defined group in relation to agriculture. Our best examples of such work by rural sociologists are provided by studies of blacks. Woofter (1930) provided an extensive early overview of the economic status of southern blacks in agriculture. Beale (1966, 1976), using historical, census, and other statistical data, gave a more recent view of "the Negro in American agriculture." Neal and Jones (1950) asserted that the reorganization of farms in the "Cotton" South was resulting in six functional types as follows: (1) three familiar, traditional types (subsistence farms, tenant-operated multiple unit farms, and small independent commercial farms), and (2) three evolving types (part-time farms, large mechanized farms, and livestock farms). Taking an historical perspective, the functional types were used to portray the effect of economic changes in agriculture on black farmers.

Finally, under our general heading of studies in which type of agriculture has provided the organizing theme, we have a small group of investigations in which some consideration other than agriculture per se served as the selection criterion but in which some elements of the agricultural arrangements proved to be, in effect, a dependent variable. All of these studies have in common the associations among religious orientations, values and beliefs, and agriculture. A good example is provided by Nelson's (1925, 1928, 1933) original studies of three Utah farm-village communities—Escalante, Ephraim, and American Fork. Although varying in size, distance from the urban center of Salt Lake City, and length of settlement, all had in common a base in irrigated agriculture and religious homogeneity (Mormon communities). All three were found to have relatively small-size landholdings and a low rate of tenancy. Nelson (1933:2728; 1952:137—138) explained that the religious and ethical idealism of the early Mormons—in particular, the doctrine of economic equality—had as one of its consequences the relatively equal distribution of land and water. Similarly, farm and home ownership has been a cardinal principle with the Mormon people (1933:2829; 1952:192) and contributed, Nelson asserted, to the low farm tenancy situation. A restudy in 1950 (Nelson, 1952) found that, despite the impact of agricultural, economic, and social changes, relatively small farms and low tenancy rates continued to prevail in Escalante and Ephraim. (No information was provided on farm size and tenancy for American Fork, which was no longer heavily dependent on agriculture.) Similarly, the importance of values and goals for shaping the agricultural organization and system has been demonstrated for such "cultural island" groupings as the Old Order Amish (Kollmorgen, 1942; Olshan, 1979), the German-Swiss (Kollmorgen, 1940), and the Hutterites (Riley and Johnson, 1970; Riley and Stewart, 1966).

SPECIALIZED STUDIES: TENURE, PART-TIME FARMING, LOW-INCOME FARMERS, AND OTHER STRUCTURAL COMPONENTS OF AGRICULTURE

Another general category of sociological investigations of agriculture up to the 1950s was the specialized research in which specific attributes or structural components such as tenure status, hired farm labor, part-time farmers, and low-income farmers were the direct object of study. Such studies were few in number prior to 1930 but increased rapidly during the depression years of the

1930s when, in response to the national need for an increased information base to cope with widespread distress in rural areas, research resources were greatly increased at the national level and, through federally funded cooperative projects, in the state agricultural experiment stations.

Tenure Status

A definite association between farm operator tenure status and a particular facet of rural life (community social participation) was discovered by Galpin (1911), almost accidentally, in the course of his first attempt at delineating the boundaries of a rural community. When Galpin placed on a map every home that went to the village of Belleville (in Jefferson County, New York) for services and activities, he placed beside each home a symbol not only for each organization or service used having the village as a meeting place but a symbol to distinguish farm renters from farm owners. One-third of the farm homes turned out to be those of cash or share tenants. For Galpin, "the startling disclosure of the survey is that the farm-tenant homes on the whole have little connection with the important associated life of this community." Subsequently, tenure was used by rural sociologists as an independent variable for a wide range of investigations, e.g., levels of farm family living and social participation. In this section, however, we limit our review to research for which tenure or other structural components were the immediate focus of attention.

Only Wisconsin followed up on the recommendation of the National Committee on Standardization of Research in Country Life (appointed at the 1917 annual meeting of the American Sociological Society) that some responsible agency in every state make a field study with emphasis on the social aspects of tenancy, especially the shifting of farm tenants. In Wisconsin, Galpin and Hoag (1919) analyzed the occupancy history over the 10-year period, 1909–18, for 500 farms in Sun Prairie Community (Dane County). Of the 500, some 246 had been constantly occupied by their owners for the last 10 years, 254 had been occupied by tenants at some time during the 10 years, and, of these, 42 had been constantly rented. In making this study, the relationship of tenancy to farm retirement was discovered. It was shown that the gradual "advance" of youth into farming during this period corresponded with a process of slow "retreat" from farming by older operators. Shortly before Galpin left Wisconsin in 1919 to head up a division of Farm Life Studies in the USDA, a 28-member group, which included Galpin, had been appointed by the secretary of agriculture to suggest fields of study to be undertaken by the unit. Among the 10 fields outlined was "social aspects of tenancy and landlordism" and "special aspects of various types of farm labor" (Taylor, 1948). Among the first cooperative projects initiated by Galpin were three on tenancy with the Agricultural Experiment Stations in Iowa, Nebraska, and Missouri. In Iowa, von Tungeln et al. (1923) interviewed 400 farm families in 1920 in a corner of Cedar County. The report included the 10-year occupancy record of the farms, as Galpin had done in Wisconsin, and the kinship ties of tenants to their landlords. But it went far beyond that in scope. It precisely related both owner and tenant status to the several stages of the agricultural ladder. Thus, 29 percent of the owners had "climbed the entire agricultural ladder," i.e., were farm born and reared, had been a hired man, and had been a tenant before attaining ownership. (One-third had skipped the hired man stage.) Among the tenants, 42 percent had passed through the hired man stage. The study included a section on the hired men employed by 32 percent of the farmers, on the hired women employed on 10 farms, and information about selected social and demographic characteristics associated with the major tenure classes. In Nebraska, a series of reports by Rankin (1923a, 1923b, 1924, 1926) resulted from interviews with 1,141 farmers in 10 areas of the state. The first 2 of these reports dealt with the family levels of living and with community relationships by tenure in detail, but in what we might consider a largely conventional way. The 1926 report pushed the analysis of the stages of the agricultural ladder for the sample of farmers to a new level, including discussion of factors involved in each stage. The 1924 report opened a line of inquiry;

it focused on 720 landlords, including the number of farms each held, the landowners' characteristics, and the business relationships with the tenants.

The Missouri study revealed such unsuspected sharp contrasts between the houses, churches, and school buildings of the landowners and those of the tenants and hired men that the report was eventually filed away, Galpin deciding that to attempt to publish it by his own unit would put the division at too much risk (Galpin, 1938:51–52). The field of tenancy was, in fact, by no means the exclusive research territory of sociologists, and Galpin dropped out of farm tenancy studies because, he told his successor, "others seemed to feel they should have a monopoly" (Taylor, 1948).

North Carolina's Commission on Farm Tenancy, a temporary association of state agencies, was also provided funds by Galpin, which were used for a study of the causes and effects of tenancy (Nelson, 1969:66–67). A survey of 1,014 farm families in 3 counties, chosen as typical of 3 major sections of the state, was made with a 15-page schedule including about 700 items. Tabulations were presented by tenure category and race in the report compiled for the commission by Taylor and Zimmerman (1922). From these early studies Brunner (1957:116–117) summarized:

> [T]here emerged a portrait of the farm tenant as a younger operator than the farm owner, with more children and a lower standard of living, who participated less in community life, who moved more than twice as often, whose education was below average, and whose communities were less progressive, especially if landlords were absentee. It was also clear that the higher the proportion of tenants in the farm population the more disadvantaged the situation was likely to be.

Another early piece of work that came out of Galpin's unit in the Department of Agriculture was a case study of the organization and policies of a large corporate estate in North Dakota's Red River Valley (Baumgartel, 1925). Except for the headquarters' unit, which used hired labor, the estate had been operated since about

1892 with some 65 tenant units averaging about 500 acres each. This large scale operation was of special interest because its policy of permanent farming and tenure improvement contrasted so sharply with many of the bonanza farming operations that once largely prevailed in the Red River Valley. In the meantime, the rate of tenancy steadily climbed to encompass 42 percent of all farms in 1930. Tenancy became an issue for public policy consideration. The times called for research on tenancy.

In *The Collapse of Cotton Tenancy,* Johnson et al. (1935) gave a nontechnical summary of field studies and statistical surveys of Cotton Belt tenancy conducted during 1933-35. The special inquiry among tenant farmers covered some 2,000 families in 8 counties in the states of Alabama, Mississippi, South Carolina, and Texas. This work did much to illuminate the precarious position of the tenant farmer in the Cotton Belt and to indicate the impact on tenants of the initial crop reduction and relief programs of the federal government. A second significant study of the early 1930s was Arthur F. Raper's *Preface to Peasantry* (1936, reprinted 1971) because it was a comprehensive and intensive investigation of tenancy in 1934 of 2 counties in the cotton-growing section of Georgia, which Raper had previously studied for his doctoral dissertation in sociology at the University of North Carolina, starting in 1927, under the auspices of the Georgia Committee on Interracial Cooperation.

By far the most comprehensive research of the decade into farm tenure was done by Schuler (1938) under the joint sponsorship of what was then the Resettlement Administration (later the Farm Security Administration) and the Bureau of Agricultural Economics, USDA. The elaborate questionnaire titled "Social Correlatives of Farm Tenure" was completed for nearly 2,500 families in counties located in 4 Corn Belt states, 9 Cotton Belt states, and a flue-cured tobacco area. Much of the data was presented in Schuler's report by 4 tenure categories for the Corn Belt and by color and 4 tenure categories for the South. Among the wide range of topics covered was the agricultural ladder, landlord-tenant relationships, mobility, social participation, levels and standards of living, and attitudes and opinions about farm issues and federal agricultural programs. The Southwest became the focus of a major research effort in land tenure with the organization in 1942 of the Southwestern Land Tenure Committee with representation from rural sociologists and agricultural economists from 5 cooperating states (Arkansas, Louisiana, Mississippi, Oklahoma, and Texas), from the USDA's Bureau of Agricultural Economics, and from the Farm Foundation. The project received grants from the General Education Board and the Farm Foundation. The broad purpose of the project, directed by Harold Hoffsommer, was to determine and measure the relationships between the tenure status of the farm family and its economic and social performance. The research problem was approached in an interdisciplinary manner, including not only rural sociology but land economics, farm management, law, and government. Intensive surveys of nearly 1,600 families were made in sample counties within four subregions. Sampling procedures for areas and families were carefully described in the final report (Hoffsommer, 1950:7–14). In addition to the introductory chapter setting forth the research problem and the summary chapter by Hoffsommer, rural sociologists also prepared the sections on tenure and family status, factors related to changes in tenure status, landlord-tenant relationships, and community and institutional factors in tenure.

During this general period, rural sociologists in Arkansas and Oklahoma were especially active in farm tenure work, some in conjunction with and some independent of the regional project. Otis D. Duncan (1940) advanced a set of 15 hypotheses to be tested by research on the sociological aspects of farm tenancy in Oklahoma. This was followed by empirical research in the state on social correlates of tenure status (McMillan, 1943; McMillan and Duncan, 1945; McMillan and Mason, 1945). Arkansas studies in the coastal plains and in the Ozarks dealt with the tenure process as well as the social and economic correlates (Charlton, 1947, 1954). State and local studies made outside the Southwest included one in eastern South Dakota (Slocum, 1942), a longitudinal study of land ownership by ethnic groups in a Minnesota marginal farming area (Deininger and Marshall, 1955), and an Iowa study of family factors in tenure experience (Rohwer, 1950). The first comprehensive analysis of the operation of the agricultural ladder in the United States was provided by Taylor and associates (1948) in the Bureau of Agricultural Economics in an analysis that included farm laborers as well as owners and tenants. Using census data, they developed estimates of the number of males 20 years old and over who were farm owners, farm tenants, and farm laborers per 1,000 males of this age gainfully employed on farms for 1880, 1900, 1920, 1930, and 1940 for the U.S., each census division, and the 48 states. They also reported developments in farm tenure status for the period 1940–47.

Other Specialized Studies

The depression era of the 1930s provided the context not only for such research as that on the cotton plantation and some other studies already mentioned, but also for a host of projects that we may describe broadly as "policy planning and evaluation." Much of this work was done by sociologists in federal agencies, often through cooperative arrangements with experiment stations. We limit our review to illustrations of studies in which the structure of agriculture, in some sense, was a major component. Here we can include a national study under the Works Progress Administration of farm operators receiving rural relief grants or rehabilitation advances in 1935 (Asch and Mangus, 1937), an analysis for the Farm Security Administration and the Bureau of Agricultural Economics of some 70,000 families on relief or accepted for the initial standard loan rural rehabilitation program in a number of states (Kirkpatrick, 1938), and a large number of state relief and rehabilitation studies made possible by the Works Progress Administration's rural research program. The situation and characteristics of low-income farms continued to get some attention after the 1930s as illustrated by Lionberger's (1948) efforts in Missouri, which had the ultimate objective of determining better ways and means of reaching low-income farmers with educational materials.

Here, too, we include research that evaluated the impact on farmers of federal government agricultural program efforts. Some were efforts by sociologists to assess the differential effects on tenure classes of the Agricultural Adjustment Administration's acreage reduction programs (e.g., Blackwell, 1934; Hoffsommer, 1935). Another example is Larson's (1947) evaluation of the standard rural rehabilitation loan program under the Resettlement Administration and the Farm Security Administration from 1935–1943. And, at the level of a single county, we have Raper's (1943) intensive study in Greene County, Georgia, of farm families and the whole set of agricultural and other governmental programs encompassed in what the USDA called a "Unified Farm Program."

A few studies were concerned with other special farm operator categories; among these, part-time farmers and farming were frequently the focus. Examples of such studies include a survey of over 1,100 white and black households in 5 industrial subregions of the Eastern Cotton Belt (Allen et al., 1937), a study of nearly 900 part-time farmers in 6 industrial areas of Pennsylvania (John, 1938), and a Rhode Island study of 1,100 households combining nonagricultural employment and agricultural production (Gordon, 1942).

Perhaps it seems odd that during the period under review in this section, into the 1950s, the family farm as such received little research, although there was an analysis of commercial farms (Skrabanek, 1954), which was confined to census data on farms by economic class, and a study of nonresident farmers (Belcher, 1954), again limited to census data. The distribution of economic and authority aspects of status among farmers by tenure and race was examined for four southern states as of 1950, again using census data to estimate these differentials (C. A. Anderson, 1954).

Hired farm labor increasingly became the object of study. Wage rates and earnings received particular attention during the 1940s (see especially Ducoff, 1945). A few studies were concerned with "regular" hired workers (e.g., Burnight et al., 1953). More were centered on migratory agricultural workers (e.g., Larson, 1968; Larson and Sharp, 1960; Metzler, 1955; Reuss et al., 1938).

The increasing mechanization of cotton and reductions in cotton acreages were the stimulus for a socioeconomic study of black laborers on cotton plantations in a Louisiana parish (Grigsby and Hoffsommer, 1941). Also in the tradition of earlier research on plantations was a study of the labor and tenancy arrangements on 100 sugar cane farms in nine Louisiana parishes (Hoffsommer, 1940).

Limited research on cooperatives and other marketing systems was fostered briefly in the environment of the 1920s and early 1930s when cooperative marketing by farmers was being vigorously advocated. In Minnesota, Zimmerman and Black (1926) not only studied farmer attitudes concerning cooperative and other marketing organizations but identified the cooperatives in each of the nine communities, selected to represent the state's agricultural and social diversity, within which farmers were interviewed. T. B. Manny of the USDA's Division of Farm Population and Rural Life was lead investigator for a study of potato marketing in Maryland and Virginia (1929), of cotton-marketing methods (1931), and of Ohio farmers' attitudes toward farmer-owned business organizations (1932).

Some areas pertaining to the structure or the sociology of agriculture received little attention during the time period under review. One example is represented by Gillette's (1946) effort to determine the reason for farm enlargement given by North Dakota farmers who increased the size of their farms during 1942–45. The leading reasons given by the farmers in his sample who responded were (1) to raise the family's level of living, and (2) to offer a place on the farm for sons. Another example is a comparison of permanent, "temporary," and new farmers over a 10-year period in 2 central New York areas (Lackey and Larson, 1959). The permanent farmers scored higher than the temporary farmers on all the socioeconomic variables measured except age. The new farmers were much more like the permanent farmers than were the temporary farmers.

CONCLUSION

For most of the first five decades of the sociology of agriculture, this area of study was largely coterminous with the sociology of rural communities. By the late 1940s and early 1950s, however, the unity of agriculture and rural communities began to break down, in both sociodemographic and scholarly terms. There came to be an increased frequency of studies that focused on agriculture and did so outside of the community studies tradition. As we discuss at greater length in the next chapter, one of the main factors that contributed to the differentiation between sociological research on agriculture and rural communities was the development of survey research methodologies and quantitative techniques. These methodologies and techniques permitted researchers to focus more specifically on farmers and farm households, particularly from a social psychological perspective. From this point forward studies of agriculture and rural communities would increasingly be conducted by separate groups of scholars.

Rural Sociological Research on the Structure of Agriculture, the Early 1950s to the Early 1970s: Behaviorism and the Social Psychology of Agricultural Activities

INTRODUCTION

Rural sociology in a sense came of age in the period of concern in this chapter. Whereas U.S. sociology prior to the Korean War had been largely devoted to Chicago School-style human ecology and, increasingly, to "grand theory" (a la Parsons, 1937, 1951), rural sociology had been largely detached from these major themes. Much of pre-1950s rural sociology had largely eschewed an explicit theoretical orientation (other than elaborating rural-urban continuum themes derived from a portion of the work of Toennies, as, for example, in the work of Sorokin and Zimmerman, 1929). And since human ecology had been almost exclusively focused on metropolitan communities (until the publication of Hawley's [1950] *Human Ecology*), there was perceived to be little of relevance in human ecology for understanding rural community dynamics.

This was all to change very dramatically beginning in the late 1940s and early 1950s. During this time there emerged a new cohort of rural sociologists—principally graduates of Cornell University, the universities of Wisconsin, Minnesota, Missouri, and Kentucky, and Iowa State University—trained in social psychology. This cohort of young rural sociologists would retain the social psychological component of the rural-urban continuum tradition but would replace its rooting in community studies with the theoretical orientations of William F. Ogburn and Robert K. Merton and the methodological innovations of Paul Lazarsfeld, Rensis Likert, Stuart Chapin, and Louis Guttman. Whereas, in pre-Korean War rural sociology, agriculture was of interest insofar as it was among the principal ensembles of institutions and activities that shaped the nature and structure of rural communities, agriculture in the social psychological-behaviorist era of rural sociology was largely construed as a situation in which farmers (and farm family members) were *actors* responding to stimuli such as new agricultural technologies, the mass media, educational and occupational opportunities, and so on (Fliegel and van Es, 1983).

This era was one in which Emile Durkheim and Max Weber became the predominant classical exemplars of sociological inquiry, based on the Parsonian (Parsons, 1937) synthesis of Durkheim and Weber in terms of an incipient "theory of action." Robert K. Merton's (1957) notion of "theories of the middle range," however, was arguably the central notion of the 1950s and 1960s era of research in sociology and rural sociology. The notion of theories of the middle range was crucial in enabling sociologists to translate the rather abstract propositions of Parsonian functionalism into hypotheses suitable for testing with micro-level data from individual, household, organizational, and related units of analysis. It is arguably the case, however, that Parsons' synthesis of Durkheim and Weber, and Merton's subsequent elaboration of a social psychological, middle-range version of Parsons, led to a scholarly tradition with only superficial similarities to the work of Durkheim and Weber (Giddens, 1971; Mills, 1959). For example, the unison of functionalism with causal analysis of micro-level data was alien to key Durkheimian notions of the analytical priority on society *sui generis* and on functional over causal analysis. Likewise, Weber's method involved comparative historical research, and Weber stridently criticized methodologies that involved superimposing the putative hypothetico-deductive approach of the natural sciences on the social sciences. Nonetheless, the Mertonian agenda of middle-range theory and research revolutionized and gave coherence to American sociology, and ultimately codified a pattern of sociological inquiry that, in many respects, remains influential to this day.

Typifying this new theoretical-methodological orientation in rural sociology at large, and dominating rural sociological research on agriculture from the Korean War to the early 1970s, was the diffusion and adoption of innovations. In many respects diffusion-adoption theory was a prototypical "theory of the middle range," in that it combined social psychological reasoning with a type of functional analysis (i.e., the notion that adoption of new technologies would contribute to positive social change). It should be noted, however, that Young (1959) made the claim, about a decade into the diffusion-adoption era of research, that much of this research was sufficiently scattered and atheoretical so that diffusion-adoption inquiry had only recently begun to approximate a theory of the middle range.

Of somewhat less importance to rural sociology as a whole and to rural sociological research on agriculture was work on the social psychology of the value-orientations of farm people and of educational and occupational aspirations and attainments. This research, however, was based on premises—middle-range theorizing, social psychological reasoning, and survey-based methods—that were essentially identical to those of diffusion-adoption tradition.

Rural sociological research on agriculture during this era was to become substantially more quantitative than was typical in the rural community studies tradition from 1900 to 1950. In particular, the use of sophisticated multivariate analyses would increase greatly during the late 1950s and 1960s as high-speed computers became available, and as large data-sets with individuals and families as the units of analysis were compiled with the support of expanded federal appropriations for social science research.

It should be emphasized again that while rural sociology from the early 1950s to the early 1970s came to be dominated by social psychological approaches, each era of rural sociological research on agriculture, including this one, has involved significant diversity. In particular, the community study approach to agriculture persisted, albeit to a decreasing degree, after 1950 (see, for example, Richardson and Larson, 1976; Smith and Zopf, 1970). Also, the research traditions that dominated in rural sociology from 1950 to 1970 have persisted to some degree up to the present. Thus some of the literature reviewed in this section was conducted and published after 1970. Nonetheless, social psychology was clearly ascendent in rural sociology from 1950 to the late 1960s and would remain unchallenged in rural sociological studies of agriculture until the early to mid-1970s.

This chapter, like rural sociological scholarship on agriculture during its social psychological era, is devoted largely to the diffusion and adoption of agricultural innovations. This is followed by two sections that discuss other foci of the social psychological-behaviorist paradigm of the period. We first discuss research on the value-orientations of farmers and then research on educational and occupational aspirations and achievements of farm people.

THE DIFFUSION AND ADOPTION OF AGRICULTURAL INNOVATIONS

Research on the adoption of innovations has had a long history going back to the work of the early anthropologists. But whereas these anthropologists typically construed the adoption of new ideas and technologies to be a disruptive influence on peasant communities in nonindustrial countries, the study of the diffusion and adoption of new farm practices in post-1950s rural sociology tended to involve no such pejorative connotations.

As Fliegel and van Es (1983:14) have noted, "briefly stated, the diffusion/adoption research tradition viewed the farmer as actor, in a farm and local community situation, responding to stimuli concerning what were *unquestionably viewed as improvements* in agricultural technology" (emphasis added). Thus this research tradition was premised not only on understanding the spread of new technologies from the vantage point of the farmer as actor, but also, in general, took a promotional posture toward technological change. Rural sociologists tended to adopt the language of their agricultural experiment stations by referring to the technologies they studied as "improved" or "recommended." Most such studies were therefore couched in terms of how the new knowledge on diffusion-adoption would enable "change agents" (extension officials and county agents, agribusiness sales representatives, the mass media, and so on) to increase the rate of adoption of these new, improved, and recommended technologies.

It is generally accepted that the first studies in the rural sociological diffusion-adoption tradition were those by Hoffer (1942) and Ryan and Gross (1943) in Michigan and Iowa, respectively. E. A. Wilkening (1949, 1950, 1952, 1954), a student of William Ogburn at the University of Chicago, has typically been credited with making the most influential early elaborations of diffusion-adoption research. Further notable contributions were made by Fliegel (1956), Beal and Bohlen (1957), Lionberger (1960), Coughenour (1960), and Rogers (1962).

Most versions of the classical diffusion model had the following components. First, as emphasized several times in the preceding, the point of departure was the social psychology of individual decision making. As Bohlen (1964:268) noted: "The adoption of a new idea or practice is not a simple unit act, but rather a complex pattern of *mental activities* combined with *actions* before an *individual* fully accepts or adopts a new idea" (emphasis added). Second, the process that individuals went through in adopting new practices or ideas was conceptualized in terms of stages (typically in terms of the stages of awareness, information, evaluation, trial, adoption); it was generally argued that whereas there is a tendency for an individual to go through the stages sequentially, some stages may be skipped and passage through a particular step is not irreversible. In particular, the earliest innovators of technologies frequently were found to skip the trial stage, and farmers often were observed to go back and forth between the information and evaluation stages (Beal and Rogers, 1960).

Third, most researchers had an explicit or implicit typology of new ideas and practices, which was generally focused on the degree of complexity of the idea, the divisibility of the product or practice, the congruence of the technology with existing practices, and the economics of the practice. The more complex the idea, the more farmers would need to alter their attitudes and beliefs and receive persuasive, timely information before adopting the innovation. Highly divisible products or practices were observed to be adopted more rapidly than less divisible ones, since a highly divisible innovation could be tried out on a small scale before full-scale adoption. Congruence of the technology with farmers' existing practices was seen to facilitate adoption. Finally, highly profitable ideas or practices were observed to be adopted more rapidly than less profitable ones.

Fourth, diffusion-adoption researchers generally posited and observed a logistical growth (or "S") curve of the cumulative percentage of adopters at each stage of the diffusion-adoption process, albeit with variations in the configuration of the curve depending upon the stage of diffusion-adoption and the type of idea or practice that was being diffused. The frequency distribution of adoption over time was found to be bell-shaped and normally distributed. The shape of the typical diffusion-adoption curve became the basis for classifying farmers as innovators, early adopters, early majority, majority, late majority, and laggards, depending upon the point at which they adopted the new idea or practice.

Fifth, much of "normal science" in the diffusion-adoption tradition took the form of determining the personal and social characteristics of farmers according to the rate, or point in time, at which they accepted a new idea or practice (or a set of practices that were the basis of "adoption scales"). Widely accepted profiles of the personal and social characteristics of innovators, early adopters, and so on were compiled based on this research (see especially Lionberger, 1960; Rogers, 1962). Finally, diffusion-adoption research tended to give major attention to communication aspects of the diffusion or new ideas or practices. Much research was done on the types of mass media and interpersonal influences that were most effective at particular stages of the diffusion-adoption process, on how different types of farmers responded to different media and communication patterns, and on how the effects of communication processes varied by the type of innovation. The following is a selective summary of major research thrusts within the general rubric of diffusion-adoption of innovations. We do not intend to be exhaustive, since even by the early 1970s there had been roughly 1,000 studies in diffusion-adoption, though not all were conducted by rural sociologists or focused on the United States (Rogers and Shoemaker, 1971). We also highlight some of the emerging criticisms of the diffusion-adoption perspective that began to appear in the 1960s and that proliferated in the 1970s. The discussion is organized in terms of 7 categories of research and inquiry: (1) the characteristics of farm practice adopters, (2) the social psychology of and role of aspirations and motivations in farm practice adoption, (3) group influences on adoption, (4) the role of communication and the media in adoption, (5) conceptual clarifications of the diffusion-adoption process, (6) methodological aspects of diffusion-adoption studies, and (7) criticisms of diffusion-adoption research and modifications of the approach in response to these criticisms. These are admittedly overlapping categories. For example, much research into the characteristics of farm practice adopters utilized social-psychological variables and took into account such factors as communication, media contact, group influences, and so on. Also, some important themes have been omitted for reasons of space. Nonetheless, these categories permit a convenient summarization of this very large literature and convey the essential flavor of the research tradition.

Characteristics of Farm Practice Adopters

One of the empirical generalizations for which adoption studies would become best known has been that farmer socioeconomic status (which has been measured according to a variety of indicators such as acres operated, acres owned, gross sales, net farm income, total family income, and so on) was positively related to adopting recommended farm practices. It is useful to note, however, that this generalization did not become broadly accepted until the middle to late 1950s. Some of the earliest studies in the diffusion-adoption tradition (e.g., Gross and Taves, 1952) failed to find that socioeconomic status was highly related to farm practice adoption. Gross and Taves (1952), for example, noted that reading state college bulletins was the single most important predictor of the adoption of 10 "extension-recommended" practices, with other consistent correlates being belonging to a cooperative, age, and frequency of trips to the nearest metropolitan center (see also Fliegel's, 1956, analysis of data collected by Wilkening in 1952 in which Fliegel showed no association between farm size and adoption). Marsh and Coleman (1955) later replicated the Gross and Taves study and reported that socioeconomic status, education, and contact with extension agents were the best predictors of 21 independent variables examined with reference to the adoption of 16 practices (see also Subcommittee for the Study of Diffusion of Farm Practices, 1955). Fliegel (1957), Coughenour (1960), Abd-Ella et al. (1981), Carlson and Dillman (1983), and other subsequent studies would later confirm that large, high socioeconomic status, young farmers with high contact with extension and other information sources and high levels of social participation tended to be the earliest adopters of new farm practices. Net worth, however, did not generally prove to be a major predictor of adoption (Photiadis, 1962), presumably because high-net-worth farmers tended to be older farmers for whom farm expansion was less important and social-psychological orientations less conducive to adoption than younger farmers. Nonetheless, it is possible to observe that over the course of 30 years of adoption research, reported correlations between various indicators of farm size, farm income, and socioeconomic status and indexes of adoption of commercial innovations became larger; this may well be explained by the fact that this period corresponded with rapid differentiation among U.S. farmers—and hence increased variability in farmers' socioeconomic statuses—which contributed to socioeconomic status becoming a more effective predictor of adoption over time.

A further component of rural sociological research into the characteristics of farm adopters was the work by Rogers (1958a) and others on developing categories of farm practice adopters and developing socioeconomic and social-psychological profiles of these categories of adopters. Rogers (1958a) reported data from Iowa and Ohio farmers indicating that adoption distributions over time tended to be bell-shaped and to approximate normality. He developed a method by which adopters of agricultural practices may be grouped into five categories—innovators, early adopters, early majority, late majority, and laggards—based on the farmer's position on the time-distribution of adoption. Rogers was thus able to codify the work of others (e.g., Subcommittee for the Study of Diffusion of Farm Practices, 1955, which had proposed tentative terminology for a series of five stages of the adoption process and for categories of adopters). Rogers' schema became widely accepted and led to a substantial amount of research on characterizing farmers at various stages of the adoption curve (see especially Rogers, 1962). It should be noted, however, that subsequent research has indicated that "S-curve" formulation of Rogers and others does not hold for all innovations; Perry et al. (1967), for example, reported data showing that the adoption curve for two insecticides in North Carolina was "J-shaped," with high rates of adoption almost immediately after the insecticides were introduced.

One of the major debates concerning the characteristics of adopters has revolved around Cancian's (1967) theory of stratification and risk taking, which has been explored through the adoption of new farm practices as an operationalization of risk. Cancian argued that the relationship between socioeconomic rank and risk taking was a curvilinear one and that, in particular, persons of "high-middle" rank would risk less than those of "low-middle" rank. Gartrell and Wilkening (1973), however, found little support for the curvilinear hypothesis of "middle-class conservatism" among a sample of Wisconsin farmers; they found that the relationship between income and innovation was essentially linear in nature. Morrison et al. (1976) also reported evidence contrary to the Cancian hypothesis with data from India. Morrison et al. have suggested as well that farm practice innovation is not unambiguously a risk-taking phenomenon, since failure to innovate involves risks as well.

The Social Psychology of Farm Practice Adoption

Along with research on the socioeconomic characteristics of farm practice adopters, inquiry into the social psychology of adoption has been one of the two most frequent foci of adoption research. The central figure in the early development of the social psychological approach to farm practice adoption research was E. A. Wilkening (1949, 1950, 1958). Wilkening (1950) reported early research results showing that several "sociopsychological" variables—farmer attitudes toward education for boys going into farming, indicators of traditional attitudes toward religion and other domains, and dependence on neighborhood and kin ties—were associated with the acceptance of improved farm practices in North Carolina. Wilkening concluded from his study that traditional attitudinal orientations led to resistance to and a lack of readiness to change, such as change reflected in accepting and adopting new practices. He called for further research into personality characteristics in relation to farm practice adoption, a call that was well heeded and led to a very large literature.

In particular, Rogers (1957) followed up on Wilkening's lead in a study of Iowa farmers. Rogers reported substantial correlations between social-psychological/personality indexes (rigidity, change orientation, innovative proneness, and adoption self-rating) and an index of adoption of new farm practices. In a later article Rogers (1958b) reported that indexes of change orientation, communication competence, and status achievement were positively correlated with a measure of the adoption of farm practices. Hoffer and Stangland (1958) found that indicators of progressive and modern attitudes were the most efficacious predictors of adopting new technologies for corn production among Michigan farmers. Dean et al. (1958) reported comparable results among a sample of North Carolina farmers. In one of the more comprehensive studies relating value-orientations to farm practice adoption, Ramsey et al. (1959) related twelve indexes of values to two practice adoption scales (one relating to dairy production and the other to the use of lime). Ramsey et al. found that an orientation toward security and an index of traditionalism were inversely related to the behavioral adoption scale (dairy), whereas there were significant correlations between the cognitive adoption (lime) scale and five value-orientations—three of which were positive (with respect to achievement, science, and material comfort) and two of which were negative (with respect to security and traditionalism). Each of the relationships, however, was reported to be modest in magnitude. More recently, Hooks et al. (1983) found very low associations between personality/social-psychological indicators and farm practice adoption. The fact that early studies reported fairly strong associations between value-orientations and farm practice adoption, whereas these correlations have proven to be smaller in more recent studies, suggests that there may have been an historical change in the bases of adoption behaviors (see van Es, 1983). This is corroborated by the observation of Perry et al. (1967) that there has been a change in the form of adoption curves as technological change has become more routinized and institutionalized. One might also add that these results might have been influenced by changes in farm structure as well.

After 1960 much social psychological research came to be devoted to the cognitive orientation of farmers toward practices of different types. Fliegel and Kivlin (1966) and Kivlin and Fliegel (1967, 1968), for example, found that the attributes of new practices are differentially perceived and considered important by different types of farmers, especially between small and large farmers. They found that complexity, a saving of discomfort, association with dairying, and divisibility for trial were the perceived characteristics of innovations that were most closely associated with adoption. Other social-psychological research has found that farmers' evaluations of new technologies in terms of their congruence with previously adopted practices influence the adoption of subsequent practices; for example, Brandner and Kearl (1964) found that previous use of hybrid corn was a more effective predictor of adopting hybrid sorghum than age, education, income, and other factors. Havens (1965) found that indicators of farmers' perceptions of adoption situations—whether they adopted involuntarily, voluntarily with uncertainty, or voluntarily by assuming risk—made a significant contribution to the explanation of adoption when five objective antecedents were controlled.

Group Influences

Virtually from the start of diffusion-adoption research there was a concern with how a farmer's involvement in various social groups influenced adoption behavior. Pedersen (1951), for example, reported in an early study that Danish and Polish-origin farmers in Wisconsin tended to adopt new farm practices at greatly different rates, with the former ethnic group doing so more rapidly than the latter; in a later Wisconsin study van den Ban (1960) found that a German Lutheran community had higher adoption rates than did a community of Calvinistic Dutch origin after taking into account farmers' differences in education, farm size, and net worth. Wilkening (1952) also conducted an early study to determine the influence of "informal leaders" in agricultural communities on farm practice adoption. Duncan and Kreitlow (1954) found that community context affected adoption behavior; adoption was most rapid among ethnically and religiously heterogeneous neighborhoods. Marsh and Coleman (1954) and Flinn (1970) found that the norms of the neighborhood or community affect the adoption decisions of farmers who reside therein.

Adoption researchers thus came to recognize that the sources of information upon which farmers relied to make adoption decisions were not confined to institutionalized sources such as extension or the mass media. Farmers' decisions were found to be affected by neighboring farmers' opinions and advice. In one of the more comprehensive papers on the role of group influences on adoption behaviors, Lionberger and Francis (1969) sought to measure and describe the views that farmers have of 2 sources of farm information: early innovators and personal influence referents. The first part of the article addressed the conceptualization and measurement of farmers' views of information sources. After a discussion of their methodological problems and solutions, the authors presented 4 clusters of multiple-item scales, the product of a factor analysis, which measure farmer views on the *utility, affectivity, practicality,* and *accessibility* of information sources. These conceptual tools were then applied in the field through interviews with 288 farmers in a southern Missouri Ozark community. Scores for innovator and influence referents for each of the cluster of variables were obtained. The results showed that "influence referents were perceived as significantly more accessible, of higher practicality, and held with more affectivity than innovator referents" (p. 207). These results are consistent with the expectation that farmers are more likely to rely more on influential people than on early innovators. However, both sources of information obtained high ratings for all scales, and innovator referents actually received slightly higher ratings for being more "up-to-date" and "scientific." Lionberger and Francis argued that the 2 sources of information played different roles in the adoption process: innovators create "awareness of new ideas and practices about farming and . . . [provide] information about them" (p. 209), whereas others may be more important in influencing the actual decision to adopt a new practice.

Mass Media and Other Information Influences on Farm Practice Adoption

Interest in the communication and information aspects of adoption behavior was also reflected at the outset of diffusion-adoption research. In one of the earliest papers on this topic, Wilkening (1950) found major differences in the sources of information on improved farm practices reported by farmers of different socioeconomic levels and in the sources reported for different types of practices. Farmers of high socioeconomic levels relied most heavily on agricultural agencies, while lower socioeconomic status farmers relied most on other farmers and on agribusiness dealers as their main sources of information. Wilkening reported that for practices, such as those relating to corn growing, associated with established farm operations, other farmers or dealers were the main information sources. However, for practices such as permanent pastures or contouring, which represented more recent innovations, the agricultural agencies and mass media were the more important information sources. Copp et al. (1958) expanded upon Wilkening's early research on the differential use of information sources in the adoption process. They found in particular that farmers for whom peer sources were most important in the early stage of adoption were less likely to move through the stages of the adoption process than were farmers citing other information sources. Coughenour (1960) found that socioeconomic status, education, and social participation are positively related to adoption largely because of their providing "situational support leading to contact with agricultural agencies" (p. 296).

Mason's (1964) study of the use of information sources in the adoption process was among the more comprehensive in delineating the impact of various types of information sources in the different stages of adoption. Mason argued that the process of adopting new farm practices occurs in several stages. This study compared the use of four types of information sources (mass media, authoritative, peer, and commercial) in the different stages of the adoption process. The results indicated that all sources of information were used to acquire technical information before adoption and to obtain supporting information for the practice after adoption. The use of authoritative sources increased rapidly as the farmer moved through the different stages of the adoption process. The use of mass media was consistently lower than for the other three sources. The results did not completely concur with other studies of the importance of mass media at different stages, but were consistent with previous observations of the differential use of the other three sources of information. Finally, Mason attempted to place his results in a theoretical model of information flow and decision making. His attempt, however, was only partly successful, for his data do little other than confirm that there are two types of information-seeking behavior: seeking information about how to implement a practice, and seeking to confirm and support the implementation after the fact.

The Conceptualization of Farm Practice Adoption

The major elements of the classical diffusion paradigm as set forth at the beginning of this chapter were developed during the early stages of adoption research. Nonetheless, a substantial amount of inquiry into diffusion-adoption processes came to be devoted to scrutinizing and revising concepts in the paradigm. Beal et al. (1957), for example, conducted a study to determine the validity of the notion of stages in the adoption process. They noted that Wilkening, in his early work in North Carolina and Wisconsin, had posited that diffusion is a process, rather than a single-unit act. Wilkening had identified four stages of the diffusion process, and his early work was followed by a report of the Subcommittee on the Diffusion and Adoption of New Farm Practices (1952) that had suggested a five-stage model. Beal et al. examined the five-stage model with data from Iowa farmers and determined, via retrospective questions about the times at which farmers became aware of, tried, and adopted new practices, that the five-stage model was valid. In particular, these data indicated clearly that adoption was not a single-unit act, since there was an average reported time lag of 1.54 years between awareness and adoption.

We noted earlier the results of a study by Perry et al. (1967) indicating that the adoption curves (heretofore presumed to be normally distributed, bell-shaped, and upon which classifications of farmers as innovators, early adopters, and so on were based) were not always observed for all innovations. Perry et al. (1967) suggested, in fact, that adoption rates of 70 percent or more within 3 years of introduction of a practice were becoming common. They concluded that "the findings of 10 to 30 years ago may no longer be generally true in an agricultural economy so highly conditioned to technological innovations" (p. 222). Bohlen (1967) likewise indicated that the 5-stage model of the adoption process may no longer be universally applicable. Several other researchers (e.g., Klonglan and Coward, 1970; Klonglan et al., 1971; Powell and Roseman, 1972) have since examined various components of the adoption process and have suggested conceptual modifications that are more consistent with previously published data.

Campbell (1966) took this reconceptualization of the adoption process one step further in his theoretical analysis of the social psychology of individual decision making. He began by recognizing that rural sociologists have long accepted the notion that adoption of new farm practices occurs in a series of stages, rather than in one immediate event. He noted, however, that even this model fails to capture the complexity and diversity of adoption decisions. Campbell criticized the model of individual adoption as currently used and suggested a different model organized around two dichotomies: problem vs. innovation-orientation, and rational vs. nonrational orientation. By combining the two dichotomies, four possible adoption types can be recognized (rational problem solving, rational-innovative, nonrational problem solving, and nonrational-innovative). Campbell noted that there are aspects of each of these ideal-types in most decisions we make. Further, there are elements of dissonance and dissonance-resolution involved in all four ideal-types, which would lead individuals to bias their rationalizations for decisions in favor of rationality. By doing so, individuals try to appear more rational than they actually are. Campbell argued that this has serious implications for research done after the decision, because the dissonance accompanying the decision no longer exists. The application of this new paradigm was seen to allow for a more sophisticated understanding of the adoption process and, if used during the early stages of adoption, could avoid some of the types of bias described above.

Shortly after the publication of Campbell's (1966) paper there began to appear a number of further critiques of the diffusion-adoption research tradition. These early criticisms were made by persons working within the diffusion-adoption paradigm, although, as we see shortly, there were to be a growing number of challenges to diffusion-adoption research from persons arguing for radically different paradigms for understanding technological change or the organization of agriculture.

Among the more trenchant critiques of the diffusion-adoption tradition was that by Valkonen (1970). Valkonen offered three major criticisms of prevailing research in adoption and outlined a new model that might avoid some of these limitations. Valkonen argued that, in general, diffusion studies pay too much attention to correlational relations and not enough to causal or theoretical interpretations. Second, the variables that are used tend to be too closely related conceptually or causally, rendering them relatively useless in developing statistical models. Third, Valkonen suggested that most diffusion research tends to isolate one or two segments of the social process of innovation; this makes "it difficult to combine the results of diffusion research with theories of social change" (p. 177). Valkonen concluded by proposing a model based on three subprocesses of adoption that he felt should help to clarify causal and theoretical relationships.

Methodological Aspects of Adoption Research

Many of the conceptually related inquiries into the diffusion-adoption model discussed above were stimulated by methodological problems in research, or involved quantitative methodologies to explore alternative theoretical constructs. There have, however, also been a number of studies that have examined methodological aspects of adoption research from the vantage points of index construction and the use of statistical procedures.

The bulk of attention to the methodology of adoption research has been focused on the suitability of adoption scales or indexes (though there has been considerable attention paid to statistical methodology; see, for example, Boyd, 1980). Rogers and Rogers (1961), for example, evaluated 28 different field studies that attempted to measure innovativeness (with adoption of farm practices scales) in terms of the validity, reliability, internal consistency, and unidimensionality of these adoption indexes. They found that these scales were reasonably valid, reliable, and internally consistent. The data indicated, however, that not all scales were unidimensional.

Coughenour (1965) utilized a quite different approach to evaluating the reliability of survey techniques for measuring adoption. Coughenour drew on a survey of Ohio farmers to ascertain dates of adoption for the use of the herbicide 2,4-D, the rat poisons Decon and Warfarin, Clintland oats, and soil tests. The same survey was repeated again in 1959 and 1962. The combination of surveys provided an opportunity to assess the reliability of the survey technique for identifying the dates of adoption of these practices. Estimates for dates of adoption for the herbicide and the rat poisons were reasonably consistent in all the surveys, but conflicting and misleading results were found for the oats and the soil samples. Coughenour concluded that survey instruments should be used only cautiously when ascertaining dates of adoption or constructing rank-order differences in average rates of adoption. Best results appeared to be obtained when the farm practice in question is less ambiguous (i.e., such as a single major purchase) and when the adoption time is within the past 10 years.

In a subsequent paper Presser (1969) attempted to evaluate different methods for measuring innovativeness. After a discussion of the concepts of innovation, innovator, and innovativeness, Presser found that most widely used adoption scales fail to measure innovativeness (or tendency to innovate). This is because they do not give weighted credit for adoption of a new practice at an earlier date. Using data from 495 Wisconsin farmers, several hypotheses were tested concerning methodological questions useful for the construction of a measure of innovativeness. It was found that the use of all adoption behavior in a scale, even when weighted, did not portray innovativeness. When restricted to the first 16 percent of adopters, the measure was improved somewhat, but a weighted score that differentially scales adoption according to "firstness" would provide the best measure of identifying farmers who are most innovative.

Critical Assessments of the Diffusion-Adoption Paradigm

As noted in more detail in Chapter 4, the early and mid-1970s witnessed several trends external and internal to rural sociology that stimulated a renewal of attention to the social impacts of technological change. Research into the social impacts of technological change had largely languished since the discontinuation of studies that were conducted on mechanization in southern agriculture from the 1930s through the 1950s (see, for example, Anderson, 1954; Bertrand, 1948, 1952; Pedersen, 1952, 1954). Among the concomitants of this increased attention to the consequences of technological change in the 1970s were concerns that: (1) the established rural sociological perspective for studying technological change, the diffusion-adoption paradigm, had largely taken a promotional posture toward technological change and had failed to scrutinize whether particular forms of new technology were socially beneficial, and (2) the diffusion-adoption paradigm had focused primarily on commercial innovations and had largely ignored conservation or environmental innovations.

Several studies in the late 1970s came to the conclusion that the classical diffusion-adoption paradigm might be limited in assessing the adoption of environmental innovations. Pampel and van Es (1977) noted that there were major disparities in the correlates of commercial innovations on one hand, and environmental-conservation innovations on the other. They concluded that "environmental innovativeness is not predicted well by demographic variables commonly used in adoption research" (p. 57). Comparable observations were made in a succeeding study by Taylor and Miller (1978).

Subsequent commentary on the applicability of the diffusion-adoption model has proceeded in two major directions. In the first, represented most clearly by Goss (1979a), it has been contended that a very crucial aspect of technological change in agriculture is its socioeconomic consequences. Since the diffusion-adoption model concerns itself largely with the processes by which the technology is diffused—and, in some versions, is biased toward promoting technological change—the model has very limited applicability to the major research questions on technological change that should be of concern to rural sociologists. Goss (1979a) thus questioned whether the diffusion model can advance rural sociological knowledge on agriculture.

The second direction of criticism of the classical diffusion-adoption model has been in terms of what some see as weaknesses and biases with regard to public policy problems such as soil conservation. Van Es (1983), for example, following on his earlier work with Pampel, has argued that "the transformation of agriculture has removed or modified most of the factors that a generation ago were thought to determine adoption and thus the diffusion process" (p. 77). Van Es argued that "under these circumstances the diffusion model is . . . largely irrelevant to determining farmer behavior" (p. 77). His conclusions to this effect were illustrated in terms of the relevance of adoption models to resource conservation in agriculture. Van Es indicated that for a variety of reasons conservation technologies tend to be very different from the commercial practices and technologies that were the subject of previous adoption research. Van Es argued, in particular, that using the adoption model to explore conservation practices involves a key bias—that the research will support a voluntarist (nonregulatory) approach to resource conservation when, in fact, this approach may not be very efficacious (see also Chapter 4). He concluded that "the [adoption] research thus threatens to find itself in the unenviable position of legitimizing a politically preferred approach to resource protection not because the research strongly supports the efficacy of the policy, but because it is the only policy approach about which the research has anything to say."

Writing in the same issue of *The Rural Sociologist* in which van Es' paper appeared, Nowak (1983a) defended the adoption approach as applied to soil and water conservation practices. Nowak argued that there have been many misconceptions about the diffusion-adoption approach and that it can be a useful basis for developing a comprehensive understanding of the overall agricultural decision-making process. In particular, Nowak strongly defended the voluntary approach to diffusing soil and water conservation technologies and argued that it deserves greater study. Nowak presented a revision of the classical diffusion model in a way that he felt lent itself better to researching conservation technologies. The model differs from the classical model in that it assigns relatively little importance to the individual social-psychological characteristics of the farmer and devotes more attention to an understanding of the structural constraints within which farmers must operate. In a further elaboration, Nowak (1987) argued that both economic factors and the fit of the particular technology to the ecological situation of the farm are, in addition to diffusion processes, important in the adoption of conservation practices. In another article Nowak (1983b) outlined four strategies for increasing the adoption of conservation technologies: conservation education, assisting in conservation efforts, increasing the social utility of conservation, and promoting local adaptation of conservation technologies (see also Nowak, 1984). Nowak also suggested how diffusion-adoption-type research can answer important questions about the contribution of each strategy to an overall strategy for soil conservation. Audriac and Beaulieu (1986) have taken Nowak's arguments one step further, especially in addressing the concerns raised by Goss (1979a) and others, by setting forth an adoption-diffusion perspective that incorporates the social consequences of technological change when analyzing the adoption of microcomputers by farmers.

THE VALUE ORIENTATIONS OF FARMERS

After research bearing on the diffusion-adoption of innovations, the second most important area of inquiry on agriculture during the 1950s, 1960s, and early 1970s pertained to the value orientations of farmers. It should be noted, nonetheless, that this area of research had major connections with that on the adoption of innovations. Much of this research was carried out by diffusion-adoption researchers, such as Fliegel, in connection with their research programs on the diffusion of innovations. Many of the themes of research on farmers' value orientations were derived from the diffusion-adoption and related paradigms deriving from domestically applied versions of modernization theory (see Harrison, 1988, for a discussion of the connections between diffusion and modernization theories in the 1950s and 1960s). Among the most common dependent variables were indicators of entrepreneurial orientations and achievement-oriented attitudes. Other nonadoption research involved the measurement and prediction of farmers' occupational and mobility aspirations, a topic which is treated more fully in the following section on the educational and occupational attainments of farm-reared persons. Nonetheless, the distinguishing feature of this research on the value orientations of farmers was that the dependent variables were indexes of value orientations rather than of the adoption of farm practices.

Much like the diffusion-adoption perspective, the principal orienting perspectives in research on farmers' value orientations were variants of modernization theory positing the centrality of traditional-modern orientations in the economic development process. Previous research on the adoption of innovations had provided very strong evidence that the principal correlates of farmers' adoption behaviors were attitudinal variables that reflected variation across the continuum from traditional to change-oriented, entrepreneurial, "progressive," and achievement-oriented values. Given the centrality of these traditional-modern attitudinal complexes to farmer behavior and performance, there came to be expanded efforts to understand the roots of variations in value-orientations.

Among the initial studies in this tradition was the research of Dean et al. (1958), which conceptualized a "rationality" variable as an intervening social psychological variable between socioeconomic characteristics of farmers and the adoption of recommended farm practices. Their North Carolina survey data supported this model. Variants of the Dean et al. model would shortly become very influential in subsequent research.

It is curious to note, however, that an early study by Fliegel (1959) indicated that rural sociologists might be oversimplifying their conceptualization and measurement of the aspirations of farmers. Fliegel found that small, low-income farmers tended to orient their aspirations toward nonfarm sources of family income rather than toward their farm enterprises. Therefore, Fliegel suggested that public programs to assist low-income farmers should be focused on nonfarm rather than farm goal orientations. Moreover, Fliegel found little relationship between farmers' incomes and their economic aspirations; the major association noted was that farmers with the highest level of aspirations tended most to reject farming as a preferred occupation. In a subsequent paper Fliegel (1960) did find that low-income farmers tended to be older and less well educated than farmers with higher incomes and that low-income farmers lacked a commercial orientation toward agriculture. Fliegel found that these low-income, noncommercially oriented farmers had a low motivation to change their farm operations. He therefore suggested that promotion of subsistence farming for low-income farm households may be the most viable strategy for those low-income farmers who wish to remain in agriculture.

Morrison's (1964) study was the first to develop a rigorous conception of achievement motivations as applied to farmers. The previous literature on achievement and related constructs had been developed on a projective basis among youth and was shown to be associated with academic and later indicators of behavioral achievement. Such constructs, however, had not been applied to farmers. Morrison's efforts to adapt such indexes to adult farmers was only moderately successful, mainly because of measurement problems. His results, however, were largely consistent with the expectation that achievement orientations were positively related to indicators of behavioral achievement.

In a related study exploring the role of social and psychological factors differentiating successful and unsuccessful farmers, Taylor (1962) found that unsuccessful farmers had a greater desire to migrate, had less schooling and special training, and were less concerned with status and prestige than were successful farmers. Taylor nonetheless found that these differences were quite modest. Barban et al. (1970) later investigated Reisman's theory of social character as applied to farmers. Contrary to expectations, they found that the distribution of the two most common character types (inner- and other-directed) had distributions among farmers that paralleled those of the urban population. They found that the inner-directed type of farmer was most prone to adopt new innovations, though there was no association between the character types and being influential to other farmers in their adoption decisions.

Among all the studies in the tradition of explaining the origins of farmers' value orientations, the largest differences revealed were those between the goal orientations of farmers and farm workers found by Rushing (1970). Rushing found that the goal orientations of farm workers tended toward basic physical and economic survival, whereas farmers were more "concerned with economic enhancement and continued monetary success, with peace, and quality of government" (p. 391). Only a minority of farm workers expressed interest in home ownership, self-employment, or occupational advancement, which have usually been taken to be components of economic-monetary-materialistic goals of the middle class and which were generally considered important by farmers.

While Rushing (1970) found farmers to be more oriented toward achievement-related, middle-class goals than farm workers, a number of studies have found that urban persons with farm backgrounds have scored lower on "individual modernity" scales than urban-reared persons (see, for example, Grasmick and Grasmick, 1978). As we see in the next section, farm-nonfarm differences in educational and occupational aspirations have been a major theme in research on mobility and behavioral achievement among farm youth and other farm personnel.

EDUCATIONAL AND OCCUPATIONAL ASPIRATIONS AND ACHIEVEMENTS AMONG FARM-REARED PEOPLE

As social psychological perspectives came to be more and more dominant in rural sociology in the 1950s and as it became more apparent that large numbers of farmers were leaving agriculture, much of the attention to agriculture among rural sociologists turned to the impact of farm origins on educational and occupational attainments in the nonfarm sectors of society. This research thrust was made possible by several simultaneous aspects of sociological research. First, it had been recognized for several decades that persons reared on farms tended to have lower occupational attainments than persons reared elsewhere (see, for example, Sorokin, 1927); thus there was a clear problematic for shaping research programs. Second, the 1940s and 1950s had witnessed major advances in theory and research in social psychology. Third, there had been rapid expansion in the statistical tools and computational routines needed for analysis of large-scale data-sets such as those that were typical in occupational attainment and mobility research.

Research on the educational and occupational aspirations and achievements of farm-reared people would lead to a relatively large literature by the end of the 1960s. It should be noted, however, that a small handful of researchers accounted for the bulk of the published research—in particular, A. O. Haller and M. A. Straus. Haller initiated a long-standing research program in the mid-1950s in which he began to explore why farm-reared people had low levels of occupational achievement. Haller (1958), for example, examined the hypothesis of S. M. Lipset (1955) that the limited occupational and educational alternatives available in rural areas lead to low educational and occupational aspirations and thus to low levels of occupational achievement. Haller found that Lipset's hypothesis was partially correct in that levels of educational and occupational aspiration have an impact on levels of occupational achievement. He found, however, that farm-nonfarm differences in levels of educational aspiration were not large enough to explain much of the overall variation in levels of occupation achievement. In particular, while it had been known for some time that rural youth intending to farm had low levels of educational aspiration, farm-nonfarm variations in this regard explain little variation in levels of occupational aspiration.

Haller (1960) explored the role of planning to farm on educational and occupation aspirations in a later study. He found that whereas planning to farm was common among farm youth and planning to farm led boys not to aspire to high levels of education (see also Burchinal, 1961; Cowhig, 1962; Haller, 1957), this "normal self-conception" may be abandoned by boys who are unusually self-reliant or inquisitive. Haller argued that the normal self-conception of planning to farm causes farm youth to make themselves aware of only a limited range of information on the availability of alternative careers. He found tentative evidence supporting the hypothesis. Haller concluded by arguing that since only a small fraction of rural youth who want to farm will be able to do so, there should be public programs to modify the conceptions of farm boys that they will be able to farm. The result of such programs was expected to be that farm boys would seek out more information on nonfarm careers and would be better prepared to enter the nonfarm job market. Further elaboration of these arguments has been reported by Haller and Wolff (1962) and Haller and Sewell (1967). Haller and Sewell (1967) and Portes et al. (1968) have also explored the social-psychological antecedents of planning to farm. In both studies they found that planning to farm was not heavily shaped by achievement-related variables and that youth planning to farm had characteristics similar to those of persons intending to enter low-status, nonfarm jobs such as blue-collar or lower white-collar occupations. Haller and Sewell (1967) did, however, find that the more "significant others" expect a farm youth to be a high achiever, the less likely he is to choose a farm, blue-collar, or lower white-collar occupation.

Straus, like Haller, began an extended research program on the educational and occupational aspirations of farm youth, particularly with regard to the intention to farm. In an early study Straus (1956) reported that farmers' sons choosing farm and nonfarm occupations differed little in terms of family structure, religious participation, proximity to urban centers, or physical or intellectual ability. He did, however, find that sons choosing to farm tended to come from high-income, owner-operated farming households that were best able to assist the sons in starting farming. Sons planning to farm tended to come from families with traditional rural values. They were overwhelmingly influenced in their occupational socialization by direct experience and primary group contacts, as opposed to secondary sources and contacts influencing sons to choose nonfarm occupations.

Straus extended this research in several subsequent studies. He (Straus, 1962) reported that the values of farm families played a major role in the socialization of youth. Farm families were found to place the greatest emphasis on work role learning (by comparison with town and nonfarm-fringe boys), while nonfarm boys' socialization involved more emphasis on individual responsibility. In a survey of 11th and 12th grade boys, Straus (1964) attempted to discern the social and psychological characteristics of farm-reared boys with different occupational aspirations. Those choosing a career in farming were compared to those choosing blue-collar and white-collar occupations. Straus tested the broader hypothesis of congruence among farm boys' occupational aspirations, backgrounds, and the social and psychological characteristics of the occupations they wish to enter.

Straus' findings revealed several characteristics that seemed to be associated with the different occupational aspirations, leading him to six major conclusions. Initially, the socioeconomic position of the family was a powerful determinant of the resources available to help a son start farming. A second conclusion was that the internal structure of the family was important. Boys who chose to go into farming had fewer siblings, better relationships with their parents, and came from more stable homes. Straus theorized that "this integration with the family provides the social structural setting within which it is psychologically possible for the son to accept the dependent relationship inherent in taking advantage of family economic resources to become established in farming" (pp. 423–24). The third conclusion was that the work, values, work role learning, and fiscal responsibility experiences differed between the two groups of boys. Farm-choice boys worked more for their parents, but were given less experience in managing their financial resources. Fourth, the educational experiences and educational goals of the boys differed according to career aspiration. Blue-collar-choice boys performed worst in school, closely followed by farm-choice boys, with white-collar-choice males performing the best and having the highest educational goals. Straus argued that "this distribution of intelligence and grades is roughly in proportion to the intellectual demands of the three groups of occupations and may, therefore, be said to represent an approximation of societal needs" (p. 42). Fifth, these groups differed in personality characteristics. Farm-choice boys depended on parents, were shy, displayed a lack of self-sufficiency, and valued stability more than change. Straus noted that most boys showed characteristics that were "remarkably consistent with the demands and lifestyles of their ultimate social class position" (p. 425). The final conclusion was that the farm-choice boys may have made their occupational decisions prematurely and may be unprepared for competition in the nonfarm job market should they fail to find employment in farming. This, according to Straus, does not disprove his broader hypothesis, but rather reveals a dysfunctional aspect of society.

In a further study Straus and Sudia (1965) examined the impacts of farm, working-class, and middle-class origins on entrepreneurial orientations. Straus and Sudia found that farm boys had lower levels of entrepreneurial orientation than either working-class or middle-class boys. Straus and Sudia stress that these results challenge the classical image of the small, independent farmer as the bulwark of individualistic entrepreneurialism. They suggested that the results indicated a dysfunctional element in the socialization of farm (and working class) boys, since their lack of an entrepreneurial orientation would adversely affect their ability to compete in the job market.

Slocum (1967), however, reported research results from a statewide study of rural high school students in Washington that were substantially at variance with those of Haller, Straus, and their associates. Slocum reported data showing that farm boys were *more* likely than nonfarm boys to expect to attend college and receive a degree. Similar results obtained for farm and nonfarm girls. Slocum argued that "the message concerning the need to leave farming has been heard and understood by the large majority of Washington farm boys and girls who are high school students [and that] those who plan to farm are evidently aware of the need for scientific knowledge as the basis for scientific farming" (p. 277).

While Slocum's paper suggested that there might be a changing milieu of structural and socialization influences on the aspirations of farm youth and their intentions to farm, there has long been evidence that few farm youth planning to farm are ultimately able to do so. Kuvlesky and Bealer (1967) utilized longitudinal data from 1,001 young males surveyed in 1942 when in high school and again in 1952. Only 21 percent of those planning to become farmers were actually farming in 1952. Lyson (1982) reported similar results from a longitudinal data-set collected about two decades later. But whereas there is evidence that farm youths' intentions to farm are a poor predictor of their later ability to enter farming, Slocum's (1967) paper did herald what has now been recognized to be a dramatic transformation of the educational structure of farm personnel. Lyson (1979) has noted a rapid increase in the mean years of education among U.S. farmers and has suggested that many aspiring farmers are now more aware of technological sophistication and capital requirements of modern agriculture and thus are viewing college as a necessary prerequisite to successful farming (see also Lyson, 1984). Recent studies of the expectation to farm, interestingly enough, have been conducted among *agricultural college or university* students. Lyson (1979) and Molnar and Dunkelberger (1981) have found that college students intending to farm are those from farm backgrounds, from actively farming and full-time farming households, and from households from which the youth are expected to be able to inherit a farm. Lancelle and Rodefeld (1980) likewise found that the social origins of youth—in particular, whether the parents owned a farm or had other resources available to assist the youth in entering agriculture—were a major factor in the attainment of ownership of large farms in Wisconsin.

CONCLUSION

By the end of its first decade diffusion-adoption research had come of age and had achieved the status of being a full-blown, middle-range theory, as noted by Young (1959). But the very year that Young made this pronouncement, an angry young sociologist at Columbia University, C. Wright Mills, published *The Sociological Imagination* (1959), a book that challenged the very notion of middle-range theorizing and associated behaviorist research. Mills criticized Parsonian "grand theory" and claimed that Merton's notion of middle-range theory had given license to a mindless "abstracted empiricism" that had stifled the sociological imagination. Mills' bombshell, though very controversial and widely discussed in the larger discipline of sociology, received relatively little attention in the rural sociological community until a decade after it was published. Diffusion-adoption work and its parallel traditions in farmers' value orientations and educational and occupational aspirations continued to be vibrant areas of inquiry well over a decade after publication of *The Sociological Imagination*. Ultimately, however, in the early and mid-1970s, these traditions were to be scrutinized by a new generation of rural sociologists influenced by the critiques of Mills (1959), Gouldner (1970), and others. This reevaluation of the dominant perspective of 1950s and 1960s rural sociology would ultimately lead to a "new rural sociology," which is the subject of the next three chapters.

The New Sociology of Agriculture, I: The Political Economy and Social Structure of Farms, Farm Households, and Farm Labor

INTRODUCTION

During the 1950s and 1960s rural sociology as a whole, and especially rural sociological analyses of agriculture, closely reflected the character of the larger sociological discipline. A distinctive division of labor between sociological theory and empirical research had emerged, with the theoretical enterprise being dominated by Parsonian functionalism and empirical research by quantitative analysis of survey data. Empirical researchers did seek guidance from the theory community, but they were by and large limited in doing so because the methodological innovations of Paul Lazarsfeld and others were primarily suited to micro units of analysis that were inappropriate for directly testing the macrosociological and macrocultural formulations of Parsons and others. To the extent that there was a linkage between structural-functionalism and quantitative research, it was largely carved out by Robert K. Merton (1957) through his notion of "theories of the middle range" and his exemplary collaboration with Paul Lazarsfeld at Columbia University in the sociology of communication, deviance, interpersonal influence, and so on.

Much the same could be said of rural sociology during the 1950s and 1960s (Gilbert, 1982; Hooks, 1986). The theoretical and empirical research enterprises in rural sociology were largely insulated from each other, save for middle-range theories such as diffusion-adoption of innovations and Merton- and Lazarsfeld-inspired conceptualizations of the processes of interpersonal influence. "General theory" in rural sociology (e.g., Loomis and Beegle, 1957) was rarely drawn upon as a direct source of hypotheses to be tested through empirical research, since the macrosociocultural character of these theories rarely lent itself to the elaboration of hypotheses suitable for testing with the new methodological tools being embraced within sociological and rural sociological circles.

The extent to which there was a disjuncture between theory and research in 1950s and 1960s sociology and rural sociology is, of course, a matter of opinion. That many sociologists did (and still would) disagree with such an assessment can be gauged by the sharp reaction to C. Wright Mills' publication of *The Sociological Imagination* (1959). Nonetheless, it is generally agreed that there came to be a crisis of sorts in American sociology coincident with —and, in many respects, as a result of—the general social ferment of the late 1960s (the Vietnam War, the Civil Rights Movement, and so on). This social ferment caused many sociologists to question whether prevailing social theory and research had the effect of reinforcing the status quo of racism, militarism, and inequality. Others came to be influenced by theoretical innovations in Europe that were nonfunctionalist, if not antifunctionalist (e.g., by J. Rex and F. Parkin). These new influences, combined with a rediscovery and reanalysis of the work of many sociologists (such as by R. Dahrendorf, R. Bendix, H. H. Gerth, A. Gouldner, and D. Wrong, in addition to Mills) who had opposed the orthodoxies of functionalism and behaviorism, led to an intellectual ferment that, in a sense, continues today. The late 1960s milieu of challenge to prevailing post-World War II sociological theories and methods culminated in the publication of Gouldner's (1970) *The Coming Crisis of Western Sociology*.

Rural sociology, however, was not to experience this intellectual ferment until the mid-1970s, and its origins were to be of a somewhat different character than those that shaped sociology at large. Perhaps the most immediate influence on the theoretical and research traditions in rural sociology was the disillusion with prevailing international development efforts that began in the early 1970s. Also, several rural sociologists deeply engaged in international development research (e.g., Havens and Flinn, 1975) became acquainted with theoretical perspectives prevalent in Latin America and other Third World countries that represented critical challenges to Western development orthodoxy (e.g., Frank, 1967). Havens' (1972) paper on development theory in *Sociologia Ruralis* was, to the best of our knowledge, the first publication by a North American rural sociologist to confront directly the theoretical and methodological orthodoxies of then-contemporary rural sociology.

Many of the concerns of internationally oriented rural sociologists came to be seen as directly parallel to agriculturally related phenomena in the United States. Critics of the "green revolution," for example, were concerned that these technologies were biased against small-holder peasants, landless agricultural laborers, and the rural poor and were ecologically destructive (Griffin, 1974; see also Lipton with Longhurst, 1985, and Pearse, 1980, for summaries of this literature). So, too, U.S. rural sociologists (e.g., Rodefeld et al., 1978) came to be concerned whether technological change in agriculture was having the effect of marginalizing family farmers and farm workers here at home. Others began to cast a critical eye on the structure of agricultural research and the role of rural sociology in the development and diffusion of new agricultural technologies (Busch, 1978; Goss, 1979a). Still others came to be concerned about the ecological impacts of modern agriculture and argued that researchers must consider ecological variables if they want to understand the social organization of and technological change in agriculture (e.g., Stockdale, 1977).

Other impetuses to the emerging intellectual ferment in rural sociology included the concerns raised by late-1960s social movements (especially the environmental, civil rights, and other social justice movements) and the writings of several prominent non-sociologists whose work came to set the agenda for rural social science. Perhaps the single most influential person in this regard was Jim Hightower (1973), who raised provocative questions about agricultural research and the land-grant universities, the effects of agricultural technology on American farmers, the status of the family farm, the rising prominence of large corporate farms, the ecological consequences of agriculture, and so on (Hooks, 1986).

While Havens and his international development colleagues began to develop alternative theoretical and methodological formulations for international rural sociology, William Heffernan (1972) and Richard Rodefeld (1974) were the first to do so for domestic rural sociology and the sociology of U.S. agriculture. In a sense, Rodefeld's work drew on theoretical postures that had been prevalent in rural sociology for decades (e.g., his conceptualization of farm structural change in terms of the increasing differentiation among capital, land, labor, and management). But while this theoretical posture was seemingly quite conventional, Rodefeld's (1974) conclusions were quite at variance with received notions of the benign character of technological and farm structural change. Rodefeld argued that the traditional family farm was undergoing a process of disintegration and was being replaced by corporate-industrial and larger-than-family farms. Rodefeld was extremely influential in rediscovering Goldschmidt's (1947) *As You Sow* and in suggesting that the demise of family farming was adversely affecting rural communities. Many of these themes appeared contemporaneously in the work of Heffernan (1972; see also Heffernan and Lasley, 1978), but Rodefeld's (1978, 1980) integration of these themes into monograph-length works enabled his formulations to be highly visible inside and outside of rural sociology.

It is important to recognize that the new sociology of agriculture as it emerged during the mid- to late 1970s was theoretically diverse. For example, Rodefeld and Heffernan had their impact by revising fairly traditional theories (e.g., of Stinchcombe, 1961) and demonstrating that seemingly "natural" trends toward structural differentiation in agriculture had adverse implications for family farmers and rural communities. Later there came to be developed a theoretical tradition in the sociology of agriculture that drew heavily on Marxist political economy and, in particular, on the classical treatments of agricultural political economy by Marx, Kautsky, and Lenin. During the same year the Rodefeld et al. volume was published, a set of articles appeared by Mann and Dickinson (1978), Friedmann (1978a, 1978b), and Newby (1978) that opened up whole new vistas in the sociological analysis of agriculture through the application of Marxist theory. This trend was consolidated with the appearance of an anthology edited by Buttel and Newby (1980), the publication of a book by Friedland et al. (1981), and an anthology by Havens et al. (1986). More recently, the political economy of agriculture has taken a neo-Weberian direction, which was stimulated by Newby (1977, 1983b), Newby et al. (1978), and Mooney (1983, 1985, 1986a). Finally, the post-1980 new sociology of agriculture has been influenced by an ecological posture that was originally codified by Dunlap and Martin (1983) and that is discussed in Chapter 4.

The new sociology of agriculture has been quite diverse theoretically, but there are several common characteristics of this reorientation of rural sociological research. First, the new sociology of agriculture has been much more ambitious theoretically than the research traditions that prevailed prior to the early 1970s, attempting to combine broad, macrosocial theorizing with the elaboration of falsifiable theoretical formulations and testable hypotheses. Second, the new sociology of agriculture has a greater representation of historical and qualitative research methods than was typical in rural sociological research on agriculture during the 1960s. Finally, the glue that has tied these diverse theoretical approaches together over the past decades has been that these perspectives have tended to be critical, albeit in diverse ways, of prevailing agricultural institutions.

But just as social psychological-behaviorist perspectives that predominated in the 1950s and 1960s did not wholly supplant the community study perspective on agriculture, so, too, the new sociology of agriculture has by no means displaced social psychological—in particular, diffusion-adoption—research. Indeed, there have been major revisions of the diffusion-adoption perspective that have enabled it to remain viable and to contribute to the understanding of agriculture. Nonetheless, the neo-Marxist, neo-Weberian, and ecological theories have been most influential in shaping the issues of concern to sociologists of agriculture for more than 10 years.

POLITICAL ECONOMY AND THE NEW SOCIOLOGY OF AGRICULTURE

The most distinctive aspect of the new sociology of agriculture in the United States has been a strong representation of and legitimacy accorded to Marxist and neo-Marxist perspectives. This has been unprecedented in U.S. rural sociology (despite the fact that Galeski, 1972, and others had developed comprehensive neo-Marxist treatments of Western agriculture well before the rise of the "new sociology of agriculture" in North America). Perhaps Steeves' (1972) article in *Rural Sociology* was the first instance in which RSS' official journal published a paper based largely on Marxist theory. It was not, however, until the late 1970s that there began to be elaborated systematic Marxist explanations of the dynamics of American agriculture by U.S. scholars.

As noted earlier, pioneering papers in this tradition were prepared by Mann and Dickinson (1978), Friedmann (1978a, 1978b), and Newby (1978). The Mann-Dickinson paper and one of the Friedmann papers (1978b) were published in the *Journal of Peasant Studies,* a British journal that had been the publishing vanguard of a revitalized political economy of peasant studies and agrarian history in Europe. The third major contribution to the development of a Marxist political economy of agriculture, that by Newby (1978), was somewhat idiosyncratic in the sense that Newby was and still is one of the most influential "neo-Weberians" in the United Kingdom. In Newby's 1978 paper he nonetheless made a strong case that the work of the German Social Democratic Party theorist of the turn of the century, Karl Kautsky, especially his book *Die Agrarfrage* (Banaji, 1980), had palpable relevance for understanding the structural dynamics of American agriculture. Newby has elaborated this argument in a further paper (1983b) in which he has suggested that a fruitful sociology of agriculture must be based upon an integration of the perspectives of Kautsky, Marx, and Weber.

What is, in retrospect, remarkable about this early phase in the development of a Marxist political economy of agriculture is that the earliest contributors to this line of scholarship had to stray very little from the classics in political economy. The Mann and Dickinson (1978) paper, for example, drew fairly directly from Marx's *Capital* and *Grundrisse* and secondarily on Lenin's work. Friedmann (1978a, 1978b) likewise drew on the work of Mandel, especially his *Marxist Economic Theory*. Newby (1978), as noted, focused largely on Kautsky's work. One should not ignore the creativity of their reformulations of these classical ideas, but there had nonetheless been a long classical tradition in the Marxist political economy of Western agriculture (see also Nakano, 1972; Djurfeldt, 1981; Thorner, 1982).

It is useful to begin this section by recalling why, aside from questions of scholarly acceptability, Marx had been almost totally ignored in analyses of changing agricultural structures by North American rural sociologists until the late 1970s. In addition to the unpopularity of Marxian ideas in the land-grant system, the key reason for the neglect of his work in the study of agriculture probably has been that Marx's stylized model of the polarization of economic enterprises (according to the laws of the centralization and concentration of capital and of proletarianization) into the antagonistic classes of capital and labor seemed to be negated by the very persistence of the family farm. Marxist sociologists of agriculture, however, came to question this dismissal of Marx in two different ways, which continue to represent the major axis of debate and orientations toward research within this emergent Marxist tradition (Buttel, 1982a). On one hand, Mann-Dickinson, Friedmann, and others have rooted their analyses in elaborations of Marx's own arguments about why one might predict that the particularities of agriculture as a production sector would cause agriculture to experience far slower and more uneven capitalist development than would other branches of industry. Newby (1978) and, more recently, de Janvry (1980), Goss et al. (1980), Friedland et al. (1981), and others have, on the other hand, raised arguments that there has been and will continue to be demonstrable capitalist development in Western agriculture, as typified by industrial agriculture in the U.S. Sunbelt and in large-scale farming in eastern England. Attempts at reconciling these two views have been made by Buttel (1980a, 1982a, 1983a), Davis (1980), Mooney (1983, 1985, 1986a), Pfeffer (1983), and Newby (1983b).

Barriers to Capitalist Transformation of Agriculture

Mann and Dickinson's (1978) pathbreaking article begins by identifying the weaknesses of prevailing subjectivist arguments (e.g., of Chayanov, 1966) as to why family farming has persisted in advanced capitalist societies (though the degree to which Chayanov eschewed structural analysis has often been exaggerated). They suggest, instead, that there are within Marx's work the major elements of a nonsubjectivist or nonvoluntarist explanation of why capitalist development, which they largely define in terms of proletarianization and the establishment of the capital-labor relation at the point of agricultural production, should proceed more slowly in agriculture than nonfarm industry. They emphasize how agriculture, because of its seasonality, tends to involve a disjuncture (or "nonidentity") between "production time" and "labor time," which creates a barrier to the routinization of the labor process around the calendar and makes agriculture less profitable than other branches of industry. Mann and Dickinson make the case that agriculture is a unique industry in that the seasonal cycle results in interruptions in the use of labor in the production process while the growing commodity is left to natural vagaries. Thus labor by those working in agriculture ("living labor") is both discontinuous and makes only a modest contribution to the overall production process. Since, in Marxist terms, only living labor creates surplus value, value is neither created nor transferred during these interruptions, thereby creating the nonidentity between production time and labor time. Hence, agriculture tends to be unprofitable and therefore relegated to family labor (or petty commodity) producers. Mann and Dickinson also suggest that agricultural commodities involve longer turnover times (production time plus circulation time [the time required to sell the commodity]) than do other industries, further reinforcing the relegation of farming to noncapitalist producers. Finally, Mann and Dickinson note that agriculture tends to involve producing perishable commodities, which increases the risk of production and therefore makes it even more unattractive to capitalists.

Mann and Dickinson (1978), however, do not claim that capitalist development is precluded in agriculture. They emphasize, in particular, that agricultural research may have the effect of reducing or eliminating the nonidentity of production time and labor time, reducing turnover time, and minimizing the perishability of agricultural commodities. They point out that there are instances of capitalist agriculture in commodities in which a combination of research advances and favorable agroclimatic circumstances have permitted the establishment of capitalist relations of production.

Friedmann's (1978a, 1978b, 1980, 1981) work, although it has taken much the same approach as Mann and Dickinson's, has proceeded along somewhat different explanatory lines. Friedmann has drawn on the Marxist theoretical tradition, but her explanation of the persistence of household forms of agricultural production (which she terms simple commodity production) rests largely on how family farms can meet the competition of—and often outcompete—capitalist farms in the hostile context of competitive markets in means of production and agricultural commodities. (Mann and Dickinson, by contrast, give more emphasis to why capitalists tend not to be interested in investing in agricultural production.)

Friedmann begins in much the same way as Mann and Dickinson, pointing toward the high degree of risk and the cyclical demand for labor in most agricultural commodity systems. She argues, however, that the crucial aspect of household forms of agricultural production is that simple commodity producers, unlike capitalists, do not have to earn a profit in order to reproduce their enterprises, i.e., remain in business. Simple commodity producers need only accomplish "simple reproduction." Capitalists, on the other hand, are forced by the logic of competition to strive to earn the average rate of profit, lest their firms become marginalized and eventually be forced out of business. Moreover, Friedmann has maintained that simple commodity producers in agriculture have a far greater flexibility than do capitalists in reducing their consumption to the subsistence level in order to survive severe market downturns. Capitalist farmers will typically tend to liquidate their assets if agricultural production is no longer able to generate the average rate of profit. Friedmann (1978a) tested this proposition empirically with historical data which show that the world-market downturn in the price of wheat in the late 1800s led to family producers in the United States and other white settler colonies being able to outcompete capitalist producers in England, Prussia, and the United States. Finally, Friedmann (1980, 1981) has noted, much as did Mann and Dickinson (1978), that there are "transformational tendencies" in simple commodity production, among them the subordination of independent producers by nonfarm capital. Thus, whereas Friedmann emphasizes the particularities of agriculture that lead to the persistence of simple commodity production in advanced capitalism, she recognizes that there are conditions that may lead to its transformation toward capitalist forms.

Along a similar line and influenced by the world systems school of political economy, McMichael (1987) analyzed the cotton plantation system of the Antebellum South, finding that this system was in transition during the period as its basis in mercantile capitalism became transformed into industrial capitalism with an accompanying need for specialized raw materials (cotton). The credit system that developed concomitantly transformed the southern plantation into a system of fully commercialized relations with all the preconditions of industrial agriculture, save for the presence of slave labor. The lack of "free" wage labor—that is, the reliance of plantations on slavery and later on sharecropping as means of labor recruitment and control—proved to be extremely significant, especially by inhibiting the technological transformation of production. McMichael concluded that understanding the transformation of the relations of agricultural production requires attending to the emerging forms of the capitalist economy, "including political relations, competitive market structures, and the organization of credit institutions" (1987:259). Related work by Gary Green (1984, 1987a) and Zey-Ferrell and McIntosh (1987) also suggests that the structural organization of the banking industry affects access to credit by farmers with farms of different sizes, and that this has implications for change in the structure and character of farms.

Simultaneously with the publication of the work of Mann-Dickinson and Friedmann, there emerged a very different neo-Marxist tradition, which stressed that U.S. and Western agriculture was rapidly going down the road of capitalist development and proletarianization—a theme to which Marx had given considerable emphasis in major portions of his work. De Janvry (1980), an agricultural economist by training and vocation but a scholar with strong ties to the sociological community, has been among the most outspoken on the issue of the demise of the family farm in advanced capitalism. Following Kautsky's *Die Agrarfrage* (Banaji, 1980) and Lenin (1974) and building on his own previous work on Latin American agriculture (de Janvry, 1981), de Janvry (1980) argued that the development of late capitalism has witnessed a startling rate of destruction of family farms and that the forces that now affect agricultural producers—rapid technological change, state subsidies of research and capital investment, and state commodity programs—make it quite implausible that the family farm can survive. De Janvry has argued that whereas agriculture tends to experience capitalist development less rapidly than other branches of industry, it is quite likely that the forces of proletarianization and state-subsidized capital accumulation in agriculture will continue to slowly but surely erode the position of the family farm and lead to its differentiation into antagonistic social classes. Thus, in de Janvry's view, independent producers are a transitional class in advanced capitalism; capitalist relations must inevitably and irreversibly penetrate family farming and lead to its demise, much as has occurred in other branches of industry in advanced capitalist societies (see de Janvry and LeVeen, 1986, for a more recent statement of this position). Newby (1978), largely writing on behalf of the neglected works of Kautsky, made many of the same points as did de Janvry.

It is useful to note in this regard, however, that Kautsky's *Die Agrarfrage* contained a series of sophisticated arguments about why there would be a *slow* pace of capitalist penetration of agriculture. Kautsky argued that capitalist penetration of agriculture, despite its slowness and unevenness, would ultimately proceed and would result in the decomposition of the German peasantry (Hussain and Tribe, 1981a, 1981b). Kautsky's work can be seen to at once recognize reasons for persistence of the peasantry, yet deny that the peasantry would survive over the long term in advanced capitalism.

The work of Friedland et al. (1981) has also been a highly visible contribution to the Kautsky and Lenin tradition, which emphasizes the primacy of analyzing emerging capital-labor relations in agriculture and the ultimate separation of independent producers from their means of production. Drawing on Marxist scholarship in the sociology of work and industry as well as on Kautsky and Lenin, Friedland et al. developed a comprehensive theoretical position on agricultural development and the selective industrialization of particular agricultural commodity sectors. While their *Manufacturing Green Gold* book was based on the California lettuce industry, Friedland and colleagues have explored several other commodity sectors in California agriculture, including tomatoes and grapes-raisins. They have given particular emphasis to the penetration of capitalist relations of production into agriculture, but have also stressed that the nature and pace of this penetration vary widely depending upon the commodity system in question (see especially Friedland, 1984a). Nonetheless, they take a posture similar to that of de Janvry—that while agriculture in general and particular commodity sectors exhibit a slow pace of capitalist penetration, capitalist relations do appear increasingly and bear many similarities to production relations in other branches of industry.

The Incorporation of Noncapitalist Agricultural Production Forms into the Capitalist Political Economy

Another thrust in the neo-Marxian political economy literature, and one that is somewhat contrary to those discussed above, has been the argument that the differentiation of agriculturalists into the capitalist and working classes may be incomplete in the foreseeable future as farm and nonfarm production become integrated into a single system incorporating different organizational forms of production. An early statement of this line of thought was that of the German Social Democrat and Marxist theoretician, Karl Kautsky (see Banaji, 1980). Kautsky argued that what was crucial to understanding the evolution of agriculture in advanced industrial societies was not simply the dominant form of ownership of agricultural enterprises, but rather the functions that were served by the emerging organizational forms of agricultural production.

This approach was developed further by Mottura and Pugliesi (1980) in an historical analysis of small holdings farmed part-time in southern Italy and the functions of smallholder agriculture in contemporary decentralized economic development. The thrust of their argument was that while most agricultural production took place on farms organized along capitalistic lines, part-time farming served as a backup alternative for the workers in industrial plants located in rural areas. In times of industrial contraction and high unemployment, displaced workers with small farms could turn temporarily to subsistence production until industrial conditions improved, thus forming a reserve labor force. This integration of agricultural and nonagricultural production spheres has been further elaborated by Bonanno (1985, 1987a), who examined the role of the state in fostering small farms as one strategy to mediate the interests of the conflicting social classes in the emerging social orders of the advanced societies, particularly Italy and the United States. In this light, various farm programs to deal with problems in the agricultural sector can be seen in part as rooted in the legitimation function served by the continuation of small farms. Small farms are also important in the decentralizing industrial system fostered by state policy. In this system, industrial firms move to rural areas where labor is not unionized and where wages are low because many potential workers have small farms producing inadequate incomes and few alternative opportunities. Work is also increasingly "informalized" in cottage industry, piecework arrangements. In such contexts, small farms serve the function as "keeper of surplus labor"—providing, at the same time, a source of low-cost labor for industry and, in the face of the tenuous employment, a source of security for the members of households with small farms.

Wenger and Buck (1988), building on this line of thought but especially on the earlier work of Andre Gunder Frank (1967), take this argument another step by examining how exploitation and superexploitation (extracting more value from workers' labor than permits reproduction of that labor) from members of farm households are necessary and dynamic features of both advanced capitalist societies and developing societies. Production organized according to obligations of kinship ("domestic relations of production") link ("articulate") in various ways with production organized along capitalist lines so that value is transferred from the domestic sphere of production to the capitalist sphere of production. This takes place in such a way as to make the domestic sphere an "interstitial domestic reserve of labor" that subsidizes the capitalist sphere either directly or indirectly through various mechanisms. For example, unpaid household labor reduces both the wages necessary for workers employed in industry and the prices of agricultural commodities required by farm families. Off-farm income from wage work helps to pay the costs of agricultural production and thus lowers the price of food for other working class families.

Farmers as Actors in a Capitalist Political Economy

Whereas the perspectives of Mann-Dickinson and Friedmann on one hand, and of de Janvry, Friedland et al., and others working in the Lenin (and, to a lesser extent, the Kautsky) traditions on the other, are, in a sense, in diametrical opposition, much of the most provocative work in the Marxist tradition in the "new sociology of agriculture" has revolved around formulations that explicitly or implicitly are attempts at synthesis. One of the most noteworthy attempts has been by Mooney.

Mooney's principal contribution has been to cast doubt as to whether the existence of conventional capital-labor relations on farms is an adequate benchmark for gauging the existence of capitalist penetration of agriculture. Following Wright (1978), Mooney (1983, 1985, 1986a, 1988) has developed a model of agrarian class structure involving "contradictory class locations" such that class positions other than family labor farmer (unity of capital and labor in the farm household), capitalist farmer, and agricultural wage labor are seen to exist (see Figure 1). In particular, Mooney sees that there are several "detours" that can be taken by farmers in order to avoid proletarianization (e.g., either being forced from agriculture or becoming hired agricultural laborers). These detours involve tenancy, contract farming, part-time farming, and debt. In each, whereas there is no capital-labor relation at the point of agricultural production, farmers are exploited by some fraction of nonagricultural capital (in tenancy, by landlords; in contract farming, by agribusiness; in part-time farming, by off-farm capitalists; and in debt, by finance capital). Thus, Mooney argues that the exploitation of farm wage workers by agrarian capitalists is only one form that capitalist penetration of agriculture can take. Moreover, Mooney sees that these detours—that is, the alternative ways in which capital acts to "strip simple commodity

Figure 1
A Model of Agricultural Class Structure

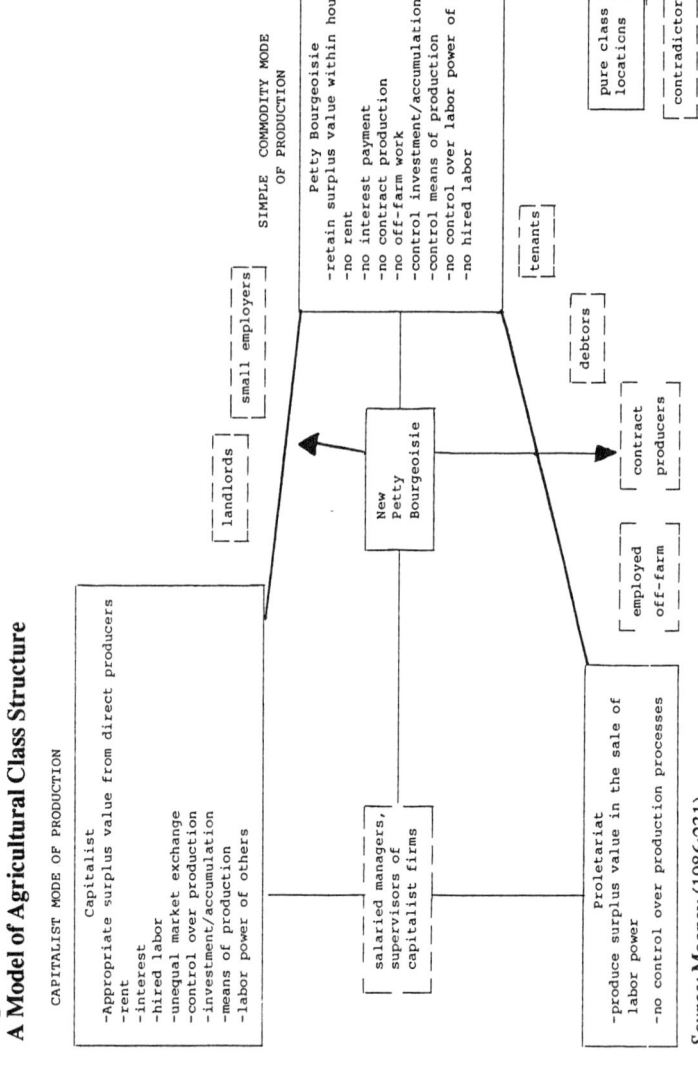

Source: Mooney (1986:231)

producers of . . . surplus value other than through the extension of wage labor" (Mooney, 1983:567)—may be more significant than full-blown capital-labor relations at the point of agricultural production. It is significant, however, that Mooney's explanation of why these contradictory class locations in agriculture tend to emerge has a subjectivist component, based on Weber's distinction between formal and substantive rationality. Mooney sees that many farmers are motivated more by forms of substantive rationality (e.g., the desire for autonomy over their work) than they are by formal capitalist rationality. Accordingly, these farmers tend to be tenacious in holding onto their farms and farm lifestyles and will often tend to take one of the four "detours" to capitalist development in order to remain in agriculture.

Mann and Dickinson (1987a), however, replied vigorously to Mooney's neo-Weberianism with two major arguments: first, that so-called contradictory class locations are really based on the same social relations of production grounds that Mann and Dickson use and, second, that Mooney has misconstrued their notion of "obstacles to capitalist development" in agriculture to be immutable barriers, so that Mooney was unable to recognize that his notion of "detours" to capitalist penetration of agriculture is similar to their own views. Mann and Dickinson thus argue that subjectivism, and the explanatory ambiguities it involves, does not yield insights beyond those afforded by a structural, neo-Marxist theory. They were also critical of Mooney's project of synthesizing Marxian and Weberian approaches on the ground that these approaches are incompatible, except on an ad hoc, eclectic basis. Mooney (1987a) added further to the debate by arguing that Mann and Dickinson have exaggerated his departure from a neo-Marxist framework—that his perspective retains Marxist insights by incorporating key Marxian categories as ideal-types within a Weberian framework. He argued that this approach overcomes the incompatibilities of the Marxian and Weberian frameworks—unless, of course, one adopts a mechanistic Marxist or Leninist perspective. His key position was that the presumption of a predictably patterned and necessary differentiation of farmers into the capitalist class and proletariat is erroneous and that subjectively meaningful human action affects the process of differentiation substantially.

With the 1980s farm crisis coming under increasing scrutiny by rural sociologists, Mooney (1986b) has extended his analytical framework to an historical examination of the state-sponsored farm credit system (Farmers Home Administration [FmHA], Commodity Credit Corporation [CCC], and the Farm Credit System [FCS]) and tax policy incentives for increasing the capitalization of agriculture. Mooney conceptualizes credit and tax policies as means of dealing with the crisis of legitimacy posed by the increasing prevalence of tenant farming produced by the Great Depression. Mooney argues that this credit and policy system created more indebted farmers who ultimately became vulnerable to financial crises in the form of rising real interest rates and declining agricultural commodity prices, a situation such as that which occurred in the 1980s (see also Chapter 4). Financial crises expose to perceptive actors the role of the state in creating the crisis, thus creating another crisis of legitimacy and providing a basis for affected farmers to mobilize against the state.

Pfeffer (1983) has taken a considerably different tack than Mooney, though Pfeffer's work has some similarities to that of Mooney in that he stakes out middle ground on the question of whether the predominant feature of agriculture in advanced capitalism is the persistence of the family labor farm on one hand, or its demise into capitalist relations of production on the other. Pfeffer conducted an historical analysis of three systems of agricultural production in the United States (industrial agriculture in California, family farming in the Great Plains, and the sharecropping system in the South prior to World War II) and demonstrated that recruitment and maintenance of access to a suitable labor force was a crucial factor shaping the disparate organizational structures of these three systems. Only in California, largely because of preexisting land concentration and of state actions to recruit and restrict the residential, educational, and occupational mobility of ethnic minority farm workers, was capitalist agriculture able to set root prior to World War II. Noting that the U.S. South had a high degree of land concentration during the entirety of the nineteenth century, Pfeffer goes on to explain why southern planters were unable to recruit a wage labor force after the Civil War and why the tying of sharecroppers to plots on the landlord's plantation through the crop-lien system was the only possible route to recruiting the labor necessary to operate a large plantation. Finally, Pfeffer demonstrates that a combination of labor scarcity, the unwillingness of immigrants to work for wages on farms, and severe declines in the price of wheat in the late nineteenth century led to the establishment and persistence of family farming in the Great Plains. Pfeffer thus suggests that while capitalist agriculture can emerge under particular circumstances, there have been several alternative forms of agricultural organization—sharecropping and family farming, in particular—that have become established due to regional and commodity variations in the ability of farmers to recruit a dependable labor force.

Still a different approach was taken by Whatmore et al. (1987a, 1987b), who have developed a theoretically based typology of farms in Britain. Their goal was to understand the effects of external pressures by nonfamily and nonfarm capitals to penetrate agriculture and how these pressures articulated with internal processes on farms. By cross-classifying levels or degrees of subsumption of internal and external relations, they developed a typology with four main categories of farm types, ranging from relatively unsubsumed ("marginal closed unit") to the "subsumed unit." The internal relations variable pertained to ownership and control of farm capital and land, control over management, and the balance of family and hired labor. The external relations variable pertained to level of dependence on industrial capitals for production inputs and purchase of farm outputs and to the degree of involvement in credit relations, especially with finance capitals. Applying this theoretically based typology to the data from three areas in southern England—an urban fringe area, an agricultural area undergoing commercial and industrial development, and a primarily agricultural area—they found that the process of subsumption of farm production relations, and thus their integration into the "wider circuits of capital," varied over time and space. Whatmore et al. concluded that farm families need to be understood as actors in the process of subsumption rather than its passive victims.

The neo-Marxian theoretical enterprise (and that of the modernization school as well) on the conversion of traditional peasant economic relations to commodity relations under capitalism has also been scrutinized by Vandergeest (1988). Among his major criticisms were that neo-Marxist approaches tend to be too unilinear, too macro-structural, too denying of human agency, too inattentive to the role of the state in the process, and too unconnected with practice (see, however, the critique by Long and van der Ploeg, 1988). He has argued, from a neo-Weberian position rooted in the work of Pierre Bourdieu, that

> all categories and theories are in the last analysis historically contingent, ideological, and interpretive social products. The world is a complex whole which can only be investigated empirically and understood through theory. It cannot be reduced to the simple working out of a model derived through deductive theory—whether that of "simple commodity production" (as [Harriet] Friedmann tends to do) or of "capitalism" (as [David] Goodman and [Michael] Redclift do). There is not a single deductive logic (such as the logic of exchange-value or accumulation) underlying or determining all relations in a capitalist formation, but there are different, historically contingent principles which we can only investigate through empirical research. (Pp. 21-22)

As we note at greater length in Chapter 5, there has recently been a tendency in the neo-Marxist and neo-Weberian literatures toward a deemphasis on "deductivist"-functionalist theoretical postures. Subjectivist perspectives such as those of Vandergeest and Mooney have been influential in leading to this reorientation, though this tendency is by no means limited to those persuaded by neo-Weberianism (see, for example, Friedmann and McMichael, 1989).

The three postures in the Marxist political economy of agricultural tradition—those emphasizing the persistence of petty commodity production, those emphasizing the inevitable differentiation of petty commodity producers into antagonistic social classes, and those seeking synthetic positions—have yielded a continuing, lively debate in the rural sociology literature. Particularly instructive is the debate over the Mann-Dickinson hypothesis (Mann and Dickinson, 1986; Mooney, 1982; Singer et al., 1983). Also of importance is Goodman and Redclift's (1985) commentary on the work of Friedmann in which Goodman and Redclift critique Friedmann for taking an overly deductive approach to petty commodity production that ignores the role of historical conjuncture and ideology. Bernstein (1986) has made a comparable argument —that generic theories of simple commodity production under advanced capitalism tend to overemphasize its "functional" aspects and downplay contradictions and the diversity of household forms of production.

It should be emphasized that theoretical and empirical treatments of the political economy of North American agriculture have not been made only by rural sociologists. Many of the pioneers in this tradition of scholarship have been nonsociologists (e.g., de Janvry, 1980; Fine, 1979, 1980; Hedley, 1981; Hussain and Tribe, 1981a, 1981b; Lianos, 1984; Murray, 1977, 1978) or sociologists who have had little or no connection with the Rural Sociological Society or the institutionalized form of rural sociology in U.S. land-grant universities (e.g., S. Mann, J. Dickinson, H. Friedmann; McMichael, 1984, 1987). Nonetheless, rural sociologists have made influential contributions to this literature.

The emerging political economy tradition in the sociology of agriculture has led to a provocative and stimulating literature. It should be mentioned, however, that those working from this perspective are just beginning to establish a distinctive research program; much of the existing literature, in fact, often tends to involve superimposing a new vocabulary on already-established data (Buttel, 1982a), such as Goss et al. (1980) set out to do. Establishment of a distinctive research tradition will probably occur slowly since conventional data sources such as censuses and sample surveys are often inapplicable to theoretical issues in the political economy of agriculture. There have, nonetheless, been several research papers in the political economy tradition (e.g., Friedmann, 1978a, 1978b, 1983; Mooney, 1985, 1986; Pfeffer, 1983) that have utilized innovative new methodologies to generate research findings that bear directly on specific hypotheses.

SUBCULTURE AND AGRICULTURAL STRUCTURE

It is useful to note that the growing interest in subjectivist approaches in the new sociology of agriculture has not been confined to those who work within the neo-Marxist and neo-Weberian traditions. Anthropologically-oriented researchers have also contributed to this literature through the examination of the effects of ethnic background on state and local level farm structure. Salamon and associates (Salamon, 1980, 1985; Salamon and Davis-Brown, 1986; Salamon and O'Rielly, 1979) have done the pathbreaking studies in the anthropological tradition in Illinois communities, though recently this work has been taken up by others. While their work was not intended to contribute to the "structure versus agency" debate (in the words of Giddens, 1979) that has raged between Mann and Dickinson (1978, 1987a, 1987b) on one hand, and Mooney (1983, 1987a, 1988) on the other, and actually predated much of this debate, it is clearly relevant to the debate. In particular, the work of Salamon and associates pertains to the role of subjective motivations in farm decision making, especially motivations conditioned by persisting subcultural variations based in differences in ethnic origins of farm families. The key finding of this line of research has been that farm families with German ethnic backgrounds tend to view farming as a way of life and hold a strong value for keeping the family farm intact. These Salamon has labeled "yeoman" farmers. In contrast, farm families with British (Yankee) ethnic backgrounds tend to be more entrepreneurially oriented, viewing farming as a way to make profits and having little attachment to farming or to particular farms. These Yankee farmers are more likely to seek growth in scale and less likely to support their local communities. This research has led to understanding differentials in farm size as a partial function of differences between these subcultural variants. Flora and Stitz (1985) found that yeoman farmers in a Kansas county generally expanded less than did Yankee farmers. Foster et al. (1987) also found support for the Salamon hypothesis in a study of a sample of Illinois farms that had been in the same families for 100 years or more.

Several other anthropological studies in the tradition of Salamon and colleagues have been reported in Chibnik (1987). Of particular importance is Barlett's (1987) article in which she criticizes notions of the demise of the family farm and of the "disappearing middle" from an anthropological perspective (see also Barlett, 1986c).

INDUSTRIAL AGRICULTURE

It was noted earlier that a number of neo-Marxist analysts of agriculture have stressed the notion that agriculture, although it exhibits a slower and more uneven pace of capitalist penetration than other branches of industry, is nonetheless likely to experience the generalization of capital-labor relations and to become industrialized along capitalist lines, much as has tended to occur in other industrial sectors. It is also widely recognized that industrial-capitalist agriculture has taken root earliest and most thoroughly in California and other areas of the Sunbelt. Accordingly, many of the most provocative analyses of industrial agriculture have been conducted by persons persuaded by this form of neo-Marxist analysis and have been focused on the Southwest, especially California. The earliest and some of the most influential rural sociological research in industrial agriculture, however, was conducted by non-Marxists and in states other than those in the

Southwest. Most notable in this regard are the studies by Heffernan (1972), Ploch (1960), and Rodefeld (1974). Heffernan, following Ploch and working largely from complex organization theory (see also Heffernan, 1984), focused on integrated poultry production in Louisiana, while Rodefeld, basing his work on a long line of Durkheimian-influenced theory on structural differentiation and specialization (e.g., Stinchcombe, 1961), focused on corporate-industrial farms in Wisconsin.

For over a decade and a half Heffernan has investigated structural change in the U.S. broiler industry and in the farm structure of one poultry-producing parish in Louisiana. Heffernan has sought to explain why there has rapidly been developed a concentrated structure of broiler processing firms, why these firms historically opted to enter into contractual relations with family farmers, and what the consequences of these contractual relations have been for farm personnel and rural communities. Heffernan (1984) has documented the very rapid pattern of structural change in the poultry industry by identifying major trends in processing and direct production. On the agribusiness side, there has been a dramatic shift toward large-scale national processing and distribution firms, the largest of which tend to be subsidiaries of large conglomerate firms. This rapid concentration of the industry was made possible by, among other factors, a small handful of firms gaining control of retail markets (e.g., supermarkets, fast-food restaurants) and entering into production contracts with farmers to ensure control over the quality and quantity of the raw product. Heffernan (1984) has explained these changes in terms of complex organization theory, emphasizing the tendency of complex organizations such as broiler processors to attempt to control "environmental conditions" external to the firm in order to reduce uncertainty.

Broiler processing firms have thus become the prototype of the integration of production, processing, and distribution functions within a handful of firms in a concentrated agribusiness industry. Heffernan (1972, 1984), drawing on the pioneering work of Ploch (1960) on integrated broiler production in Maine, has given principal emphasis to the structure of contractually integrated poultry farming in a Louisiana parish. Here the farmer enters into a contract with the processing-distribution firm and, in the process, relinquishes virtually all entrepreneurial control over the farming operation; the processor supplies chicks and feed and specifies most aspects of the production process.

Heffernan noted that the integrated processing firms have tended to focus their procurement and contracting activities on areas in which farmers had few economic alternatives to contractual production of poultry as a way to sustain the family farm and remain in the community. Heffernan has emphasized the consequences of contractually integrated poultry production for patterns of community social participation. He found that while family-farmer contractees and owners of larger (larger-than-family or industrial) operations differed little in terms of community social participation, hired workers on industrial farms exhibited very low rates of participation (Heffernan, 1972). Heffernan (1982) has accordingly suggested that expanded contractual integration in agriculture might have detrimental consequences for rural communities (see Chapter 4).

Rodefeld's (1974) study was focused on legally incorporated farms in Wisconsin. Recognizing that not all legally incorporated farms were "corporate"—that is, industrial or capitalist—farms, Rodefeld developed a typology of farm types based on control over land, capital, labor, and management, a reduced form of which (based on land and labor) has been used most extensively in Rodefeld's work (see, for example, Rodefeld, 1978, 1980). This typology, which has been widely applied in other research, appears in Table 1. Similar to Heffernan's results, Rodefeld found that members of family-type, legally incorporated farms in Wisconsin had substantially higher levels of participation in voluntary associations and other community social activities than did workers on larger-than-family and industrial-type farms (see also Martinson et al., 1976). Rodefeld also documented the growing prevalence of large, nonfamily farms in the US over the preceding decades and suggested that this trend would have adverse implications for agricultural communities.

Table 1
Farm Types Based on Classification by Their Amount of Land and Capital Ownership and Amount of Labor Performed by the Farm Operational Manager and Family

Amount of Land and Capital Ownership by Operator	Amount of Labor Provided by Operator	
	Most or All	Least or None
Most or All	Family type	Larger-than-family type
Least or None	Tenant-type	Industrial-type

Source: After Rodefeld (1978, Fig.1, p. 159).

Much of the research on industrial agriculture conducted since the Ploch, Heffernan, and Rodefeld studies has been based on the emerging neo-Marxist tradition and has focused on dependent variables other than community social participation. The most notable studies in this regard have been by Friedland and coworkers. The Friedland et al. (1981) book, which is referred to several times for its contributions to the neo-Marxist theoretical perspective, was also devoted to depicting the social organization of lettuce production in California and to projecting the possible consequences of lettuce harvest mechanization. Drawing on their earlier research into tomato production (Friedland and Barton, 1975), they argue that the nature of the lettuce commodity system is largely shaped by the characteristics of the commodity (especially perishability) and by the vagaries of control over the agricultural wage labor force (see also Majka and Majka, 1982). Lettuce production has become highly concentrated in the hands of a small number of integrated grower-shipper firms that directly control production, processing, and distribution. Profitability of and competition among firms in this labor-intensive commodity system have been based on access to and control over cheap wage labor, chiefly provided in recent decades by Mexican nationals (legal and illegal) and by Mexican Americans.

Friedland et al. (1981) emphasize the evolution of the labor process in lettuce production since the termination of the bracero program in 1964, which many grower-shippers feared would lead to rising labor costs. Friedland and colleagues note, however, that grower-shippers in the lettuce sector were able to develop new strategies of labor recruitment and control—a combination of "ground crews" employing primarily legal and illegal Mexican immigrants and paid on a piece-rate system, and "wrap crews" employing primarily women and other citizens paid on an hourly basis—in the aftermath of the termination of the bracero program. In particular, unlike California tomato producers who rapidly mechanized harvest operations in the late 1970s, lettuce producers eschewed harvest mechanization for a number of reasons, though they used the threat of mechanization in an attempt to discipline the labor force during the years of uncertainty following 1964 (Friedland, 1980).

Thomas (1981a, 1981b, 1985) has provided much greater detail on the labor process in California lettuce production and on the structure, recruitment, and remuneration of the wage labor force. In particular, Thomas (1981a) has explored constraints on unionization of the lettuce harvest labor force, the effects of grower manipulation of citizenship and gender status of workers (Thomas, 1981b), and the interaction of citizenship and gender in the labor process (Thomas, 1985).

Friedland et al. (1981) conclude by constructing a model in which two factors are seen to influence the rate and nature of technological change in lettuce production. These factors are the supply and control of labor on one hand, and the economic structure of the industry on the other. It is emphasized that these two variables may exhibit an interactive effect. The examples of processing tomatoes and lettuce production are used to illustrate the ways that unique structures of the two industries can lead to diverse responses to changes in the supply of labor. Accordingly, Friedland et al. stress the need to study capitalist development in agriculture on a commodity system basis. Furthermore, Friedland et al. argue that the interactive nature of technological changes casts doubt on technological determinist theories and theories of labor force homogenization.

In a subsequent article, Friedland (1984a) has argued for adopting a commodity systems focus in the sociology of agriculture in general, rather than only for industrial-capitalist agriculture. Friedland outlines a general methodology for commodity systems analysis (CSA) and provides examples from previous studies by him and his colleagues to illustrate its relevance. Friedland argues that the increasingly specialized character of American agriculture makes the use of commodity systems analyses particularly appropriate; in many sectors "discrete commodity systems . . . are conceptually and socially distinct" (p. 223). Typical commodity studies use historical, institutional, quantitative, and qualitative research tools to discern the complex nature of the production of a given commodity. Friedland identifies five major areas that should be important foci in any commodity system analysis. Initially, these studies should analyze (1) the nature of the production process, (2) the economic and social organization of growers, (3) the use and management of labor, (4) the role of scientific research and extension activities, and (5) the structure of marketing and distribution networks. Friedland presents examples from studies of three commodities—processing tomatoes, iceberg lettuce, and grapes—in California to illustrate the diversity of different crops with respect to these five foci. He concludes by noting that the commodity systems approach should not be the only one used to develop a mature sociology of agriculture. Importantly, most existing commodity studies have been done in the Sunbelt states, so that extending CSA to other regions and commodity spheres would likely require modifications in the CSA methodology.

A noteworthy preliminary extension of commodity systems analysis into a non-Sunbelt context is Gilbert and Akor's (1986, 1988) comparative studies of dairying in Wisconsin and California, the first and second most important dairy states in the United States, respectively, which together account for 28 percent of the U.S. milk supply. Gilbert and Akor note that whereas U.S. dairy farming as a whole has become more concentrated and specialized since World War II, the Lake States region, which includes Wisconsin, and the Northeast have exhibited continuity of family-operated dairy farming (independent commodity production), while dairying in the Southwest states has largely been industrial-capitalist in character. Family-operated dairies in the Lake and Northeast states, which produce their own feed and hire relatively little labor, still predominate in terms of aggregate U.S. milk production. Dairy production in the Southwest and other Sunbelt states, however, has grown very rapidly over the past three decades. These large-scale industrial-capitalist dairy farms in the Sunbelt states generally are "drylot" farms, which do not produce feed and are very capital-intensive, highly specialized, and rely heavily on hired, nonfamily labor.

Gilbert and Akor examine the hypothesis that this dual, regionally based structure of dairy farming is undergoing a process of convergence into a single homogeneous structure. They note, however, that instead of convergence, census data for the period from 1950 to 1982 reveal continuing divergence into two very different farm structures. They conclude by identifying the factors that have contributed to increased divergence between California and Wisconsin dairying; these factors are argued to include differences in labor markets, natural resource bases, climate, dominant ethnic farming groups, and state policy. Thus, while California and Wisconsin dairying has been affected by common forms of technological change, technology has not affected these two dairy regions in a homogeneous way that has led to convergence of farm structures. Gilbert and Akor (1988) thus suggest that regional variations in land use, labor supply, ethnic subcultures, and other variables make it essential to undertake comparative regional analyses of agricultural commodity systems.

THE AGRICULTURAL WAGE LABOR FORCE

As noted earlier, much of the attention of sociologists who have researched industrial agriculture has been focused on issues relating to the hired agricultural labor force. In this book, however, we treat the agricultural wage labor force as a distinct topic, since the bulk of this labor force in the United States (in terms of hours of annual labor) is white, works full-time, and works outside of the industrial agricultural sector (according to the criteria in Table 1). In this section we make some observations on research into the structure of the hired agricultural labor force in both industrial and nonindustrial agriculture.

It is useful to make several preliminary points about the U.S. agricultural wage labor force before proceeding with an overview of the relevant literature. First, as Friedland (1984b) has noted, federal government data sources on the structure of the hired agricultural work force are notoriously inadequate, so that one cannot even develop a satisfactory profile of the socioeconomic characteristics of the employers of these workers. Second, there are many popular misconceptions about the hired agricultural labor force—presumably, at least in part, because federal data sources are so poor. As noted earlier, the vast majority of hired workers are white and work full-time (rather than being largely migratory Hispanics and blacks). Further, the proportion of total hours of labor in agriculture accounted for by hired workers has either been stable (at about 25–27 percent from the turn of the century to the early 1970s) or increased (to about 35 percent by the early 1980s) (Smith and Coltrane, 1981); thus technological change has been much more effective than often realized in displacing family labor than it has in displacing hired workers (Perelman, 1977; Perry, 1982). Perry (1982) and Friedland (1984b) have, in fact, noted that trends in agriculture toward concentration and very large, specialized farms may well lead to increases in the magnitude of the agricultural wage labor force despite the displacement effects of agricultural mechanization. Friedland (1984b) has reported data showing that, in the 1970s, each state, with the single exception of Connecticut, experienced an increase in the number of hired workers per farm. Third, our knowledge of the structure of the wage labor force in industrial agriculture is far superior to that for the labor force of family-proprietor farmers (Newby and Buttel, 1980).

Because several useful summaries of the literature on the wage labor force in industrial agriculture exist, we make only a few general comments here. Thomas-Lycklama a Niejholt (1980), a Dutch sociologist, prepared a useful study of the East Coast migrant labor stream—one of the three major such streams along with the mid-continent and West Coast streams—based on survey data collected among hired workers in 1970 and on documentary data. She has made several observations that parallel those made by Friedland et al. (1981), Thomas (1985), and others who have studied farm labor in the Southwest. First, the key element in migrant agricultural labor markets tends not to be labor sufficiency (i.e., enough labor to meet demand), but rather labor surplus, which creates cheap labor. Second, agricultural mechanization, whereas it has historically decreased aggregate demand for migratory labor, has not eliminated this demand; in particular, mechanization, since it is typically accompanied by specialization, tends to result in seasonal bulges in labor demand and continued dependence on abundant, cheap, mobile labor. Mechanization thus creates demand for a large number of workers to be employed for very brief periods of time. Some large growers, however, have shifted from an "external" labor force, dominated by migrant workers, to a more permanent, "internalized" labor force where agroclimatic and technical conditions permit (see also Friedland et al., 1981). Third, migrant workers tend to migrate much shorter distances than often assumed; of the workers studied by Thomas-Lycklama a Niejholt, about 50 percent worked in only one state or two, rather than migrating incrementally along the entire East Coast migratory stream from Florida to the Northeast. Fourth, she reported that migratory farm workers are not uniformly disadvantaged. There are substantial income differentials, which are largely explained by ethnic-racial status. Mexicans were the most disadvantaged, followed by West Indians, Puerto Ricans, blacks, and whites. She also found that migratory workers, who are predominantly nonwhite, tend to receive lower wages than nonmigratory workers, who are predominantly white. It should be noted, however, that Thomas (1985) has reported evidence that, in the lettuce harvest wage labor force in California, citizenship and gender tend to be the principal bases of wage differentials, with noncitizens and women receiving lower wages than citizens and males. Thomas has stressed that subordinate status in terms of citizenship and gender are resources utilized by employers to discipline the lettuce harvest labor force. Thomas (1985), Friedland et al. (1981), and Majka and Majka (1982) along with Thomas-Lycklama a Niejholt (1980) have also stressed the role of state policy in facilitating labor surplus, curbing the establishment and militancy of farm labor unions, and permitting the payment of relatively low wages.

As suggested earlier, while there have been hundreds of studies by sociologists and nonsociologists of the hired labor force in industrial agriculture, little attention has been given to the largely permanent, full-time, white workers recruited by family-proprietor farms from the community or surrounding region in the nonindustrial agricultural regions. There have, however, been three such studies—one in England by Newby (1977; Newby et al., 1978) and two in the United States (Barlett, 1986a; Perry, 1982)—that provide an encouraging basis for future research in this area.

Newby's studies of petty capitalist agriculture in England began with several theoretical and empirical issues relating to the relations between large farmers and their hired workers. Whereas farm workers make relatively low wages and perform demanding work, they nonetheless tend not to be politically radical, to be dissatisfied with their work, to join labor unions, or to otherwise dissent from the discipline and authority of their employers. Newby explored the role of paternalistic controls in enabling capitalist farmers to maintain a relatively docile labor force despite low wages and low levels of living. He has emphasized the fact that farmers tend to recruit workers who have agricultural backgrounds and are from the local area, thereby reducing the impersonality that typically exists in urban-industrial labor markets. Employers also tend to provide part of their workers' compensation in the form of housing on the farm, which further ties the worker to the employer. Finally, Newby observed a close correspondence between workers' sociopolitical values and images of the class structure and those of their farmer employers. He suggests that workers have internalized many of the ideological constructions of their employers and have remained deferential rather than rebellious toward them.

Barlett (1986a), largely following Newby's (1977) research design, has studied the full-time hired labor force in a region of Georgia and has made several observations that closely parallel those in Newby's study of English farm workers. The descriptive component of Barlett's study revealed data that contradict many widely held assumptions about full-time hired agricultural laborers in the South. Only about 60 percent were black, and, given their average age of 35, most were neither tied to one farm for a long time nor spent the majority of their careers as farm workers. Similar to Newby's (1977) sample of farm workers, 82 percent had connections to agriculture before beginning work as a hired farm worker; 27 percent of their fathers were farm owners, 23 percent sharecroppers, and 32 percent farm workers. Barlett, however, found that these workers tended to have low educational backgrounds (though no lower than national averages for farm workers), work very long hours, and earn low wages, consistent with observations in other regions of the country. Most farm workers, however, had few or no brothers or sisters in farm work, suggesting that they are less "trapped" in farm work than usually supposed.

Barlett's analysis of the attitudes of farm workers toward their jobs was also similar to Newby's. Newby (1977) reported that workers on large capitalist farms in England had much more positive attitudes toward their work than did industrial workers. Barlett reports very similar job satisfaction data for the sample of Georgia farm workers. Barlett also found that these Georgia farm workers were similar to Newby's sample in that they tended to have personalistic ties to their employers—frequently referring to their relationships with employers in family-like terms—and generally had a strong identification with the farm, the employer, and fellow workers.

Perry (1982) utilized quantitative analysis of census and USDA data on hired labor to explore a major anomaly in the conceptualization of hired farm workers. On one hand, Perry notes that many observers see hired labor in agriculture as low-opportunity-cost, "salvage" labor and that technological change is reducing the need for such workers in agriculture. On the other hand, Perry cites data, such as those referred to earlier, indicating a trend for an increasing proportion of hired farm workers to be employed full-time and for the share of hired labor in total labor demand on farms to increase at the expense of family labor. He has argued for a reconceptualization of the role of hired labor in agriculture. Following Braverman (1974), Perry suggests that the use of hired labor should be viewed from the vantage point of the rationalization of U.S. agriculture, which causes farmers to adjust their use of labor, technology, land, and other resources in order to produce a profitable set of commodities with manageable risk. Perry also follows Braverman in arguing that the role of technological change in affecting the use of labor will tend to be contradictory, given the imperatives of the rationalization process. On one hand, technological change may result in the simplification and deskilling of work, which encourages the use of cheap, unskilled wage labor (as opposed to family labor and more highly skilled hired workers). On the other hand, technological change may tend to create greater complexity in the labor process, which will encourage the use of more highly skilled labor such as farm family members and permanent workers. Perry's analysis of state-level census data suggests that the paradox of displacement of "salvage" labor by mechanization at the same time that hired agricultural labor is increasing in importance in U.S. agriculture can be accounted for by these two simultaneous and contradictory trends resulting from rationalization and technological change.

SMALL FARMS AND PART-TIME FARMING

The nature, social bases, and socioeconomic consequences of "small" farms and part-time farming are, in a sense, among the most longstanding foci in rural sociological research on agriculture (see, e.g., Bertrand, 1967). Nevertheless, sociological analysis of small-scale agriculture and part-time farming received substantially increased attention and exhibited considerable theoretical reformulation in the 1970s and 1980s for several reasons. First, as noted earlier, spearheaded by the writings of Hightower (1973) and others on the demise of "small" farms, there was a startling renaissance of concern with the status and prospects of small family farms, which had greatly subsided a few decades earlier in the aftermath of the apparent resolution of the depression-induced increase in tenancy. Second, quite ironically, several observers began to document the fact that the 1970s had witnessed an unprecedented trend toward the stability and persistence of small farms; in most regions the absolute number of farms with fewer than 50 acres has increased over the past one to two decades (see Harper et al., 1980). Third, it became apparent that much of the reason for the enhanced viability of small farms was the growing access of farm households to off-farm jobs and income; indeed, the U.S. Department of Agriculture (1979, 1981) began to note that, in most years, the majority of farm households' aggregate income came from nonfarm sources and that there had been a slow but steady increase in the prevalence of off-farm labor market participation among farm families since World War II.

Small and part-time farms are treated here as a particular focal point in the new sociology of agriculture, a tack that has been taken by many others (see, e.g., Coughenour and Wimberley, 1982). Whereas there is a key connection between small-scale agriculture and part-time farming—the fact that part-time farming has in recent decades been much more common among "small" than among "medium-size" or "large" farms (see, e.g., Bertrand, 1967; Fuller, 1984; Wimberley, 1983)—the two phenomena, however, are by no means equivalent. In particular, some "small farms"— which provisionally can be referred to here as low-sales-volume farms, with about $50,000 or less in gross annual sales volume— have little or no off-farm income and, accordingly, have long been overrepresented among rural poverty groups in the United States and elsewhere. Moreover, in all advanced capitalist societies, especially the UK, part-time farming occurs across the whole spectrum of sizes of family-proprietor farms; in the UK it has been quite common for the operators of very large farms to have off-farm occupations, especially the operation of small businesses related to agriculture (see especially Gasson, 1967, 1983, 1986). Thus small-scale and part-time farming, although tending to be significantly related, are by no means coterminous. Further, the analysis of neither small nor part-time farming has been dominated or influenced by neo-Marxist postures nearly as much as other areas in the new sociology of agriculture. In the huge literature on these topics there have been theoretical and empirical neo-Marxist works (e.g., Bonanno, 1985, 1987a; Cavazzani, 1979; Sivini, 1976), but these approaches have been a distinct minority component of the literature.

It is useful to begin with a very generalized model of the recent evolution of U.S. agriculture to situate the theoretical and empirical issues relating to small and part-time farms. Over the past decade or so there has been growing acceptance of the notion that U.S. agriculture has followed a dualistic or bimodal pattern of development since the early 1970s (see, for example, Buttel, 1981, 1983a; Green and Heffernan, 1984; Tweeten and Huffman, 1980). There is evidence that prior to the late 1960s (and thus preceding the phase of dualistic development) there was a singular pattern of increased concentration and differentiation in U.S. agriculture in which there was a direct association between size of farm and its persistence or viability; thus large farms increased in numbers, acreage, assets, and so on at the expense of small farms, particularly small tenant farms without the means to acquire off-farm income (Cochrane, 1979). Farm operators with access to off-farm income were thought to be largely in a transitional status, either into or out of agriculture.

It is now suggested that a more complicated or dualistic pattern of concentration and differentiation has emerged. The stylized facts of this association are, first, that large farms—including large family-type, larger-than-family, and industrial farms in Rodefeld's (1978) terms (see Table 1)—are, much as in previous decades, exhibiting a demonstrable increase in their shares of aggregate production, sales, assets, profits, use of hired labor, and so on.

Second, however, it is argued that small farms are increasing in numbers and holding their own in terms of acreage and aggregate production. This bolstered status of small farms is considered to be made possible largely by access of their operators and other family members to off-farm wage income. U.S. small farmers have been noted to have, on average, total family incomes in excess of those of medium-sized farmers and the U.S. median family income (USDA, 1981) because of the higher than average educational attainments of members of small farm households and their consequent ability to acquire highly remunerative off-farm work. While outside of the South small farmers have tended to have higher educational levels than larger, full-time operators for several decades, the educational disparities between small, part-time and larger, full-time operators are suggested to have increased. This has often been explained in terms of the 1970s "population turnaround" in which well-educated persons, many of urban origin, were attracted to farm residential situations for lifestyle reasons. Finally, it is asserted that there has been a "disappearing middle" —that medium-size (traditional family-type) farms have decreased in numbers and in shares of aggregate output, assets, profits, and the like. It has been suggested that these medium-size farms enjoy neither the advantages of bigness or of smallness. In particular, "middle farmers," because they have operations too large to be farmed on a part-time basis, tend to lack the labor resources (and often the educational qualifications) to participate effectively in off-farm labor markets. Thus "the middle" is tending to "disappear," albeit slowly. Approximately 5, 70, and 25 percent of U.S. farms are seen to lie, respectively, in the "large," "small," and "medium" categories.

These stylized facts appear to be largely accurate, although Ehrensaft et al. (1984), and Barlett (1984, 1986c, 1987) have raised empirical and theoretical objections to the disappearing middle thesis. Salamon and Davis-Brown's (1986) findings suggest that the "disappearing middle" may have come more from certain segments of the farm population (the more risk-accepting, entrepreneurial farmers) and less from other segments (the "yeoman" farmers whose key goals are preserving their family farms). Similarly, this conclusion may not hold for black farmers whose limited access to credit for land purchases and mechanization led to rapid declines in the total number of black farmers (Hickey and Hickey, 1987). Nonetheless, there has been general confirmation of this empirical model for the U.S. farm sector (Edwards et al., 1985), which provides a preliminary framework for placing the phenomena of small and part-time farming in historical context (see Buttel and LaRamee, 1990, for an overview of the "disappearing middle" debate).

As Coughenour and Wimberley (1982:349) have noted, "most American farm families live on small and part-time farms." Thus in the sense of understanding the composition of the U.S. farm sector, it is essential to account for the status of and trends in small-scale and part-time agriculture. As noted earlier, a dramatically different context of research on small farms emerged in the mid- to late1970s. This context can now be seen as contradictory; at the same time that there had been a rekindling of concern with the status and prospects of the small-scale farm that had been unprecedented since the Great Depression, there was a correspondingly unprecedented increase in the numbers of small farms in most regions of the country.

The changing context of the decline and persistence of small-scale agriculture strongly influenced the conduct of research on small farms. There emerged a number of studies examining the factors leading to small farm decline, persistence, survival, adaptation, and so on (Gladwin and Zabawa, 1984; Voth et al., 1983; Williams and Bjergo, 1982). The dominant finding in this research was that small farmers pursue multiple strategies for survival—access to off-farm income; minimizing debt; direct marketing of high-value, specialty crops; and so on—and that the choice of strategies was related to the socioeconomic characteristics of the farm, farm operator, and farm household members.

Recognition of the diversity of small farmers and their survival strategies set forth a related line of inquiry: documenting the internal differentiation among small farmers and generating typologies of small farms and small farming households. Major studies in this genre include Buttel and Gertler (1982), Schulman et al. (1985), Muñoz (1984), Schroeder et al. (1985), and Heffernan et al. (1982). These studies have typically found that gross sales (or other indicators of scale), age, education, motivations for farming, household composition, off-farm occupation, and off-farm income are important dimensions of internal stratification among small farmers.

A third cluster of research activities relating to small farms has been to explore small farmers' sociopolitical attitudes. One major area of inquiry has been in documenting the motivations of small-scale farm operators and their family members (see especially Schroeder et al., 1983, 1985). Another focus of attitudinal research has been on the political orientations of small farmers. Research to date has generally not reported that small farmers have dramatically different political orientations than large farmers on either general dimensions of political ideology or orientations toward agricultural politics (Buttel et al., 1982; Coughenour and Christenson, 1983). It has been demonstrated, however, that there are major differences in political orientations among small farmers that are primarily accounted for by off-farm occupation, total family income, and race (Coughenour and Christenson, 1983; Schulman and Luginbuhl, 1985).

Finally, there has been a nagging concern among rural sociological researchers as to how small farms should be defined. Gross farm sales has for a very long time been the principal scale variable used by the Census of Agriculture in collecting and reporting data, and our macrosociological knowledge base on trends in the structure of small-scale farming is largely based on gross sales data. Nonetheless, it is widely recognized that gross farm sales have significant limitations as a measure of scale or "smallness." For example, many economists would prefer value-added over gross sales as a measure of scale. But in the absence of a convenient measure of value-added (or some other concept preferable to gross annual sales) for census and survey research purposes, some arbitrary criterion based on gross sales, sometimes combined with a total family income criterion, has continued to be the measurement convention in small-farm research. Nonetheless, as Carlin and Crecink (1979) have shown, alternative definitions of small farms have significant implications for the numbers and characteristics of farmers and farm households included in that category.

Part-time farming research in the United States was initiated during the Great Depression of the 1930s, mainly by agricultural economists and to a lesser extent by rural sociologists (see Chapter 1), and was part of the concern about "agricultural adjustment" that prevailed in USDA and land-grant university circles. It was observed that many farmers were attempting to survive depression conditions and avoid (or extricate themselves from) tenancy by acquiring off-farm income. As was also to become the case in the 1980s, part-time farming came to be widely advocated as a partial solution to the difficult problems of the agricultural depression of the 1930s. In the decades up until the early and mid-1970s, however, it was recognized that "agricultural recovery," which typically was conceptualized in terms of increased owner-operation of farms, did not correspond to a decrease in part-time farming. Indeed, coincident with agricultural recovery from the late 1930s to the 1960s was an unprecedented exodus of farmers from the land—a new "agricultural adjustment" problem born of expansion, dynamism, and what latter-day neo-Marxists would refer to as differentiation, rather than depression and decline—that again called for part-time farming as an adjustment mechanism. Whereas in the 1930s farm size and part-time farming did not appear to be strongly correlated, by the 1950s it was widely recognized that there had emerged a strong inverse association of gross farm sales and various indicators of the involvement of the operator in off-farm work. Among many researchers, especially agricultural economists, the principal research concern, on which there was a decade of conflicting results, was with whether part-time farmers were as efficient as full-time farmers.

Whereas rural sociologists were a minority among researchers on part-time farming during this period, Fuguitt in particular made several important contributions to the literature that continue to be drawn upon today. Fuguitt (1959) first demonstrated that part-time farming represented a combination of "push-pull" factors—that the prevalence of part-time farming was positively related to off-farm employment opportunities and inversely related to opportunities in agriculture. Fuguitt (1961, 1965) then established that there were categories of part-time farmers (based on farm and nonfarm origin and on farmers' aspirations) with distinctly different social characteristics.

Fuller (1984) has noted that after 1975 research attention to part-time farming increased dramatically and that several new issues occupied the attention of rural sociologists and kindred social scientists. Definitional matters received major attention after 1975; in particular, there came to be dissatisfaction with conceptualizing part-time farming in terms of the presence or absence, or the number of days, of off-farm work by the operator—the way that off-farm employment data have traditionally been collected and reported in census sources. A consensus began to emerge on conceptualizing part-time farming in terms of the activities of the farming household rather than the farm operator (Cavazzani and Fuller, 1982; Kada, 1980). There also continued to be typological research, following Fuguitt's (1961) efforts (e.g., Mage, 1982). Further, there was a significant amount of research on mobility into and out of part-time farming, on the significance of differences in the off-farm occupations that are held, on the implications of part-time farming for rural communities (Heffernan et al., 1981), and especially on the motivations of part-time farmers (e.g., Barlett, 1986b; Coughenour and Christenson, 1983; Schroeder et al., 1985). Finally, there has emerged a significant political economy tradition in small and part-time farming research that has explored issues such as the rooting of part-time farming in the concentration and differentiation process (Buttel, 1982b), the roles that part-time farming plays in accumulation and legitimation in the agricultural and larger economy (Bonanno, 1985, 1987a; Cavazzani, 1979; Sivini, 1976; Wenger and Buck, 1988; but see Barlett, 1986b), the role of off-farm work in the sexual division of farm household labor (Sachs, 1983), and the "embourgeoisiement" thesis—that part-time farming, by enabling smaller farmers to avoid proletarianization, may blunt the emergence of radicalism by subordinate groups in the agrarian class structure (Buttel, 1982b; Buttel and Larson, 1982).

In light of excellent review articles on the status of part-time farming research (especially Cavazzani and Fuller, 1982; Fuller, 1984), there is a less pressing need to summarize what has been a voluminous literature. Instead, we will comment on some "metathemes" in this literature that have not yet been the subject of thorough reviews.

First, there is a general tendency for the literature on part-time farming to be polarized into highly structural (if not structuralist in the Althusserian-Marxist sense) and highly voluntarist accounts. Structural(ist) accounts see part-time farming in almost teleological fashion—that the dynamics of capitalism lead inexorably to agrarian proletarianization in (among others) the form of part-time farming, which provides a mechanism for sustaining profitable capital accumulation in farm, and especially nonfarm, industry by providing a low-wage labor reserve. The subjective motivations and experiences of part-time farming households are thus ignored and viewed to be epiphenomena of larger laws of motion of capitalist development. This approach has historically been prominent in Italian rural sociology circles (see Bonanno, 1985, for a useful summary and reformulation). Voluntarist accounts, on the other hand, have largely focused on the motivations of members of part-time farming households—especially their desire to remain in farming and to fulfill lifestyle aspirations. To the degree that nonsubjective factors are considered, they are treated as an "opportunity structure" and not as a social structure that is rooted in the historical and material dynamics of agriculture. Fuller (1984) has made a related diagnosis of the state of research on part-time farming—namely that despite widespread social science research on part-time farming, as yet there exists no satisfactory explanatory theory. Fuller attributes this to the fact that there has been disproportionate attention to the "farming" aspects of part-time farming and too little attention to the family and other nonfarming aspects of rural life. We would suggest that the frontier of research in part-time farming should lie in integrating objective and subjective aspects of these phenomena, which should help to stimulate the theoretical thinking that Fuller has found lacking.

A second metatheme that can be distilled from the part-time farming literature concerns the need for a truly comparative approach to part-time farming research. This observation is, in a sense, ironic, since there has probably been more cross-national comparative observation of part-time farming than in any other subject matter in the sociology of agriculture (see Cavazzani and Fuller, 1982). But while cross-national variations in part-time farming are widely recognized, these divergent systems of part-time farming have yet to be explained theoretically. This suggests the need for a comparative, integrative perspective on agricultural and rural development, which, like de Janvry's (1980) rendering of Lenin's classical schema of "roads of agricultural development," would examine the interrelations between agriculture and the larger, nonfarm rural economy and society. A major step in this theoretical direction has been taken by Bonanno (1985, 1987a), though his focus has been more on the persistence and role of small farms than on part-time farming per se. Nonetheless, much work remains to be done to explore part-time farming and other aspects of agrarian structure from the vantage point of the dynamics of agrarian and regional-development dualism.

GENDER AND AGRICULTURE

The role of women in U.S. agriculture was by no means a new area of inquiry when interest in this topic soared in the late 1970s and early 1980s. Wilkening (1954, 1981a), in particular, had sustained a major research program on the work roles of farm women and men since the early 1950s. And for several decades there had been a substantial amount of attention paid to rural and agricultural family structures (see, e.g., Bertrand, 1958a). Nonetheless, rural sociological research on gender and agriculture was to embrace distinctly different themes in the era of the "new sociology of agriculture" (see also Ross, 1985). Whereas there have been a number of foci in this new tradition of research, the dominant cast of roughly 20 recent studies has been to explore the "invisibility" of women in U.S. agriculture, to paraphrase the title of Sachs' (1983) recent book-length work in this area (see also Long, 1984; Reimer, 1986).

Research on gender and agriculture has fallen into four major categories, which basically have represented stages in the development of knowledge on the role of women on American farms. The first category is that of cross-sectional descriptive studies that have sought to document the nature and extent of farm women's involvement in on-farm, household, and off-farm tasks. The second is a set of studies that have attempted to assess changes in women's involvement in on-farm, household, and off-farm tasks by utilizing longitudinal research designs. The third category is that of studies exploring the interrelations between the on-farm, household, and off-farm roles of farm men and women. The final category is that of comprehensive theoretical and empirical approaches that attempt to understand how the institutions of capitalism and patriarchy interact to shape the involvement of men and women in various work roles.

The first descriptive phase of research on gender relations in agriculture was initiated by Joyce and Leadley (1977), who summarized the existing literature on rural women, both farm and nonfarm. Joyce and Leadley lamented the lack of research on rural farm and nonfarm women and set forth an agenda for research (see also Flora and Johnson, 1978). Soon thereafter a number of studies would be conducted in which many of the basic parameters of women's participation in farm, off-farm, and household activities were clarified.

Because census data have included little information on farm women and thus have seriously underestimated the economic contribution of women to farming operations (Haney, 1982; Wilkening and Ahrens, 1979), the knowledge base on the productive activities of farm women has been greatest and most longstanding in terms of off-farm employment. It had been recognized for quite some time that farm women were increasing their participation in off-farm labor markets (see, e.g., Bokemeier and Coughenour, 1980; Bokemeier et al. 1983; Sweet, 1972), and that women's off-farm earnings were often crucial in ensuring the viability of farms. It was also recognized, however, that farm women's off-farm jobs typically were concentrated in low-skill, low-wage sectors of the economy (Brown and O'Leary, 1979) and tended to involve less-than-full-time or otherwise intermittent employment (Rosenfeld, 1985).

Subsequent descriptive studies on farm women's work roles focused primarily on their on-farm and household work and its relationships with off-farm employment. One of the most extensive studies was by Jones and Rosenfeld (1981), who used 1980 national survey data to profile farm women's involvement in farm work, off-farm employment, community activities, and several USDA programs. They found a high incidence of women's involvement in most agricultural production tasks, including those typically considered to be "men's work" (e.g., harvesting crops and doing field work). Over three-quarters of farm women were found to play a role in bookkeeping and other financial management tasks on the farm. Slightly over 30 percent of the farm women (60 percent of whom worked less than 40 hours per week) reported off-farm employment.

A further major descriptive study was Salant's (1983) survey of farm households in 29 rural counties in Mississippi and Tennessee. She concluded that farm women are extensively involved in on- and off-farm work; over half of the women reported employment either on-, off-, or both on- and off-farm, about 75 percent of whom worked off-farm. Women's off-farm labor force participation was found to be related to age and family life cycle. The off-farm income earned by farm women made a major contribution to the income of households in the survey—in many cases enabling the family to rise above poverty-level status—despite the fact that farm women's employment was largely in low-wage jobs. Women who worked on-farm primarily did so as unpaid family laborers. Only

3 percent of the women in the sample were principal farm operators. Salant did not, however, find any support for the hypothesis that women who work on-farm tend to do so to free the labor of men in order to acquire more lucrative off-farm jobs.

Another important descriptive study is that of Fassinger and Schwarzweller (1984), which was based on a 1979 sample survey of 124 farm households in Michigan. Fassinger and Schwarzweller found that farm size was positively related to the amount and proportion of time spent by farm men and women in on-farm work. Farm size was inversely related to men's off-farm employment but had no association with women's off-farm employment. They found that men's time devoted to on-farm work was positively associated with women's on-farm work. Fassinger and Schwarzweller found a very high degree of division of labor by gender for both farm and household tasks. On the farm, women were more likely to assist with financial and recordkeeping aspects of the business and to plant and maintain a vegetable garden. Men, on the other hand, were primarily involved in field operations, the purchase of farm inputs and machinery, and the repair of machinery and farm buildings. The lion's share of household tasks was performed by women regardless of the scale of the farm.

Kalbacher's (1985) study was the first comprehensive report profiling the role of women farmers in American agriculture (but see Sachs, 1983, for preliminary data). Kalbacher used 1978 census results and data from a 1979 Farm Finance Survey to present a statistical profile of women farm operators. About 5.2 percent of all U.S. farm operators, or 128,000 farmers, were women in 1978—representing a near-doubling of the number of female farmers since 1970 and a tripling since 1950. Female-operated farms were located disproportionately in the South, and tended more often to be owner-operated, part-time, and smaller than male-operated farms. Female farm operators were also older and more likely to be in a racial-minority group than their male counterparts. But whereas women farmers were less likely than men to report farming as their principal occupation, their average off-farm income was significantly less, resulting in a much lower average household income for women farmers, though female-operated farms typically had lower debt and more favorable debt-asset ratios than did male-operated farms.

A further examination of the role of farm women in the United States was conducted by Tigges and Rosenfeld (1987) in their study of differences between men and women among "independent" farmers using a national sample. The independent farmer was defined as "a woman or man who has managerial responsibility for the farm operation and lacks a spouse's regular farm labor" (p. 345). They found that, unlike independent farming men who were similar to men whose wives participated in farming, independent farming women tended to have lower net farm incomes and total family incomes than did other women. Part of these differences were explained by differences in type of farm, class, and life-cycle situation variables. Tigges and Rosenfeld concluded that independent women farmers tended to enter farming by default (as upon the death of a spouse) rather than seeking to enter farming on their own.

After several years of descriptive studies documenting the variety of contributions of women to U.S. farm households, the attention of several researchers shifted to changes in these roles over time. The most important study in this regard has been by Wilkening (1981b) in which he presented data from a 1978 mail survey of Wisconsin farm families, personal interviews with farm couples completed in 1979, and data from a 1962 study carried out in the same region. The data reveal that families remain the most important source of labor on Wisconsin farms, particularly on dairy farms that dominate in Wisconsin. Nonetheless, Wilkening found that both farm men and women now contribute less time to the farm operation than they did in 1962. Off-farm employment by one of the spouses was significant in the late 1970s on about one-quarter of the farms, and off-farm work was associated with low levels of gross farm and high levels of total family income, but was unrelated to stage in the family life cycle. While Wilkening found that farm women have not played an increased role in farm production activities since 1962, the data did show that farm women have begun to assume major responsibilities for recordkeeping and other financial aspects of Wisconsin farm operations. Women were reported to be equal partners in making important farm decisions on about half of the farms, a slight increase since 1962. Farm women remained largely responsible for the vast majority of household work during the study period.

Testing part of a theory about the sexual division of labor and authority in farm households, Bokemeier and Garkovich (1987) found that farm women's self-concepts relating to their identification with their farms' operations were complex in their sources, including scale of farm, farm background, women's human capital, and family characteristics. They identified four roles for farm women, ranging from little or no involvement and authority to full partnership: homemaker, "ag" helper, business manager, and full "ag" partner.

A quite different study oriented toward assessing change in women's and men's work roles was conducted by Gladwin (1985) in North Florida. Gladwin was concerned with exploring an extension of the Boserup (1970) hypothesis that the capitalization and intensification of agriculture are inversely associated with the level of participation of women in farm activities (see Stratigaki, 1988, for a related finding for Greece). Specifically, Gladwin examined the reverse hypothesis—that a decrease in intensification, or marginalization, of agriculture will be associated with an increase in female labor with survey and census data. Gladwin reported that women are now involved to a greater extent in farm production than in the 1920s and 1930s and that the majority of farm women think of themselves as "farmers" rather than farm wives. But she also reported that off-farm work has become more important for both men and women on North Florida farms. About 88 percent of the farms were part-time farms with significant off-farm income supporting the farm family. These part-time farms tended to produce crops or livestock requiring relatively little labor. Gladwin concluded that there is an association between labor intensification and the growing participation of women in farm work, since the few highly capitalized farms in the region received comparably less labor from women in the farm family than did the more numerous part-time, less-capitalized farms.

The third category of research on gender and agriculture has been that of assessing the mutual interrelations of men's and women's on-farm and off-farm work and how these associations are affected by the scale of the farm. One such study, by Fassinger and Schwarzweller (1984), found that men's and women's on-farm work were positively associated, and each was positively related to farm size. Also, men's off-farm work was found to be positively associated with farm scale, while women's off-farm work was not related to the size of the farm.

Coughenour and Swanson (1983) examined 1979 Kentucky farm survey data to explore the associations between farm size and the work status of farm men and women. They did so, however, in a manner different from the previous literature; whereas previous studies have seen men's and women's work statuses as a function of farm size, Coughenour and Swanson suggest that the opposite direction of causality may be important. They explored this hypothesis by developing a four-category farm-type typology based on men's and women's work statuses. They found that there was a modest association between farm types and size of farm (measured by acreage and gross sales). They explored this association further in terms of "exchanges" between men's and women's on- and off-farm labor. They found, for example, that farms in which the woman has off-farm employment forfeited some of the woman's on-farm labor (and hence its contribution to farm size and sales) but gained in income relative to other farms. They also found that the allocation of men's labor—either on-farm, which was positively associated with farm size and sales, or off-farm, which was inversely associated with farm size and sales—was a stronger determinant of the size structure of farms than was the allocation pattern of women's labor. Nonetheless, they did find that the women's role in farming had significant effects—in particular, that women's off-farm work, which reduced or eliminated her on-farm labor input, tended to be inversely associated with the size and sales position of the farm despite the fact that women's off-farm work provided additional capital for the farm operation (see also Coughenour, 1984a).

Buttel and Gillespie (1984) examined the interdependencies of average weekly hours of on-farm and off-farm work by farm men and women, the use of hired labor, and the size of farm with 1979 New York farm survey data. They found that farm men and women tend to specialize mutually in either on-farm or off-farm work, with these interdependencies being greatest among small farm households. It was also found that hired labor tends to be substituted for women's on-farm labor input, with this inverse association between hired labor and women's on-farm work being greatest among larger, commercial-scale farms. The results of the Buttel-Gillespie study were largely corroborated by a replication and extension using data from tobacco-, peanut-, and soybean-producing farms in North Carolina by Simpson et al. (1988). The extension pertained to distinguishing between production of commodities that is "organized around" individual units ("small batch") and those whose production is coordinated as a "continuous process" (p. 147). Dairy and tobacco were presented as examples of the former type and soybeans and peanuts as examples of the latter type. Simpson et al. found that crop production organized as continuous processes tended to make farm women's work more independent of farm men's than was the case for crop production organized around small batches, and thus technological change in the production of "continuous process" crops had different effects on men and women.

Rigorous analysis of gender relations on U.S. farms is a sufficiently new focus of research that, save for the pioneering book by Sachs (1983), there has been little effort to incorporate gender relations phenomena into a comprehensive theory of farm structural change. Sachs' book thus is the single representative in the fourth category of research on farm gender relations and the gender division of farm household labor.

Sachs' (1983) book is a wide-ranging treatment of research on farm women from a variety of disciplines and in both First World and Third World contexts. For present purposes, Sachs' treatment of U.S. farm women receives principal emphasis. As indicated in the title of her book, one of Sachs' key arguments is that while women have historically made significant contributions to agricultural (and, increasingly, off-farm) labor, these contributions have been overlooked and undervalued. Whereas Sachs roots her analysis in the new political economy tradition referred to at the beginning of this chapter, she contends that the invisibility of the women's role in agriculture, and the subordination of women in the agricultural labor process, cannot be explained with reference to the dynamics of capitalist development alone. She argues that the simultaneous contribution of women to agriculture along with their invisibility and subordination must be viewed through the dynamics of capitalism and patriarchy, which is defined as a "set of social relations which has a material base and in which there are hierarchical relations between men, and solidarity among them, which enable them to control women" (1983:70, 71). She emphasizes, moreover, that patriarchical relations preceded (although they have been transformed by) capitalism and thus cannot be seen as a direct consequence of capitalist development.

Sachs begins by demonstrating that at each major stage of agricultural development from the seventeenth century to the present women have played important roles in facilitating the viability of U.S. farms. Until the twentieth century the importance of women was typically seen to be in producing and processing food for home consumption. There was a traditional division of labor between men and women in which men did the majority of the field work, but this division of labor would often break down during busy seasons when women would do "male" tasks. With the industrialization of U.S. society and further commercialization of agriculture, women's subsistence production activities diminished in importance. Women accordingly tended to increase their on-farm and/or off-farm work. These patterns, however, varied substantially by region, with women's direct involvement in farming being greatest in the South and West. Sachs notes that one constant historical feature of women's roles in farm households has been in their performing the bulk of household tasks. Women have become somewhat more involved in farm decision making, but Sachs suggests that their decision-making roles have been secondary to their labor contributions to the farm operation and household.

Sachs' analysis then turns to the historical development of a "domestic ideology"—that women are naturally "domestic" beings and more suited to household work than men—in U.S. society in general and in agriculture in particular. She argues that keeping women in domestic roles has facilitated the development of capitalism by maintaining a reserve labor force and creating a consumptive domestic class. Sachs suggests that the family farm, particularly because it is based on the nuclear family, has been one of the most pervasive mechanisms through which patriarchal relations have been maintained on U.S. farms. She then explores how this patriarchal order has been reflected in the sexual division of labor on farms and in the social relations of women-operated farms.

Sachs' (1983) book has been exemplary in identifying how gender relations on U.S. farms have been shaped by the twin forces of patriarchy and capitalist development. Her work remains the most comprehensive theoretical statement and overview of empirical evidence on farm gender relations that has yet appeared. Sachs' book is wide-ranging but brief, suggesting that further elaborations and critiques will increase our theoretical and empirical understanding of farm gender relations and the gender division of farm and rural labor (some of which can be found in Haney and Knowles, 1988). In particular, several ambiguities remain in the literature. At an empirical level, while the past decade of research has established a number of frequently supported generalizations about the structuring of farm women's work roles, there are a number of conflicting results. Some observers, for example, argue that women make major contributions to farm work, whereas others see a clear division of labor such that women participate very little in farm tasks. Other empirical controversies may well arise from the fact that most of the major studies in the field have been based on data from a single state. Thus further research is needed to clarify these empirical patterns and to incorporate them in a larger theoretical perspective—a major component of which will likely revolve around establishing and explaining differential patterns of women's work roles across farming regions. Some of this theorizing and comparative research is, however, taking place in Europe (see Gasson, 1988; Whatmore, 1988). Berlan Darque (1988), for example, has analyzed in detail the gender relations on farms in France and has made some initial notes toward a theory of variations in gender differences in the household, child-rearing, and farm work.

CONCLUSION

This chapter focuses on several themes in the "new rural sociology" or "new sociology of agriculture," and does so by placing particular stress on the role of neo-Marxist and neo-Weberian perspectives. It is by no means the case, however, that these new theoretical perspectives dominate the sociology of agriculture in the United States. There, in fact, has been an increase in the theoretical diversity of research on American agriculture. The community studies (e.g., Larson, 1981; Smith, 1974) and behaviorist (e.g., Schroeder et al., 1985) traditions of previous decades persist, and the newer critical tradition is itself very diverse. Neo-Marxism and neo-Weberianism, however, have come to be increasingly central to the sociology of agriculture in the late 1980s, particularly through their strong influence on defining research problems.

In the next chapter we examine several other foci in the new sociology of agriculture. Each of these foci represents the growing attention paid by sociologists to the "environment" of modern agriculture.

4

The New Sociology of Agriculture, II: The Environment of Agriculture

The tack we have taken in developing two chapters on recent research in the sociology of agriculture has been to make an (admittedly arbitrary) dichotomization of research on the basis of whether it focuses on the "internal" dynamics and characteristics of agriculture on one hand, or on the "external environment" of agriculture on the other. This chapter, in focusing on the "environment" of agriculture, employs this expression both metaphorically and literally. More specifically, we begin by focusing on four selected aspects of the metaphorical or social "environment" of agriculture—technological change, the sociology of agricultural research, the impacts of farm structural change on rural communities, and the farm crisis. We then turn to several areas of inquiry in which agriculture is explored in terms of the natural or physical environment. As noted earlier, the dual theme of the ecological consequences of agriculture and the role of environmental factors in affecting the structure of agriculture has been one of two key lines of theoretical development—the other being neo-Marxist and neo-Weberian-derived versions of the political economy of agriculture—that have spearheaded the "new sociology of agriculture" since the early and mid-1970s.

THE IMPACT OF TECHNOLOGICAL CHANGE ON AGRICULTURE

Technological change is among a small handful of topics in what is now referred to as the sociology of agriculture—along with part-time farming and analysis of the farm family—that have received attention during all three major phases in rural sociology. From the 1930s through the 1950s there were several major studies by sociologists of the impacts of technological change, most of which centered on the rapid mechanization of southern agriculture that began during the Great Depression (Bertrand, 1948, 1958b; Pedersen, 1954; Pederson and Raper, 1954; Raper, 1946; Williams, 1939). The concern of many of the early rural sociologists with the socioeconomic consequences of technological change, however, largely lapsed during the succeeding phase of rural sociology in which the diffusion-adoption perspective was dominant. In the era of the "new sociology of agriculture," we again see a rekindling of concern with the social consequences of technological change. Moreover, interest in the consequences of technological change has become expressed in more social structural terms and, as demonstrated later, has become more closely integrated with analyses of the genesis of new agricultural technologies.

Several other important observations can be made on the rural sociological literature on technological change in agriculture over the past decade. First, mechanization has received the lion's share of attention; technological change in the forms of improved varieties of crops and breeds of livestock or of agricultural chemicals has been the focus of only a few major ex post studies. Second, as Berardi (1981) has observed, there are many problems in decomposing the effects of technological change on farm structure from the effects of other variables such as public policy or changing wage rates; therefore, rural sociologists have often relied heavily on the primary research of others (e.g., agricultural economists and geographers with complementary expertise in assessing technological impacts) when developing comprehensive assessments of the socioeconomic impacts of technological change.

Third, the conceptualization of technological change in agriculture by rural sociologists has been heavily influenced by the work of the agricultural economist, Willard Cochrane (1958, 1979), who developed a theory of the "treadmill of technology" in the late 1950s (see, in particular, LeVeen, 1978, for a nontechnical summary of Cochrane's theory). Briefly, Cochrane's theory of technological change builds on a key observation from rural sociological research on the diffusion-adoption of innovations—that large farmers who are entrepreneurial and nonrisk-averse tend to be the first to adopt new agricultural technologies. By adopting early, these farmers enjoy "innovators' rents" because of their ability to reduce their average per unit production costs. Cochrane posits that after these innovators and early adopters have employed the new agricultural technology, aggregate output of the particular commodity involved will begin to increase and prices will decline disproportionately (because agricultural commodities tend to have a low price elasticity of demand). Declining prices then begin to force nonadopters to utilize the technology. These subsequent adopters gain very little from the technology; they adopt it merely to be able to stay in business. Slow adopters or nonadopters will tend to be forced out of agriculture because they can no longer compete due to their high average costs of production. Cochrane considers the technological change process to be a "treadmill" in that the majority of farmers, who receive little or no benefit from the technology, are nonetheless forced to continue to adopt new agricultural technologies in order to stay in business. Cochrane has also observed that the benefits of technological change tend over the long term to be realized in the form of rising land values, particularly if there are commodity programs in effect to cushion a commodity sector from declining crop prices caused by increases in output. The benefits of technological change (innovators' rents from early adoption) tend to be reinvested in farm land, causing increases in land prices and benefiting large landowners over smaller property owners and tenants. These effects, in Cochrane's view, are heightened when commodity programs support crop prices, thereby increasing the level of innovators' rents and intensifying the extent to which these benefits are capitalized in asset values.

Cochrane's theory of the treadmill of technology has been widely accepted in recent rural sociological work as an orienting perspective because it has effectively linked knowledge from diverse origins (rural sociological research on diffusion-adoption, agricultural economics research on technological change, and so on). Cochrane's theory, however, has its limits—in particular, its inapplicability to industrial agriculture, as noted by LeVeen (1978). Moreover, the notion of the treadmill of technology gives little attention to the origins of technology, that is, to why technologies that have displaced labor or benefited larger operators over smaller ones have been developed, a topic that, as discussed below, has recently come to be a major research issue for those working in the sociology of agricultural science. Nonetheless, with the exception of sociologists of agriculture who have focused on industrial agriculture (e.g., Friedland and Barton, 1975; Friedland et al., 1981), rural sociologists have yet to develop a distinctly sociological theory of technological change and its socioeconomic consequences.

While rural sociologists have not yet developed a comprehensive and distinctly sociological theory of technological change and its consequences applicable to both family farming and industrial agriculture, the new sociology of agriculture as applied to technological change has made some significant advances. Several of the most important of these advances are summarized below.

Among the most significant research papers on the topic of technological change in agriculture were two published in the late 1970s that dealt with limitations of the classical diffusion-adoption model. The first, by Pampel and van Es (1977), was an otherwise traditional adoption study that included, in addition to "commercial-profitable" innovations that were the major focus of previous diffusion-adoption studies, a set of "environmental innovations" such as contour farming, terracing, sod waterways, and use of rotation cover and reduced tillage. Pampel and van Es discovered that the correlates of adoption of environmental innovations were far different than those of commercial innovations. For example, while large-scale farmers were observed to be the earliest adopters of commercial technologies, there was no significant relationship between farm size and the adoption of environmental innovations. They concluded their study by cautioning rural sociologists that the diffusion-adoption tradition, because it had ignored dimensions of innovative behavior such as the adoption of environmental-conservation technologies, "may have provided within rural sociology a field of knowledge with a narrow empirical foundation on which to base its generalizations" (Pampel and van Es, 1977:69). They also emphasized that given the tendency of most environmental innovations to be unprofitable, it was not clear that voluntary strategies to achieve soil conservation and related environmental goals would be successful.

Writing two years after the Pampel and van Es study, Goss (1979a) focused more systematically on the limitations of diffusion-adoption research. The principal failings of diffusion-adoption research, in Goss' view, were (1) that it was uncritical, if not promotional, toward patterns of technological change that may be detrimental to the interests of society and/or farmers, and (2) that the focusing of research effort on the adoption component of the technology change process had caused rural sociologists to ignore the consequences of technological change for various groups in society. Goss summarized the early 1970s literature critical of the Green Revolution and pointed out that the Green Revolution had been initiated with the same promotional orientation toward technology that had predominated during the heyday of the diffusion-adoption tradition in U.S. rural sociology. He noted that many social scientists who had once worked within the diffusion-adoption tradition in international agricultural activities had begun to recognize the limits of the adoption paradigm (e.g., Rogers, 1976). He argued, however, that this point had not been well recognized in domestic rural sociology and that rural sociology must begin to develop a more comprehensive program of research on the consequences of technological change in agriculture.

In a manner similar to Goss' exegesis of the Green Revolution literature in terms of the impacts of technological change on social groups and classes in agriculture, Stockdale (1977), in an influential article, raised comparable issues in terms of the ecological aspects of modern agricultural technology. Noting that the contribution of technological change to American agricultural productivity had often been held up as a model for other nations to emulate, Stockdale argued that social scientists had tended to ignore the adverse ecological impacts of energy-intensive technology in the United States and elsewhere. Like Goss, Stockdale called for an expanded program of research on technological change in agriculture that would emphasize the social and ecological consequences of new agricultural technologies.

Among the most innovative thrusts in sociological research on technological change in agriculture have been the series of books, monographs, and articles published by Friedland and associates (especially Friedland and Barton, 1975; Friedland et al., 1981). Friedland and his colleagues have focused on technological change in industrial agriculture in California and have identified a number of components of the technological change process that have tended to be ignored in the earlier rural sociological literature. As noted earlier, Friedland has focused on several commodity systems (chiefly tomatoes, lettuce, and grapes) and has found that the social organization of each commodity system—and hence the structural context of technological change—is distinctive. Nonetheless, Friedland and his associates have demonstrated that the technological change process in industrial agriculture generally is heavily influenced by considerations of the cost of, access to, and control over labor and by the relationships of grower organizations with public and private components of the agricultural research system. They have also demonstrated that the nature of the technological change process and its consequences depend upon the structure of the commodity system. For example, in the aftermath of the termination of the bracero program in 1964, a mechanical tomato harvester technology was widely adopted in California, displacing three-quarters of California tomato producers and the bulk of their agricultural wage labor forces. In lettuce, however, grower-shippers were able to utilize the threat of lettuce harvest mechanization to discipline the labor force and to avoid the costly process of harvest mechanization.

A further component of the recent rural sociological literature on technological change, one to which Friedland (1984b) and Friedland and associates (1981) have made major contributions, is social impact assessment of new agricultural technologies (see especially Berardi and Geisler, 1984). Social impact assessments of new agricultural technologies are a distinctive type of research in that they often tend to rely primarily on secondary data or on the results from the published literature (see, e.g., Geisler et al., 1984) rather than on primary research and data collection; this is particularly the case if the assessment must be prepared over a short period of time. (Some social impact assessment efforts, such as that by Friedland et al., 1981, have, however, involved extensive primary data collection and analysis.) Other distinctive aspects of social impact assessment of new agricultural technologies are, first, that the assessment is ex ante (rather than ex post, as in most previous rural sociological research on technological change) and, second, that the orientation toward these emerging technologies tends to be questioning and skeptical, rather than accepting and promotional. Rural sociologists who have conducted social impact assessments of new technologies have approached their subject matter from the vantage point that most new technologies tend to involve an unequal distribution of costs and benefits and that advance projections of these patterns of the distribution of costs and benefits can enable social scientists and affected groups to redress these distributional impacts more effectively.

An example of the type of knowledge base that has been developed, in part, as a building block for social-impact assessment research is Berardi's (1981) comprehensive review of the impacts of agricultural mechanization. Berardi reviewed the results of over 180 studies of agricultural mechanization in the United States and elsewhere and summarized the major empirical regularities in studies of a variety of types of mechanization in a diversity of commodity systems. She concluded by pointing out that the rich literature on agricultural mechanization—most of it prepared by nonsociologists—is sufficient so that sociologists may contemplate conducting rigorous ex ante studies of the impacts of new mechanical technologies in agriculture (see also Copp, 1983). Unfortunately, as noted earlier, sociological knowledge on the socioeconomic impacts of mechanization is far greater than that on "biochemical" technologies (plant varieties, fertilizers, insecticides, herbicides, and so on). There have only recently been sociological studies (e.g., Kloppenburg, 1984, 1988a) that have delivered on Stockdale's (1977) and Berardi's (1981) admonitions in the area of biochemical technologies in plant and animal agriculture. It is likely, however, that the great attention that has already been paid by rural sociologists to emerging biotechnologies in agriculture will result in a sustained research program into the socioeconomic consequences of these new technologies (see, e.g., Molnar and Kinnucan, 1985, 1989).

It should be noted in closing, however, that while there is great merit in inventorying the results of existing studies on various facets of technological change—as, for example, Berardi (1981) has done—sociologists should exercise caution, as technological change should not be assumed to have invariant consequences across time and space. In particular, as noted above, there have been some major recent changes in the structure of U.S. agriculture that one might expect will have significant effects on the technological change process and its consequences (Buttel and Geisler, 1989). For example, instead of technological change tending to result in the decline of small farms, as it did during the bulk of the post-World War II period, it may be quite likely that new agricultural technologies such as biotechnology-derived plant varieties, growth regulators, and bovine growth hormone may tend to result in the disproportionate demise of medium-sized, full-time family farmers. Thus future rural sociological research on technological change in agriculture must be cognizant of ongoing changes in the structure of agriculture and how these changes affect the types of agricultural technologies that are employed, the processes of technological change, and their consequences.

THE SOCIOLOGY OF AGRICULTURAL SCIENCE

We noted several times in the preceding that the era of the new sociology of agriculture was initiated in the aftermath of a distinctly new political milieu of agricultural science and research. Hightower's *Hard Tomatoes, Hard Times,* although sensational in tone and misleading on several aspects of the public agricultural research system (Buttel, 1985a), attracted a great deal of attention from defenders and critics of the land-grant research system. Most importantly, Hightower's book (along with contemporary ecological criticism of U.S. agricultural technology) opened up several new lines of social science inquiry into the structure and functioning of the public agricultural research system (Hadwiger, 1982).

Probably in no other state did public agricultural science become as controversial as in California after the publication of Hightower's book. The California Agricultural Experiment Station has long had close relationships with industrial farmers and other segments of agribusiness and had been held directly responsible in the eyes of many for developing new technologies, such as the tomato harvester, which had resulted in the rapid loss of tomato farmers and the displacement of hired farm workers. It was thus not surprising that the initial sociological inquiries into the conduct of public agricultural science were conducted in California.

The first set of studies by Fujimoto and others (Fujimoto and Fiske, 1975; Fujimoto and Kopper, 1975) at the University of California, Davis, were directly inspired by Hightower and were largely focused on how agricultural scientists made research problem choices. In particular, Fujimoto and colleagues devoted attention to how research problem choices were determined by "internal" factors (such as tenure and promotion considerations) and "external" factors (such as the influence of agribusiness interests and grants). They found on the basis of personal interviews with scientists that external factors were quite important, though internal factors also exerted major influence on scientists' research priorities. The second set of studies focused on California was initiated by Friedland and associates (1981), who examined the processes by which agricultural commodity groups organized to exert influence on individual scientists, departments, and the University of California system as a whole in order to ensure the development and availability of technologies that would enhance their profitability. Friedland and associates gave particular attention to how the responses of University of California research officials and scientists came to emphasize mechanization and mechanization-related technology that enabled growers to displace farm workers (Friedland and Barton, 1975) or to enhance the control of growers over their hired labor force (Friedland, 1980; Friedland et al., 1981). Based on the results of several years of research during the 1970s, Friedland and Kappel (1979) published a short, but still influential, monograph calling attention to biases in the public agricultural research system and outlining mechanisms by which social scientists and groups adversely affected by particular types of agricultural research could achieve changes in the land-grant system.

Shortly after the California studies were initiated, a research group at the University of Kentucky led by William B. Lacy and Lawrence Busch began a program of inquiry into the sociology of agricultural science that continues to make major contributions to a sociological understanding of the processes by which new agricultural technologies are generated. The first publication of this group, by Busch (1978), was a theoretical critique of the prevailing conception of scientific knowledge by researchers in the diffusion-adoption tradition. Subsequent publications by the Lacy-Busch group have focused on a variety of aspects of the structure and functioning of public agricultural research activities.

Two books published by the Lacy-Busch group have had particular impact on rural sociology and the larger social science community (see especially Hadwiger, 1982; Ruttan, 1982) exploring agricultural research. The first, *Science and Agricultural Development,* edited by Busch (1981) and containing several papers by his research colleagues, was the first book-length treatment of agricultural research in the tradition of the new sociology of agriculture. The chapters in the Busch anthology most germane to the sociology of agricultural science are the following: Randolph and Sachs (1981) compared the establishment of medical and agricultural science, emphasizing how a reductionist orientation and technocratic ideology had been developed in each during the process of institutionalization. Busch and Lacy (1981) summarized the existing literature and their preliminary research on sources of influence in research problem choices in the agricultural sciences. Striving to further the social scientific conceptualization of agricultural science and technology as social products, they explored two rival social science views of the social construction and social structure of science. One, the "internalist" view deriving from Merton's (1973) work, *Sociology of Science,* essentially holds that the outcomes of the scientific research process are determined by the "norms of science," held by practitioners and reinforced within scientific institutions, and by the very subject matter itself. The other perspective, the "externalist" view, argues that the outcomes of the research process are largely shaped by the institutions, interests, and availability of resources that originate and are determined outside of scientific disciplines and research institutions. They suggest that both perspectives have a certain validity: "[T]he internal and external positions are best viewed as distinct strata in the life-worlds of practicing scientists. Thus, for each discipline and institution, science is a continuous process of multilevel negotiation regarding the sources of influence on research" (Busch and Lacy, 1981:113). A final paper in the Busch (1981) collection of particular relevance to the new sociology of agriculture was Busch and Sachs' (1981), which employed a world-systems framework derived from Wallerstein (1974) to examine the establishment of the agricultural sciences in the First and Third Worlds since the seventeenth century.

Busch and Lacy are known best for their book, *Science, Agri-*

culture, and the Politics of Research (Busch and Lacy, 1983), which summarized an ambitious study of research problem choice through the use of historical methods, personal interviews, and sample survey data. Following several introductory chapters that discuss the establishment of public agricultural research, the organization of the public agricultural research system, the social demography of agricultural scientists, and the structure of communication in the agricultural sciences, they explore three major sources of influences on agricultural research: disciplinary, organizational, and extra-organizational. Busch and Lacy found scientific disciplines and disciplinary organizations to be powerful and growing influences over scientists' research problem choices. Scientific disciplines affect scientists' research choices in a variety of ways, particularly through controlling peer-reviewed journals and establishing the norms adopted by land-grant universities and the Agricultural Research Service (ARS) in tenure and promotion decisions. Busch and Lacy also found dramatic differences among the agricultural science disciplines according to the degree to which they emphasize basic or applied research, the rate at which they accept papers in scientific journals, their norms for scientific productivity, and the degree to which scientists exhibit consensus on what are "hot" topics in the field (see also Buttel, 1985a).

Organizational context—including ARS vs. land-grant university context and the institutional prestige of the land-grant institution—was found to be a significant influence on research problem choices. Busch and Lacy found that ARS scientists were more highly constrained in their problem choices than land-grant agricultural scientists. They also found that institutional prestige was positively related to the degree to which extra-organizational influences and constraints on research choices were manifest. Among the extra-organizational influences, granting agencies and organizations (those hiring scientists on a short-term consultancy basis) were the most direct and pervasive. Whereas there were very large differences among the disciplines in the extent to which their scientists relied heavily on extramural support, Busch and Lacy emphasize that fiscal constraints on public research appropriations are increasing the pressures on scientists to obtain grants and contracts from government agencies, agribusiness firms, foundations, and so on; accordingly, scientists are becoming less autonomous in their research problem choices.

Until the early 1980s, only a small community of rural sociologists were interested in the sociology of agricultural science. This was to change dramatically, however, in the aftermath of a workshop on biotechnology in the summer of 1982 at the University of Kentucky organized by B. Koppel, Busch, and Lacy. Since that conference there has been growing attention to a variety of facets of biotechnology as key focal points of research in the sociology of agricultural science. This research on biotechnology now represents a large literature, and the approaches developed therein have begun to substantially influence how rural sociologists are exploring other types of agricultural technology such as information technologies (Goe, 1986). This new line of research has been salutary in yet another respect; sociologists interested in biotechnology have begun to make major progress in uniting the sociology of agricultural science with sociological research on technological change and social impact assessment of new agricultural technologies (see, in particular, Kloppenburg, 1984; Molnar et al., 1985).

The wide-ranging and potentially integrative character of research on biotechnology, agricultural research, and agricultural change is amply illustrated by rural sociologists having given major attention to no less than 10 major themes under this rubric. With regard to the first, the politics of the evolution of the public agricultural research system, Buttel (1986a) and Kenney and Kloppenburg (1983) found that the basic science discoveries (especially recombinant DNA) relating to biotechnology, the promise of biotechnology to agribusiness firms for developing new input commodities, and federal government concern with the U.S. competitive position in the "high technologies" have rekindled scrutiny of the land-grant and ARS systems for placing too little emphasis on basic biological research. The result was a changing political climate of public agricultural research that has led to rapid expansion of biotechnology programs in the public agricultural research institutions and to a deemphasis on traditional, applied research. These changes in the research emphases of public agricultural research institutions have stimulated a second area of research in the sociology of biotechnology: industry-university relationships and the changing division of labor between public and private research. Buttel et al. (1986a,b), for example, have found that industrial funding of agricultural research at the land-grant universities has increased significantly and this has generated new concerns that agribusiness firms are acquiring excessive influence on research priorities in public research institutions. Lacy and Busch (1989) have identified a large number of likely impacts of closer industry-university relationships in agricultural biotechnology: further decline of public plant breeding (especially varietal releases), greater concentration of scientific talent at a small number of land-grant universities, decreased autonomy of public researchers in establishing their own research agendas, increased secrecy, and greater restrictions on the free flow of scientific information.

A third area of research relating to biotechnology has been on agribusiness reorganization. Kenney (1986), Kloppenburg (1988a), and Buttel et al. (1984) have noted that the rise of biotechnology research has reinforced or led directly to major structural reorganization in the agribusiness industries. With the passage of the Plant Variety Protection Act of 1970, the ability of private firms to acquire patent-like protection for new crop varieties increased the perceived profit potential of seed companies, leading to the incorporation of most major independent seed companies into multinational corporations as wholly owned subsidiaries or joint-venture partners. Biotechnology reinforced this trend, since seeds are projected to become the major commercial vehicle for plant biotechnology; moreover, the basic sciences underlying biotechnology (molecular and cell biology) are quite similar to those that will ultimately be applied in other areas of agricultural inputs such as agricultural chemicals, innoculants, and animal pharmaceuticals. Thus biotechnology has increased the benefits of uniting chemical and plant breeding product lines within integrated multinational firms that manufacture several agricultural input products. Kenney (1986) has given particular attention to the role of small venture-capital or start-up companies in biotechnology and has analyzed the processes by which they have developed linkages with large companies.

Goodman et al. (1987) have stressed that biotechnology will have two distinct applications in agriculture—"appropriationism" and "substitutionism"—with different consequences for structural reorganization of the food and agricultural industries. By "appropriationism" Goodman et al. mean the use of biotechnology to develop new inputs, such as new crop varieties and animal breeds, for agricultural production. Appropriationist applications of agricultural biotechnology will tend to result in the integration of agricultural input manufacturing with comparable product lines in other life science industries such as chemicals and pharmaceuticals. "Substitutionism," on the other hand, refers to the use of biotechnology to substitute for existing products. Substitutionism will therefore have the effect of severing existing production "chains," in which specific raw materials are employed to produce particular final products (e.g., substituting single-cell proteins for vegetable proteins as animal feed supplements). The implications of "substitutionist" applications of biotechnology will also include shifting food and fiber production from the farm to the factory (e.g., substituting industrial tissue-cultured thaumatin for cane sugar). Substitutionist applications will tend to lead to integration of the food and fiber processing and chemical industries.

Fourth, several researchers have examined how biotechnology has affected and will continue to affect plant breeding, including but not limited to public-sector plant breeding. Kloppenburg (1988a) has conducted an extensive historical analysis of plant breeding and the seed industry in the United States. He has argued that the trends under way as a direct and indirect result of biotechnology promise to increase the penetration of agribusiness interests into land-grant university plant breeding programs and to complete the shift, under way since the late 1930s, to curtail the role of land-grant plant breeders in developing public-domain finished plant varieties. Hansen et al. (1986) have reached similar conclusions on the basis of interviews with plant breeders and biotechnology researchers across the public and private sectors. Hansen et al. have noted as well that the increased importance of biotechnology in public-sector plant breeding programs, combined with new avenues for agribusiness influence, will tend to result in the demise of public plant breeding efforts for minor crops.

A fifth area of inquiry in biotechnology, agriculture, and agricultural research has been on the role of intellectual property restrictions and other proprietary considerations in affecting research priorities and the nature of the new technologies that are developed. Kloppenburg (1988a), for example, has called attention to private-sector plant breeding firms' longstanding concern about the perceived inadequacy of intellectual property institutions to protect their investments in plant breeding. In the absence of such restrictions for sexually reproduced crops prior to 1970, most seed companies focused primarily on hybrid seeds (largely hybrid corn), which, because of their reproductive instability, afforded a "natural," biological protection against farmers saving their own seeds and circumventing annual purchases of seeds from private companies. Kloppenburg has noted, however, that the elaboration of new legal means of privatizing plant research has increased corporate interest in plant biotechnology. Kloppenburg (1988a), Kenney (1986), and Hansen et al. (1986) have suggested that the role of intellectual property restrictions, combined with the fact that most agricultural input firms have both seed and chemical product lines, may lead to the development of "seed-chemical packages" that tie the farmer more directly to purchased, capital-intensive inputs.

Sixth, Kloppenburg and Buttel (1987) have begun to explore the relationships between the public and private sectors in terms of recently developed "theories of the state" (see, for example, Carnoy, 1984; Evans et al., 1985). They have begun this task by conceptualizing public agricultural research and government commodity programs as reflecting contradictions of state intervention.

They note public agricultural research with state intervention has tended historically to be expanded during times of socioeconomic crisis. Agricultural research, however, can be seen to set the stage for future crises in the agricultural economy by creating long-term increases in agricultural productivity. They discuss the emergence and resolution of these contradictions in the context of the Great Depression and the current era of biotechnology and farm crisis (see also Buttel and Busch, 1988; Gillespie and Buttel, 1989).

A seventh area of research pursued within the rubric of biotechnology has been the implications of this new trajectory of research for genetic resources. Kloppenburg (1988a) and Hansen et al. (1986) have argued that the increased role of intellectual property restrictions combined with the new opportunities for private firms in developing new purchased input commodities will tend to lead to a decline in germplasm flows between the public and private sectors. In the absence of greatly expanded public and quasi-public appropriations for germplasm preservation, these trends are seen to threaten the genetic resource base and perhaps to constrain plant improvement in the future. Kloppenburg and Kleinman (1987, 1988) have also examined the forces, including the rise of biotechnology, that have led to North-South conflict over control over crop germplasm (see also the related articles in Kloppenburg, 1988b).

Eighth, as noted earlier, considerable attention has been focused on how new biotechnology-related inputs such as bovine growth hormone, herbicide-tolerant crop varieties, nitrogen-fixing cereal grains, and so on might affect the structure of agriculture in the future. Kenney et al. (1982) have emphasized that agricultural biotechnologies are potentially quite diverse and that how these new technologies will affect farm structures depends heavily on the research priorities that are established. Molnar and Kinnucan (1985), basing their work on existing theories of and evidence on technological change in agriculture, argue that larger farmers will likely be the first to adopt—and thus be the major beneficiaries of —the new biotechnologies. Kloppenburg (1984) has developed a preliminary ex ante assessment of how new biotechnologies applied to corn might affect U.S. farm structure over the coming decades. Buttel (1986b) has focused on the first major biotechnology to be applied in agriculture: bovine growth hormone, which can be produced in large quantities by genetically modified bacteria and which increases milk production per cow by up to 25 percent. He has argued that this biotechnology will likely reinforce longstanding structural trends toward a dualistic farm structure. The Molnar and Kinnucan (1989) anthology contains several important papers on ex ante assessment of new agricultural biotechnology inputs.

A ninth area of biotechnology-related research has been in providing preliminary assessments of how biotechnology might affect the nonfarm economy of nonmetropolitan areas (Buttel, 1985b, 1986c). Finally, Buttel et al. (1985), Kenney and Buttel (1985), and Koppel (1985) have done research into the implications of biotechnology for international agricultural research and agrarian transformation in Third World countries (see also Research and Information System for the Non-Aligned and Other Developing Countries, 1988, and Sasson, 1988, for useful summaries of the literature).

The sociology of agricultural research, especially its recent focus on biotechnology, has been conducted within the "new sociology of agriculture" tradition to a greater extent than any other area of inquiry, save perhaps for the state and agriculture (see Chapter 5). In particular, the sociology of agricultural research, although involving some quantitative analysis (e.g., Busch and Lacy, 1983), has been at the heart of trends in the new sociology of agriculture that have created legitimacy for exploring issues that are largely accessible only through historical-qualitative research methods. Especially in biotechnology, the impacts of which on farm structure will generally not be manifest for a decade or more, quantitative research based on primary data is virtually impossible, and the quantitative research that has been done often suffers from spurious precision (Buttel and Geisler, 1989). Given the importance of understanding the likely impacts of these new technologies, the work that is being done is of high priority. Some rural sociologists, however, will feel less than comfortable with a research tradition in which quantitative methodology and the putative precision it affords are largely absent. Nonetheless, the sociology of agricultural research and biotechnology has been among the most innovative and stimulating areas of recent research in rural sociology and will no doubt have a major impact on rural sociological inquiry in the decades to come.

AGRICULTURE AND THE RURAL COMMUNITY

Perhaps in no other area of the "new sociology of agriculture" is there so much apparent continuity with the pre-Korean War tradition of rural sociological research as in research on farm structure and rural communities. The early rural sociologists primarily conceived of agriculture as one of the major institutional ensembles affecting rural community life and, especially during the 1930s, devoted much of their research effort relating to agriculture to understanding the implications of agricultural structural changes for rural community life and viability. The conceptualization of agriculture and rural community interactions and the methodologies for exploring these interactions in pre-Korean War and post-1970 rural sociological research, however, exhibit dramatic differences. Whereas most of the early rural sociologists tended to be less interested in agriculture per se and were principally concerned with understanding rural community institutions, contemporary researchers have tended to be more interested in structural change in agriculture and have deemphasized understanding the totality of the fabric of rural social life (Larson, 1981). The research tools and data sources of these two generations of rural sociological researchers are also dramatically different. The early rural sociologists relied on rural social surveys, while the bulk of contemporary research is based on county-level census data. A further difference between the early and contemporary rural sociologists of agriculture in their work relating to rural communities concerns the pivot of the latter studies around Goldschmidt's (1947/1978a) *As You Sow*. This is somewhat ironic in that Goldschmidt's study was anthropological and qualitative, whereas the research conducted since 1970 that has drawn on Goldschmidt's work has largely been quantitative and has involved far less "anthropological" detail on rural communities than did Goldschmidt's. Rodefeld (1974) is generally credited with the "rediscovery" and popularization of Goldschmidt's pioneering work among rural sociologists, though Heffernan (1972) made important contributions to elevating "Goldschmidt-style" research to a prominent position in rural sociology. Nonetheless, after Rodefeld's refocusing of rural sociological attention on the Goldschmidt thesis (see especially Rodefeld et al., 1978), Goldschmidt's book has been virtually an obligatory citation in research articles on this topic. Despite some trenchant criticisms of Goldschmidt's perspective and research methodology (see Goss, 1979b; Hayes and Olmstead, 1984; LeVeen, 1979), Goldschmidt's general hypotheses remain accepted theoretically and thus continue to shape, if not dominate, research on farm structure and rural communities within the "new sociology of agriculture."

Briefly, Goldschmidt's thesis was that there are differences in the quality of rural community life depending upon the social organization of agriculture and its attendant occupational structure. Goldschmidt observed that the quality of rural life in two carefully matched California communities in the San Joaquin Valley differed dramatically and that these differences were largely accounted for by the organization of agriculture. He argued that Dinuba, a community surrounded by "family" farms, had a greater number of businesses, a larger retail sales volume, a higher per capita income, and a greater diversity of social, educational, recreational, and cultural institutions than did Arvin, a community surrounded by large, industrial, corporate farms. These differences were principally accounted for by an intervening variable—community occupational composition—that was seen to be strongly influenced by the social organization of agriculture and which directly contributed to the dramatic variations in indicators of the quality of life. Goldschmidt reported that the high ratio of laborers

The Environment of Agriculture 147

to other occupational groups in Arvin accounted for its low level of community viability relative to Dinuba. From these observations Goldschmidt inferred that the rise of large-scale corporate agriculture then underway in California and elsewhere would have adverse implications for rural communities.

Goldschmidt's study received essentially no further attention until it was referred to in a 1968 hearing on corporation farming before the Senate Select Committee on Small Business. LaRose (1973) and Sonka and Heady (1974) soon reported further data consistent with the Goldschmidt study. In addition to Rodefeld's and Heffernan's efforts to resurrect Goldschmidt's work in rural sociological circles, there was a major research effort by the Small Farm Viability Project (1977) in California, drawing largely on Isao Fujimoto's unpublished research, which presented a larger restudy of the Goldschmidt thesis. The results largely supported Goldschmidt's findings of over three decades earlier. Flora and Conboy (1977) also reported results consistent with the thesis. Since that time there have been numerous studies in the new sociology of agriculture tradition that have explored the Goldschmidt thesis in a number of contexts (see Buttel, 1982c, 1983b; Heffernan, 1982, for overviews).

Several observations can be made on the conduct of recent research in the Goldschmidt tradition, what we might call "neo-Goldschmidt" research. First, it must be stressed that contemporary rural sociological researchers have taken considerable liberties with Goldschmidt's (1947) formulations. As noted earlier, Goldschmidt's method was a comparative anthropological case study of two communities and eschewed quantitative analysis of the sort that has predominated in the subsequent rural sociological literature. Also, Goldschmidt's analysis focused on several aspects of the property relations and control over labor, such as absentee ownership and use of ethnic minority laborers, rather than farm size, which has been the most important farm structural indicator in the neo-Goldschmidt tradition. In that regard it is important to stress that the "family" farms of Dinuba were by no means "small" farms; in fact, the family farms of Dinuba were generally larger in gross sales terms than most large farms in the Midwest today.

Second, neo-Goldschmidt research has largely focused on a single direction of causality—the impact of agricultural structure on rural communities—and has largely ignored other types of interrelations between agriculture and rural communities (Heffernan, 1982; Larson, 1981). Third, most studies have been based on Census of Agriculture data and have employed county-level data as a proxy for community characteristics (see MacCannell and Dolber-Smith, 1986, and Swanson, 1982, for significant exceptions, and Swanson, 1982, for a discussion of the consequences of this methodological convention), though some researchers (e.g., Korsching, 1984; Rodefeld, 1974) have utilized survey data to infer community quality of life consequences of changing agricultural structures. Fourth, despite obvious major regional variations in farm structures and in rural communities and their economies, there has, until very recently, been a virtual lack of a comparative perspective on farm and community structures. Goldschmidt (1978b) and Harris and Gilbert (1982) are partial exceptions to this generalization, since they have done research using states as the unit of analysis, though this procedure compounds the aggregation bias problems. Very recently, nonetheless, there has appeared a series of regionally based studies of the effects of farm structure on rural community viability and quality of life commissioned by the Office of Technology Assessment. These studies are Buttel et al. (1988), Skees and Swanson (1988), Flora and Flora (1988), MacCannell (1988), and van Es et al. (1988) as published in abridged form in Swanson (1988). These five studies were very briefly summarized in the main report (Office of Technology Assessment, 1986: Chapter 11). Together they indicate strongly that there are pronounced regional variations in how changing farm structures affect rural communities (see also Wimberley, 1987).

The impacts of farm structural changes on rural communities are generally most pronounced in the Great Plains and industrial agriculture states (California, Arizona, Texas, and Florida), less so in the South and Midwest, and very little in the Northeast. There is evidence that the degree to which farm structure affects rural communities is directly associated with the dependence of the rural community on agriculture (Green, 1985; Larson, 1981). The general model pursued in these neo-Goldschmidt studies has been to estimate coefficients for a causal chain in which farm structural change indicators are seen to affect the composition of the farm population (e.g., as measured by indicators of the size of the farm population, the proportion of full-time hired workers) and the size and composition of the rural population. These clusters of variables are then seen to affect indicators of the quality of life in rural-agricultural communities (e.g., proportion of families in poverty, median family income, per capital retail sales, unemployment rate). This general model is sometimes supplemented by technological factors as antecedents of farm structure, since technological change is considered to be one of the major factors influencing farm structural change. More recently, studies in this genre have gone beyond the cross-sectional census data designs that predominated from the mid-1970s to the early 1980s and have included measures of change, where appropriate, in variables in the model (Gilles and Dalecki, 1988; Reif, 1987). One limit to studies that use census and other data based on single-year assessments of farm income is that net farm incomes are highly variable over the short-run; for example, as many as 20 percent of farms with annual sales of over $250,000 had poverty-level incomes in 1986.

Heffernan (1982:340) has effectively summarized the general configuration of results in the neo-Goldschmidt literature by noting that "all relevant research to date suggests that a corporate type of agriculture results in a reduction in the quality of [community] life for at least some people, especially the hired workers in rural communities." As such, the results continue to lend support to the Goldschmidt thesis. But there have recently been several expressions of dissatisfaction with Goldschmidt's perspective and with the generalizations that have been made from research in this tradition. A major theoretical concern is that Goldschmidt and many researchers working in this tradition have taken large-scale and corporate agriculture to be basically synonymous (Goss, 1979b) when, in fact, not all large-scale farms are corporate or industrial-type farms. Much more important than industrial-type farms in farm numbers and shares of sales, assets, and profits are larger-than-family farms (see Table 1 in Chapter 3). Empirically, as Goldschmidt-style research has been done in the Midwest and other traditional family farming areas, there have been admonitions (e.g., by Korsching, 1984; van Es et al., 1988) that large-scale agriculture, especially of a nonindustrial character, does not necessarily lead to adverse impacts on rural communities (see also Swanson, 1988), though some studies (e.g., Gilles and Dalecki, 1988) note that increased scale of production could have detrimental impacts on community services.

A further area of dissatisfaction with research on farm structure and rural communities is that the treatment of farm structure in this literature has generally failed to incorporate new concepts relating to agricultural dualism (Buttel, 1983b). Typically farm size or scale is operationalized as a single variable representing a central tendency measure of farm size, which was a suitable procedure when there was a singular process of differentiation among farms. But with the emerging dualism in U.S. farm structure since the late 1970s, there has been little change in mean acres per farm since the 1969 census. This measure of central tendency thus ignores the processes of dualism that have contributed to increased concentration with apparent stability in average acres per farm since the late 1960s.

The neo-Goldschmidt conceptualization of an agricultural structure in which particular communities can be characterized along a continuum of farm sizes ranging from small to large has also been questioned by Wimberley (1987) who, using multiple indicators from county-level Census of Agriculture data and a longitudinal design, found that there are instead three continua relating to degree of "corporate-commercial" agriculture, "large-farm-area" agriculture, and "small-farm" agriculture. Using Wimberley's measures and including sources of off-farm employment as well, Reif (1987) found that large-farm-area agriculture

The Environment of Agriculture 151

and core-industry structures were related both to family poverty and income inequality in counties. Thus, while studies of the impacts of changing farm structures on rural communities have been a productive area of research in the new sociology agriculture, a number of research frontiers for the future are suggested by recent criticism. There is a need to diversify the methodological approach, consider alternative directions of causality, introduce more sophistication in terms of the measurement of change in farm structure, and expand recent efforts at comparative regional and interdisciplinary research (Nuckton et al., 1982). The work of Vail (1982) represents an encouraging thrust in this direction. Vail has conducted extensive research on the relationships between agriculture and rural communities in Maine in which a variety of factors of demonstrated importance—the reciprocal relations between agriculture and rural communities, the role of an increasingly dualistic agrarian structure, nonfarm aspects of agriculture, and the historically specific nature of farm-community interactions—have been incorporated into a single study.

THE FARM CRISIS OF THE 1980s

The notion that American agriculture is no longer (if it ever was) isolated from the remainder of the political economy was driven home clearly by the farm crisis of the 1980s. This crisis was brought by the conjunction of a number of factors in the 1970s, including: accelerated demand for grain on world markets, public policies that encouraged massive capital investments and expansion of production, and a political-economic context that encouraged land speculation (see Buttel 1987, 1989b). The farm crisis emerged in the 1980s for a number of reasons. Global agricultural export markets shrank, in large part due to the global recession. Farm commodity prices and ultimately net farm incomes (exclusive of federal commodity program payments and price supports) declined due to the glutting of world grain markets. Reagan administration fiscal and monetary policies led to high real interest rates, which were especially detrimental to agriculture because of its interest rate sensitivity; accordingly, debt-asset ratios among farmers increased rapidly. The 1980s also witnessed the emergence of new Third World agricultural export competitors (e.g., Argentina, Brazil) because of the global debt crisis and these countries' need to increase exports in order to repay foreign loans. Further, federal fiscal austerity eroded the federal government's ability to maintain farm incomes through commodity programs (even though commodity program expenditures soared during the decade). The result was a massive decapitalization of American agriculture, especially in the Midwest and Great Plains, as farmland prices in the states most affected by the crisis declined by over 50 percent.

This crisis attracted a good deal of attention by the mass media and by agricultural economists. It was not, however, until the middle of the decade that much was published about the farm crisis by rural sociologists. Most of this research can be divided into four categories: (1) neo-Marxian (and related neo-Weberian) analyses of the continuing penetration of capitalism into and the role of the state in agriculture, (2) analyses of the differences in the characteristics between farm(er)s that were and were not experiencing "financial stress," (3) studies of the effects of farm financial crisis and failure on the farm families whose enterprises were affected, and (4) studies of public reactions to the farm crisis.

The neo-Marxian (and neo-Weberian) approaches have largely focused on understanding continuing cycles of crises in agriculture under capitalism. Although these analyses focus heavily on the political and economic context of agriculture, they are not fundamentally different from what is discussed in Chapter 3 and therefore are not discussed specifically here. Examples of this genre specifically focused on the crisis of the 1980s include Berlan (1990), Bonanno (1987b), Mooney (1986b, 1987b), McIntosh and Zey-Ferrell (1986), Zey-Ferrell and McIntosh (1987), Goodman and Redclift (1989), and Buttel (1989b). We also briefly examine the farm crisis in Chapter 5 from a methodological angle—namely, the growing tendency in the political economy of agriculture to stress periods of agricultural crisis as key "test cases" for assessing theories of agrarian transition.

Studies in the second category, analyses of the characteristics of farms with various levels of "farm financial stress," deal more with the effects of the political and economic environment of agriculture on farms of different characteristics. These studies have produced inconsistent results due to regional (Buttel, 1987), ethnic (Salamon and Davis-Brown, 1986), and other variations within the farming population. For example, farm-size variables were found to be directly correlated with financial difficulty on Iowa farms (Bultena et al., 1986) and unrelated for Texas and North Dakota farms (Murdock et al., 1986). Yet aggregate national data revealed that larger farms were more profitable (Brooks et al., 1986), a relationship that obscured the underlying failure of many middle-size farms (Bonanno, 1987b). Farm families with fewer years of farming and younger ages were affected more severely (Bultena et al., 1986; Campbell et al., 1984; Murdock et al., 1986; Smith, 1987). However, Murdock et al. (1986) found the cohort that had started farming between the end of World War II and the mid-1960s also had higher rates of financial difficulties, suggesting a life-cycle effect for those farm families bringing another generation into the farm. The literature does, however, show agreement on the relationship between other variables and financial crisis. For example, higher debt-to-asset ratios brought by low commodity prices in a time of deflation of asset values were associated with financial problems (Brooks et al., 1986; Bultena et al., 1986; Murdock et al., 1986).

The third category, analysis of the effects of the farm financial crisis and failure on the farm families whose enterprises were affected directly, has largely been the work of William and Judith Heffernan (1986), who have conducted in-depth interviews among Missouri farm families who were in severe financial crisis or had been displaced from agriculture. These families experienced a host of difficulties beyond the simple loss of their farms and the disorientation that accompanies the loss of a valued way of life. Among their major results are the following: Many farm families felt socially isolated and were not well-prepared for participation in nonfarm labor markets. Local employment opportunities were often unavailable, and tax laws devastated some families economically after they had attempted to leave farming with some resources with which to start a new life. While the long-term effects of farm failure for these families were not yet known, it was clear that some families were adapting to their new situations successfully while others were at risk of suffering long-term poverty. Graham's (1986) study of displaced farm families in New York State bears out these findings. This category of studies has implications for the mutual effects of agriculture and its environment as the displaced farm families affect local labor markets and community social structures.

The final category of research on the 1980s farm crisis, on public reactions to the crisis, is best represented by Lyson's (1986) research on public apathy. Drawing on theories of public opinion formation, Lyson demonstrates that several factors led to a surprisingly high degree of apathy by nonfarm people toward the farm crisis, despite the massive media attention the crisis attracted. He notes that there has been a trend toward farmers and consumers having very little direct contact and that the relationship between food prices and farm income has become concealed. Most importantly, Americans have come to view "bad news" from the farm sector—the cost-price squeeze, high debt loads, and the loss of family farms—as being normal. Thus the American public, though "interested and concerned" (1986:501) about the economic woes of farmers, exhibited apathy toward the farm crisis.

A major neglected area in the rural sociology literature on the farm crisis to date is studies of the effects of the farm crisis on rural communities. This topic pertains, in particular, to how conditions in agriculture affect its environment, especially at the local level. Financial losses to local agribusiness firms when farms fail, losses of farm families in local rural market areas, declining property tax revenues due to deflated farm asset values, and other problems associated with the declining prosperity of agriculture have likely had severe effects on local services and on the local social fabric.

Unfortunately, studies of these have remained the province of agricultural economists (see, for example, Chicoine, 1987; Ginder et al., 1985; Stone, 1987).

IMPACTS OF AGRICULTURE ON THE ENVIRONMENT: THE CASE OF SOIL EROSION AND CONSERVATION*

Environmental problems are by no means new to American agriculture. The Dustbowl episode of the 1930s was but one of several historical instances in which concern has been raised about the environmental performance of U.S. farmers. Nonetheless, current controversies about the management of agricultural resources in the United States date largely from the rise of the environmental movement in the 1960s and have included issues relating to soil erosion, the use of agricultural pesticides, energy and water consumption, and the like (Buttel, 1980b). The soil conservation implications of American agriculture have remained among the most longstanding agricultural-environmental issues of concern to rural sociologists and is given principal emphasis in the section that follows.

As noted earlier, the majority of U.S. farms are family proprietorships in which there is household or family ownership and management of the land and water resources. Accordingly, the logical point of departure in understanding the soil erosion problem in agriculture has been to conduct micro-level research on the individual, farm firm, and ecological factors associated with soil erosion rates or the utilization of soil conservation technologies. This has been a productive line of research, but it has also become a controversial one, with the major controversies centering around theoretical approach, the relationships between micro and macro levels of analysis, and the public policy inferences that should be drawn from social science research.

* This section is adapted from Buttel et al., 1987.

Conceptual Issues in Research on Soil Erosion and Conservation

One of the most crucial aspects of soil erosion research is the very conceptualization of why soil erosion is a socioeconomic problem. Traditionally this has not been an issue, since sustained high levels of soil loss were presumed to irreversibly degrade the productivity of agricultural resources. Accordingly, if the soil erosion problem is conceptualized as medium to long-term land productivity decline detrimental to the interests of farmers (see, e.g., Korsching and Nowak, 1983), it would follow that conservation should be achieved through voluntary farmer compliance (rather than through mandatory regulation) based on the logic of the long-term interests of farmers. Historically, federal and state government policy thus has emphasized education of farmers and modest levels of financial inducements (such as Agricultural Stabilization and Conservation Service cost-sharing programs) to lever farmer decision making. But it has been increasingly recognized that the proportion of prime U.S. farmland that stands to be irrevocably degraded by soil erosion is relatively small (Batie, 1983) and that the "off-site" costs of soil erosion—the impacts of soil erosion and run-off on water and land resources of a farmer's parcel—are very significant and may very well be in excess of the on-site costs (Clark et al., 1985; Crosson and Brubaker, 1982).

These alternative conceptualizations of the soil erosion problem —productivity loss versus destruction of off-site water and land resources—have very profound implications for appropriate types of social science research and for public policy. To the degree that soil erosion primarily results in land productivity losses, research should focus on individual- and farm-level factors that influence resource management, and public policy should incorporate these research findings in order to develop educational and incentive programs to achieve soil conservation through farmer self-interest. To the degree that soil erosion is primarily a problem because of off-site costs, farmers cannot be expected to conserve because the long-term productivity benefits of conservation are small, and research at a more macro level (e.g., to determine the degree to which farmers' incentive structures and resource management behaviors are congruent with the public's interests in clean, navigable waters) would be most appropriate.

Debate over the appropriate kind of analysis in soil conservation research has been closely related to, and in many respects was stimulated by, debate over the adoption-diffusion approach. Pampel and van Es (1977) as noted earlier, reported that the correlates of adoption of conservation technologies tended to be different from those of commercial nonconservation technologies. They also suggested that effective conservation practices will tend not to be profitable for farmers, so that to achieve the public interest in soil conservation voluntary compliance among farmers may be insufficient. The issues raised by Pampel and van Es have continued to pervade the erosion and conservation literature. Many researchers (e.g., Carlson et al., 1981; Coughenour, 1985; Nowak, 1984, 1985) have conducted their research by seeking to revise the microsociological diffusion of innovations approach, while others (e..g., Buttel and Swanson, 1986; Napier et al., 1984; Swanson et al., 1985; van Es, 1984) have argued that the constraints to soil conservation behavior tend to be more macro in nature and that the diffusion of innovations approach will be inadequate.

Prior to 1970 soil and water conservation technologies and practices were generally understood to be a diverse collection of cropping patterns (crop rotations, contour planting, strip cropping, cover cropping, sod waterways, filter strips) and physical and biomass structures (terraces, sediment retention basins, diversion channels, animal waste structures, and hedge rows). Since that time, however, soil and water conservation has, for the majority of researchers and policymakers, come to be largely conterminous with the adoption and use of no-till and related conservation and reduced tillage equipment, which enables farmers to leave a mulch layer of residue on the soil to reduce runoff and sediment losses.

Two observations can be made with regard to traditional and reduced-tillage equipment approaches to soil and water conservation in agriculture. First, these two approaches, while by no means incompatible, are nonetheless quite different and will tend to apply most appropriately to different types of farm operations (Geisler et al., 1984). Traditional cropping practices and structures are often most attractive to smaller, more diversified farmers, while reduced tillage tends to be most attractive to larger, more highly mechanized producers of row crops (Nowak, 1984). Second, reduced tillage, although acknowledged to be effective in reducing erosion in row-crop monocultures, has become somewhat controversial. One controversial aspect of the reduced-tillage approach has been that it requires increased use of herbicides, which may lead to contamination of water and thereby negate some of the runoff reduction benefits of reduced tillage. Many studies have indicated, moreover, that reduced tillage practices have been adopted by farmers largely because of labor savings rather than because of the ability of the technology to reduce soil erosion (van Es and Notier, 1985). Indeed, the farmers who have been most likely to adopt no-till and other reduced tillage technologies have been found to be large operators with highly specialized operations involving practices such as continuous cropping and row-crop monocultures (Carlson et al., 1981; Choi and Coughenour, 1979; Nowak, 1984). Thus farmer-adopters of such conservation technologies ironically represent the major trends in U.S. farm structure that have been demonstrated to lead to environmental degradation in agriculture (Buttel, 1984a; Buttel and Swanson, 1986; see below). However, farmer perceptions of a threat to soil productivity may lead to adoption of soil-conserving innovations, whereas stewardship-related motivations may have little effect on motivations to prevent other kinds of consequences such as off-site pollution (van Es and Tsoukalas, 1987).

Summary of Empirical Research

Sociological knowledge of soil conservation has advanced rapidly, and there are now a number of demonstrated empirical generalizations, mainly at the micro level, but increasingly so at the macro level. One set of factors that has been found to affect the utilization of soil conservation practices consists of the agroclimatic characteristics of farms and farming regions. The adoption of reduced tillage technologies has been most rapid in regions of the country with the most erodible soils (van Es and Notier, 1985). Also, within a particular region, adoption of soil conservation practices is generally greatest on the most erosion-prone lands (see, e.g., Coughenour, 1985; Nowak, 1985; but see Norris and Batie, 1985, for a contrary finding).

It has also been found that farmer attitudes toward soil erosion (their perceptions of the severity of erosion on their farm or of the urgency of controlling erosion) have minimal (Norris and Batie, 1985; Nowak, 1984, 1985)—or, at most, modest (Coughenour, 1985)—impacts on conservation behaviors. Farmers thus tend to utilize conservation practices independent of their perceptions of the extent of erosion on their farms. Farmer attitudes regarding stewardship obligations toward the land have been found to have significant but modest positive impacts on the adoption of conservation practices (Coughenour, 1985; Napier and Forster, 1982; Nowak, 1985).

As noted earlier, most studies have found that indicators of farm size and income (gross farm sales, net worth, use of hired labor, acres, etc.) are positively related to the adoption of soil conservation practices. Heffernan and Green (1986) have also found that farm size is inversely related to the extent of soil erosion, which they attribute more than do most researchers to larger farmers having higher quality, more gently sloped lands. The impact of farm size on conservation practices appears to be greatest for reduced tillage practices than for traditional cropping and structures practices (Nowak, 1985). Evidence indicates that the tendency for larger farmers to adopt conservation practices earlier and more extensively than smaller farmers is reduced when public education and cost-sharing programs are in effect (Nowak and Korsching, 1983). It has also consistently been found that educational level of the farmer is positively related to adoption of soil conservation practices (Carlson et al., 1981; Coughenour, 1985).

Whereas the vast majority of rural sociological studies on soil erosion and conservation have been focused on dependent variables such as erosion rates or adoption of conservation technologies, Korsching and Nowak (1983) have been among the few to examine the correlates of farmers' views on alternative soil conservation policies. Korsching and Nowak examined farmers' attitudes toward four conservation policies: economic incentives, economic penalties, legal regulations, and educational programs. They found that farm legal organizational complexity, total acres in crops, gross farm income, use of hired labor, and managerial complexity were positively related to favorable attitudes toward economic incentives. None of the independent variables they examined was related to perceived acceptability of economic penalties. Use of hired labor, managerial capacity, use of credit, and use of "best management practices" were positively related to favorable attitudes toward legal regulations. Finally, use of hired labor and managerial capacity were positively related to favorability toward educational programs. These results thus suggest that farm size generally is positively related to farmer support for the principal, widely discussed public policy strategies for achieving soil and water conservation. It should be noted, however, that these results contrast with those of Buttel et al. (1981), who found that gross farm income and number of hired workers were unrelated to concern with soil erosion among samples of Michigan and New York farm operators. They also found that gross farm income had a moderately strong inverse relationship to concern with pollution from agricultural chemicals.

The relationship between land tenure and adoption of conservation practices has been among the most inconsistent in the literature. It has long been argued that tenancy should be a barrier to soil conservation since a tenant would have little interest in the long-term productivity of land owned by someone else and because leasing arrangements are often short-term, unstable, and uncertain. Nonetheless, while some studies have reported that tenancy inhibits the adoption of conservation practices (e.g., Norris and Batie, 1985), other studies have found no such relationship (e.g., Coughenour, 1985; Nowak, 1985). The tendency toward little or no difference in practices used on owned versus rented land probably is attributable to the fact that many farmers combine land ownership and rental and use the same practices on all of their land. Results regarding the impact of farm debt level on conservation behavior have also been mixed. It has been argued that high debt loads would inhibit the adoption of conservation practices, since current income is much more valuable than long-term productivity benefits for farmers facing high debt service payments and financial stress. Several studies have found support for this argument (e.g., Norris and Batie, 1985; Nowak, 1985), but other studies (e.g., Ervin and Ervin, 1982) have found no such relationship.

A much more consistent predictor of adoption of conservation practices has been the farmer's propensity to undertake risk. Nowak (1985) and Carlson et al. (1981), for example, have found a very strong positive relationship between risk propensity and the adoption and effective use of conservation tillage technology. It should be noted, however, that risk propensity is much more strongly related to adoption of conservation tillage than it is to traditional cropping practices and structures (Nowak, 1985). Recent research has also found that public programs can have significant impact on farmer soil conservation behavior. Cost-sharing, attendance at conservation field days, having a Soil Conservation Service farm plan, and access to and use of information sources regarding conservation technologies have been found to be positively related to the adoption of conservation practices (see, for example, Choi and Coughenour, 1979; Nowak and Korsching, 1983).

Two observations can be made on the empirical studies that have been reviewed above. First, these studies have generated a relatively consistent picture of the types of farm operators who are most likely to adopt soil conservation practices—namely, large, well-educated, nonrisk-averse farmers who have access to public cost-sharing and conservation information programs. Second, these data are, in the main, consistent with the diffusion of innovations approach. But these empirical results and their consistency with the diffusion of innovations model must also be considered along with several macro-level observations that suggest limitations to this model.

One such macro-level observation is that after $15 to $30 billion of federal spending on soil conservation programs since the 1930s (Clark et al., 1985:215), there has been no clear trend toward reduced soil erosion levels (see, for example, Batie, 1983:33). And it has been estimated that even by 2010, only 50 to 60 percent of the nation's cropland will be farmed with minimum tillage (Crosson, 1981:31). Thus if the diffusion of innovations approach is to be gauged, at least in part, on the basis of the efficacy of public information and subsidy programs to reduce erosion levels significantly, critics of the diffusion approach may have a point when they argue that voluntary programs based on influencing farmer decision-making will tend to be overwhelmed by powerful macro-level forces leading to land degradation.

It is generally agreed that the major macrostructural trends in U.S. agriculture have been toward fewer and larger commercial farms, increased mechanization, increased specialization, and endemic overcapacity (Buttel, 1983a, 1984a). These trends, singly and in combination, have been demonstrated to constrain soil conservation efforts. In particular, trends toward specialization as manifested in continuous cropping, cessation of crop rotations, row crop monocultures, and the separation of crop from livestock production have been found to severely exacerbate soil erosion problems (Pimentel et al., 1976). Thus, ironically, the very types of farmers who have been demonstrated to be most likely to adopt soil conservation practices are those who represent major farm structural trends that constrain soil conservation efforts. And given that farmers who have adopted conservation tillage have tended to do so for reasons other than soil conservation, one might question the permanency of the gains that have been made in reducing erosion on a voluntary basis.

Another macrostructural consideration in soil erosion research and policy concerns the cycles of overproduction, expansion, and instability that have affected agriculture in the past and are likely to do so in the future (Buttel, 1984b). For reasons that are largely inherent to agriculture as a production sector—high risk, the supply of land being fixed, the discontinuous nature of labor demand, and low price and income elasticities of demand for agricultural commodities (Buttel, 1983a; Buttel and Swanson, 1986)—agriculture tends to have low rates of return. The tendency toward overproduction and cost-price squeeze leads farmers to have short-term planning horizons and to heavily discount long-term returns such as those from soil conservation. And even during occasional periods, such as the 1970s, when farming becomes relatively profitable, the operation of land markets tends to discourage soil conservation practices. As farmers bid above-normal profits into local land markets and land prices increase, these higher land prices tend to encourage farmers to use land-productivity-maximizing technologies such as petrochemicals and result in exacerbation of trends toward specialization and monoculture, the principal causes of land degradation (Castle, 1984:105–161; Heady, 1984:16–17).

In sum, recent research on soil erosion and conservation has converged on a number of widely recognized generalizations, especially at the micro level of analysis. There has also been significant progress in recognizing the importance of both the micro and macro levels of analysis and in understanding their interrelations. Further work along this line can be said to represent the most promising frontier for future research on resource management and behavior in agriculture.

THE "NEW ENVIRONMENTAL DEBATES"

Environmentally related issues have been of concern to rural sociologists not only in terms of how agricultural structures and practices affect environmental quality. Indeed, over the past few years ecological phenomena have come to be viewed as explanatory variables—and, in some formulations, as an alternative explanatory theory—in relation to agricultural structures. This work, however, has been very controversial, with much of the literature having been devoted to debates and commentaries. In this concluding portion of the chapter we will explore three of the more important debates that have ensued as a result of the development of new, innovative ecological perspectives.

The first such new environmental debate, that between Dunlap and Martin (1983) and Coughenour (1984b), was based largely on two previous ones. In the first of the previous debates, Ashby and Coward (1980) commented on an article by Gartrell and Gartrell (1979), which was devoted to explaining adoption behavior in the Indian state of Andhra Pradesh. Ashby and Coward (1980:520) noted that "there is considerable research evidence available which shows that there can be dramatic changes in farmer adoption behavior with relatively minor differences in agrosocioeconomic conditions which affect the appropriateness of a technology to a particular farming environment." They argued that Gartrell and Gartrell (1979) failed to take these environmental factors into account despite the fact that there is considerable agroclimatic, geological, and topographic variation in the study area and suggested that the results reported might well be the spurious results of agroecological variations in the study area (see also Ashby, 1982, for a subsequent empirical study that stresses the relationships between ecological factors and technological change in peasant agriculture). Gartrell and Gartrell (1980) responded to Ashby and Coward's criticism in several respects. First, they argued that their methodology (use of an innovativeness index) enabled them to sidestep the issue of site-specificity for a particular innovation. Second, they argued against a principal emphasis on physical factors in isolation from the socioeconomic context of agriculture. Third, they reanalyzed their data to determine if there were demonstrable effects of environmental variables and reported that "neither controls for district or village nor analysis restricted to cultivators of the same crop leads us to significantly alter our conclusions" (1980:529).

The second previous debate that contributed to that between Dunlap and Martin (1983) and Coughenour (1984b) related to a series of studies on energy use in U.S. agriculture. Buttel and Larson (1979) used state-level census data to explore the hypothesis that farm size is positively correlated with the energy intensity of crop production. The data were found to support this hypothesis and others relating to variables such as the prevalence of legally incorporated farms. Gilles (1980), however, was critical of the study for its failure to include environmental and climatic variables. Gilles reanalyzed the Buttel-Larson (1979) data and found that irrigation, which he considered to be an indicator of climate, was most closely related to the energy intensity of crop production and that the relationships between farm size and energy use were spurious when irrigation was controlled. Larson and Buttel (1980) replied by arguing that Gilles' irrigation variable was more an indicator of capital-intensity of agriculture than of climatic conditions. Larson and Buttel measured climate at the state level in terms of mean annual rainfall and found that inclusion of this variable in the model did not alter their conclusions. Heaton and Brown (1982), however, explored the relationship between farm size and energy intensity by using a longitudinal analysis of county-level data and reported results largely consistent with those of Gilles.

Building on these two previous debates, Dunlap and Martin (1983) made a strong case that sociologists cannot adequately understand phenomena such as farm structure and technological change without considering the role of environmental variables. They developed a tentative model for "bringing the environment into the study of agriculture" and made several suggestions for future research directions. In particular, they argued for a conception of agricultural systems as ecological systems that involves environmental as well as social levels of causation in the analysis of farm structure and structural change.

Coughenour (1984b) concedes the lack of systematic attention to such factors in most research on agriculture, but he suggests that there have been a number of recent developments that have represented major progress in incorporating social-ecological concepts. Coughenour (1984b:1–2) nonetheless argues that

[a]lthough Dunlap and Martin correctly identify a gap in present research on the sociology of agriculture, I believe

their diagnosis of the problem is only partially accurate. The main causes of neglect of the environment are twofold. Foremost is the neglect by agricultural sociologists of the process of agricultural commodity production. The main way environmental factors impinge on agriculture and vice versa is through the process of food production. It is through consideration of the inputs or resources for agricultural production that environmental variables come into view. Another reason for inattention to environmental factors is the neglect by environmental sociologists themselves of two issues: the environment as resources for the production of commodities and the effects of competition for resources on the organization of the productive process.

Coughenour then proceeds to outline a theoretical perspective on agricultural production at the farm level that includes environmental variables. He does so by (1) developing concepts that link farming with the biophysical environment, (2) conceptualizing the interaction of farmers with the environment through the commodity production process, (3) conceptualizing the ways that farmers deal with environmental variability and change, and (4) distinguishing between the individual and aggregate-collective levels of farmers' responses to variability and change.

A second major new environmental debate was that between Field and Johnson (1986) and Dunlap (1986). The former argued that there has been a long tradition of rural sociological research that continues to provide a useful orienting perspective on the role of environmental factors in rural social change. They note at several points in their paper that ostensibly new "ecological" theories, such as developed by Dunlap and Martin (1983), are not particularly novel and have, in effect, "reinvented the wheel."

Dunlap (1986) responded with a vigorous defense of his work with Martin (1983) and his related work (e.g., Dunlap and Catton, 1979). He stressed that while there is much of value in the older rural sociological literature, it is not consistently relevant to the study of ecological variables within a sociology of agriculture. Dunlap reiterated that sociologists have tended to ignore physical and ecological factors in their studies of agriculture and that the inclusion of such variables can greatly increase the ability of sociologists to explain certain phenomena. Dunlap contended, moreover, that the ultimate significance of an ecological approach is that it directly challenges existing paradigms, including those used by the pioneering rural sociologists, and helps to expand the boundaries of sociological discourse. Dunlap concluded by arguing that Field and Johnson (1986) have given a misleading impression of the roots of environmental sociology and have underestimated the neglect of ecological variables in recent work in the sociology of agriculture (see also Field and Burch, 1988).

The third major new environmental debate has been between Albrecht and Murdock (1984) and Swanson and Busch (1985). Albrecht and Murdock (1984) developed an ecological approach, based on a modification of human ecology (see, for example, Micklin and Choldin, 1984), to explain the incidence of part-time farming within the universe of U.S. counties. They conceptualized part-time farming as "a form of adaptation reflecting the ability of a population of farm operators to access simultaneously two or more environmental niches reflecting farm and nonfarm forms of sustenance diversity and to compete for environmental resources" (Albrecht and Murdock, 1984:394). In particular, they saw part-time farming as a "relatively successful form of adaptation (rather than an indication of partial failure) to the changes affecting agriculture" (1984:394). They found that 55 percent of the variance in the incidence of part-time farming is explained by six ecological variables (percent of total acreage harvested, farm mechanization, farm diversity, nonfarm labor force participation, nonfarm technology, and nonfarm sustenance diversity), most of which is found to be attributable to the percent of total acreage in the county in harvested cropland and nonfarm sustenance diversity. They (1984:406) concluded that "counties with the highest prevalence of part-time farmers are those with a marginal environmental base for agricultural production and a diverse nonfarm sustenance base."

Swanson and Busch (1985) were sharply critical of the Albrecht-Murdock study on several grounds. First, although they concede that ecological models may help to explain some variation in part-time farming, other conventional social and economic models are held to be much more effective predictive tools. Second, Albrecht and Murdock, in their view, have confused and failed to distinguish between the socioeconomic and natural environments, adding ambiguity to their conclusions. Third, Swanson and Busch claim that the Albrecht-Murdock model relies on cross-sectional data and cannot infer change in the "social formation" of part-time farming. Fourth, Albrecht and Murdock are said to assume a unilinear conception of social and technological change and to confuse the process by which full-time operators become part-time. Further, Swanson and Busch object to Albrecht and Murdock's portrayal of part-time farming as an adaptive process, which ignores the fact that part-time farming may represent an unstable and undesirable situation for many farm families.

Albrecht and Murdock (1985) have defended their original study against Swanson and Busch's criticism. They restate and elaborate their human ecological theory, pointing out that the original paper was intended more as a theoretical piece to stimulate discussion than a comprehensive analysis of part-time farming per se. Albrecht and Murdock respond to Swanson-Busch's criticism of their conceptual framework and methodological procedures and explore other aspects of human-ecological theory (e.g., the distinction between technological developments that involve either commensalistic or symbiotic relationships) that may be applicable to aspects of farm structure other than part-time farming.

Albrecht and Murdock's (1985:451) response to Swanson and Busch involved a vigorous defense of the proposition that human ecological theory is useful in integrating the analysis of social and nonsocial (biophysical-environmental) phenomena and in researching "the adaptations of a society to a changing resource base." This posture, while having a very general similarity to that of Dunlap and Martin (1983), is nonetheless quite distinctive in certain respects. The notion of "adaptation," which has been integral to human ecology, but also to Parsonian and other versions of functionalism, has been largely avoided in Dunlap's work. In fact, one of the key premises in Dunlap's other elaborations of his ecological perspective is that social structures and processes may tend to result in profound ecological disruption, thereby undermining the society's resource base (or leading to a lack of "adaptation," to use Albrecht and Murdock's expression). Thus, it should be stressed that the ecological perspectives that have been developed over the past five or so years are themselves quite diverse. Dunlap (1986), in particular, has stressed that the "new environmental paradigm" involves assumptions and premises that reflect trenchant criticism of traditional sociological theory. Dunlap's criticisms presumably would extend to human ecological theory, which has been largely based on Durkheim and involves assumptions very similar to those of much structural-functionalism of the 1950s. Albrecht, Murdock, and their associates, nonetheless, must be credited with having developed a perspective that has lent itself well to systematic empirical research involving a variety of phenomena relating to the structure of agriculture.

CONCLUSION

Swanson and Busch (1985), in a footnote to their comment on Albrecht and Murdock (1984), noted that rural sociology has not had a tradition of scholarly dialogue and criticism. We would argue, however, that one of the most useful long-term legacies of the establishment of this new sociology (or "sociologies") of agriculture has been its stimulation of critical dialogue among researchers. We noted in Chapter 3, for example, that a constructive debate among proponents of alternative versions of the political economy of agriculture has emerged over the "Mann-Dickinson thesis" and a number of other issues. Thus the emerging dialogue is multifaceted, including critical commentary among as well as within "paradigms," to use Dunlap's (1986) expression. This cannot help but be an immensely positive trend in the sociology of agriculture and in rural sociology as a whole.

5

The New Political Economy of Agriculture: An Evaluation

INTRODUCTION

In Chapters 3 and 4 we stress the important role that the political economy tradition has played in the development of the sociology of agriculture. This chapter focuses on the political economy tradition by stressing some of its most recent intellectual trends as it has entered its more mature phase in the late 1980s. We begin by identifying nine trends in the sociology of agriculture that we see as being highly positive. The remaining sections are devoted to six areas of inquiry that have, in our view, been neglected and that are crucial to the further development of the sociology of agriculture.

MAJOR THEORETICAL TRENDS IN THE SOCIOLOGY OF AGRICULTURE

Trend #1: There has been a decreased dominance of deductive theories of agrarian structure and an emergence of new theoretical strategies for understanding the diversity of agricultural forms in time and space. As noted in Chapter 3, the early years of the sociology of agriculture (roughly from the mid-1970s to the mid-1980s) were dominated by a search for theories appropriate for understanding modern agrarian structures. In large part, this era consisted of rediscovering a number of classical approaches to agrarian development, particularly those of Marx, Lenin, Kautsky, and Chayanov (Newby, 1983). Each of these four major classical theorists' perspectives on agriculture was principally deductivist in nature, in that each focused on identifying a singular logic of the development of agricultural systems. For Lenin, for example, the basic logic of agricultural development was the linkage between class structure and social differentiation in agriculture and the development of the home market under capitalism, along either the Prussian or American "roads." For Kautsky, the key dynamic was the penetration of the forces of urban-industrial capital into agriculture and the slow, but sure demise of the peasantry (though, for reasons particular to agriculture, the peasantry would be able to eke out a meager existence for an extended period).

These deductive theories of agrarian structure were useful in their time, and they still have value for setting the broad parameters of inquiry. But deductive theories of agrarian structure also have their limits, particularly when they are applied to research which aims to test the "correctness" of one or more such theories. One such limit is that deductive theories tend to be based on the teleology of "necessity" arguments (see Booth, 1985, for a parallel argument pertaining to the sociology of development literature). That is, these explanatory arguments explicitly or implicitly involve postulating a logical end point of development, movement toward which is ultimately explained by the necessity of these dynamics becoming manifest (e.g., to underwrite urban-industrial capital accumulation or to rationalize agricultural production). Second, abstract deductive arguments tend to lack robustness in explaining variation across time and space. This variation tends to be approached from the vantage point of the general model and its postulated tendencies; variation that does not conform to the tendencies deduced from the model is thus "explained away"—for example, by recourse to seeing variation as reflecting differences in stages of development, as being a "blocked transition," or as reflecting exogenous forces that "interfere" with the basic logic of change. Changes that do not correspond with the model are alternatively viewed as being "exceptional"—and hence not theoretically interesting—rather than being theorized in their own right.

Third, prevailing deductive theories (with the significant exception of Kautsky's) tend to see the forces of agricultural change as being largely endogenous to agriculture (e.g., the uniqueness of agriculture, the inherent tendency toward differentiation). These theories are generally applied to confirming the centrality of what is theorized to be the predominant tendency of agricultural change under capitalism, when in fact there may be many—often contradictory—situational or conjunctural tendencies, many of which are exogenous to agriculture.

It is useful to recognize that classical deductive theories of agrarian structure were largely based on evidence from backward, but rapidly changing European countries (Russia, Prussian Germany) in the nineteenth and early twentieth centuries. For this reason, these theories, at least implicitly, were concerned to account for simultaneous agricultural backwardness and the rapid unleashing of the forces of capitalism—particularly in terms of the fate of peasantries as an historical legacy of feudalism. These conditions, however, were quite unlike those of the white settler colonies and much of Northwest Europe. This does not mean that the classical theories of agrarian structure are without use for understanding a wide range of agrarian circumstances. But these theories presume a fundamental homology of capitalism and capitalist social relations across a wide swath of the world economy, an assumption that has become increasingly problematic as the nation-states and economic formations of the world have become increasingly diverse in the late twentieth century.

Mouzelis (1976) was the first analyst to recognize the limits of deductive approaches to explaining agrarian structures. Several years later Goodman and Redclift (1982) pushed the argument a bit further in their seminal work on Latin American agrarian structure and development theory. More recently, Goodman et al. (1984, 1987), Lehmann (1986), and Redclift (1986) have expanded upon this notion, particularly in terms of explaining the persistence of family-sized farming units under conditions of rapid technological change.[1] Marsden et al. (1987) and Whatmore et al. (1987a, 1987b) have done exemplary empirical work on explaining the diversity of agricultural production forms in British agriculture. These new theoretical developments have sensitized sociologists to the prospects of being better able to explain the specificities of agrarian structures in time and space. Time is conceptualized not merely as the unfolding of the process of capitalist development, but rather in terms of long cycles of expansion and contraction, changing relationships between agriculture and industry, or the shift from one "regime of accumulation" to another. Space is accordingly treated not merely as a traditional-modern continuum, corresponding with stages of agrarian transition, but also in terms of center-periphery structures, uneven development, the "production of space," and historical legacies of regional production systems (Marsden et al., 1986, 1987).

Trend #2: Agriculture is increasingly being conceptualized in a more encompassing way, both "vertically" in terms of commodity systems and "horizontally" in terms of "rural social structure." One of the tendencies of deductive modes of theorizing agrarian structures has been the reification of agriculture as a sector or sphere. As such, agriculture typically was conceptualized, implicitly if not explicitly, as a relatively isolated or autonomous sector, the major tendencies in which should be viewed as being caused by forces endogenous to agriculture.

At the same time, the activities undertaken by agriculturalists have long been recognized as being a changing constellation, as the provision of inputs and processing of outputs have become industrialized and "differentiated away" from agriculture. Agriculture under advanced capitalism is, in a sense, a residual category, consisting of the activities implicated in natural production processes that do not lend themselves to large-scale, industrial production (Goodman et al., 1987). This reality has given rise to the "commodity systems approach" a la Friedland (1984), the goal of which is to understand agricultural commodity production as a system in which technical and manufactured inputs are incorporated into a labor process in which commodities are produced, processed, and marketed in distinctive industrial structures. The commodity systems method has become increasingly widespread, and is now no longer confined to neo-Marxist perspectives. The linkages between agriculture and the larger rural social structure have only recently received attention. In part, this is an historical legacy of the fact that the "new sociology of agriculture" of the mid- and late 1970s was founded on a critique of some of the conventional notions of rural sociological theory, particularly its rural community studies tradition which tended to ignore agriculture in preference to abstractions such as "rural society." Newby's (1980) "trend report" on rural sociology, however, underscored the pitfalls of viewing agriculture as an autonomous or distinct sector in a vacuum of the larger rural social relations in which it is embedded. Swanson's (1988) *Agriculture and Community Change in the U.S.* is a useful step in the direction of considering agricultural structures in the context of regional economic variations. What is needed is not a return to the traditional rural sociological notion of rural social structure. Rather, there is a need for reconceptualization of the notion of "rural social structures": a more comprehensive treatment of the spatial division of labor (Massey, 1984) and of the class, political, and labor market structures of agricultural communities and regions.

Trend #3: We have reached the limits of conceptualizing "the" structure of agriculture in the U.S. In a strong sense, there is no such thing as *the* structure of U.S. agriculture. To be sure, we can examine the overall tendencies of change in U.S. (or Canadian, British, and so on) agriculture and say something meaningful about long-term trends. But these exercises have clear limits, since few local or regional agricultural systems will conform uniformly to these overall patterns. Put somewhat differently, the degree to which there is consistency in patterns of change across diverse regions should be taken to be an empirical question, and not be assumed a priori in national "structure of agriculture" research. Again, the Swanson (1988) anthology is a useful first step in transcending these limitations.

But recognizing that there are several historical and contemporary systems of agriculture in the United States and other countries is not sufficient to address the limitations of older approaches. There has been growing recognition that these variations have systematic origins in several forces. One, as demonstrated by Pfeffer (1983), is the historical legacies of regionally specific production systems (e.g., the southern plantation system, large-scale capitalist production of high-value horticultural crops in the West, and family farming in the Great Plains). A second is the world market characteristics of particular agricultural commodities such as cotton and wheat (Friedmann, 1982; McMichael, 1987; Mann, 1987). A third force, one that remains largely unexplored in rural sociology, is that of the spatial organization of production. As Massey (1984) has demonstrated, space is much more than a plane along which production systems vary; instead, the process of organizing production creates distinctive spatial divisions of labor. Rural sociologists, however, have yet to take the notion of spatial divisions of agricultural and nonagricultural labor seriously and to understand this source of regional variation in agricultural production systems, as, for example, Walker (1985) has done for nonagricultural production systems.

Trend #4: There is increased attention being paid to international food and agricultural regimes and to international commodity complexes. Harriet Friedmann (1982), drawing upon nearly a decade of research by the *International Organization* school of the theory of "international regimes" (see Krasner, 1983, 1986, for more recent statements), was the first to tease out systematically the relationships between extant international food regimes and agricultural structures. In particular, Friedmann demystified the notion of "the world market," showing how the post-World War II foreign-aid-based international food regime and global food trade were dominated by U.S. foreign policy (i.e., disposal of surplus food commodities on concessionary terms to client states to serve foreign policy goals).

More recently, there have been several outstanding papers that have continued in the tradition set forth by Friedmann. Among them is Sanderson's (1986) provocative analysis of the emerging phenomenon of the "world steer." By the "world steer," Sanderson means the trend toward international standardization of cattle production, exchange, distribution, and consumption under the supervision of an "international cattle complex" that seeks to cheapen and rationalize beef procurement through multiple sourcing (particularly in low-production-cost zones of Central America). Friedmann and McMichael (1989) have prepared an impressive comparative-historical analysis of two major international food and agriculture regimes (the settler-colonial regime of the nineteenth century and the foreign-aid-based regime following World War II).[2]

These authors, along with Goodman et al. (1987), have also begun to focus attention on the processes by which international commodity complexes such as the maize/soya/quality meat and fats-oils complexes are formed. These complexes, though dominated by large private firms with an interest in deepening world trade in these commodities, nonetheless have a quasi-state character in that they play a leading role in the standardization process referred to by Sanderson.[3]

Trend #5: There has been growing recognition of the importance of research and technological change in agriculture and of the need to theorize the technological component of agriculture endogenously. Since the publication of Hightower's (1973) *Hard Tomatoes, Hard Times,* increased attention has been paid to the role of agricultural research. This research was to become much more systematic after the appearance of pioneering publications by Hadwiger (1982) and Busch and Lacy (1983). Since that time the sociology of agricultural research and technological change in agriculture has blossomed considerably.

There have been four particularly notable attempts to theorize the role of public and private agricultural research in relation to agricultural change. The first, by de Janvry and Dethier (1985), although focused principally on Third World agriculture, is of considerable relevance for understanding the macropolitics of agricultural research and its links with structural change in agriculture. De Janvry and Dethier have stressed the roles of state autonomy and the formation of class-based agricultural lobbies on the determination of public agricultural research priorities. Goodman et al. (1987) have developed a bold new perspective on agricultural research and farm structure, centered around the concepts of appropriationism and substitutionism and on a theory of agriculture as a natural production process that tends to present barriers to industrialization. Goodman et al. have also developed an innovative theory of the tendency toward family farming under conditions of rapid technological change in agriculture and have provided a useful overview of the development of biotechnology. Kloppenburg (1988a) has developed an historical analysis of plant breeding, culminating with its emergent biotechnology stage, and the antecedents and farm structural consequences of plant breeding research. Finally, Kenney et al. (1989) have sought to conceptualize post-World War II western agriculture (especially U.S. midwestern agriculture) in terms of the social and technological relations of "Fordism" (see Lipietz, 1987).

As noted in Chapter 4, it is in the area of (public) agricultural research that rural sociologists have made the most progress toward systematically understanding agricultural politics. Much of this recent work has focused on the rise and significance of biotechnology, attention which is clearly warranted given that biotechnology will be one of the major technical forces to affect agriculture in the coming decades. There are, however, reasons for concern that the new cadre of sociologists taking agricultural research and technological change (especially biotechnology) seriously may have begun to err by exaggerating the degree to which biotechnology may be "revolutionary" or "epoch-making" in the neo-Schumpeterian sense (Buttel, 1989a).

Trend #6: There has continued to be a steady flow of innovative work on gender and farm households. There has probably been no area of work in the sociology of agriculture that has experienced such steady elaboration as gender and agriculture. Stimulated by the pioneering work of Sachs (1983), there has been continual progress in the sociology of gender and agriculture, culminating most recently in the publication of the Haney-Knowles (1988) anthology.

Trend #7: There has been increased attention to the use of historical methods and to understanding the historical roots of contemporary agricultural problems. While the discipline of sociology has recently been characterized by the emergence of historical sociology as a virtual growth industry, constraints on rural sociologists in the land-grant system (Friedland, 1982) have militated against the development of historical methods in the sociology of agriculture. There have, nonetheless, been some notable efforts in this regard, which may well represent slow but sure momentum in this direction. It remains the case, however, that most of the major historical analyses of agriculture in a sociological vein continue to be written by "nonrural" sociologists, such as Moore (1966), Skocpol (1979), Wallerstein (1974), Billings (1979), and so on (Buttel and McMichael, 1988).

An excellent exemplar of the approach and promise of an historical sociology of agriculture is McMichael's (1984) *Settlers and the Agrarian Question,* an analysis of the development of Australian agriculture as the world economy in the nineteenth century was transformed into a regime dominated by industrial capital. Other notable efforts have been those by McMichael (1987) and Mann (1987, 1989) on, respectively, the antebellum and postbellum southern plantation system. Also, as pointed out elsewhere in this chapter, some of the more notable historical analyses of agriculture have been in the area of agricultural research (e.g., Kloppenburg, 1988a) and agricultural policy (e.g., Howe and Gilbert, 1988).

Trend #8: There is a growing tendency to utilize periods of agrarian crisis as key test cases for examining sociological propositions about agricultural change. It has often been noted that the basic agricultural policy apparatus in the United States in the late 1980s continues to be that implemented during the New Deal, and most New Deal agriculturally related legislation is still in effect. This observation highlights the importance of understanding social changes during periods of crisis and explains the growing attention to historical and contemporary crises of agriculture in the sociology of agriculture.

We note in the previous chapter that while rural sociologists were slow to initiate research on the 1980s farm crisis, several important studies were conducted in the mid-1980s. Most of these studies, however, have given relatively little attention to farm crisis in historical and comparative perspective. Only recently has such work appeared.

The focus on agrarian structural, political, and technological changes during crisis periods has been pursued in several ways. Berlan (1990), for example, has attempted to understand the long-term contradictions of western agricultural development that gave rise to the "farm crisis" of the 1980s in the United States and elsewhere across the globe. The forthcoming anthology edited by Goodman and Redclift (1989) seeks to do so from a comparative perspective. As noted elsewhere in this chapter, Howe and Gilbert (1988) have examined agricultural policy formation during the 1930s crisis in ways that throw light on "state-centered" and "class-struggle" theories of the state, as well as help us to understand the dynamics and significance of these policies in their own right. Finally, Kenney et al. (1989) have sought to place agrarian social change and the current crisis in the context of "social structures of accumulation" and the role of technologies in undergirding these structures.

Trend #9: There has been increased attention to the "sphere of circulation" in understanding the forces that affect production structures in agriculture. Reacting against neoclassical economic theory's emphasis on "tastes and preferences" and world-systems theory's stress on markets as the key force of expansion of the world capitalist economy, many sociologists of agriculture persuaded by neo-Marxism have tended to eschew the sphere of circulation as a key explanatory factor (see, for example, Mann, 1987). It can be argued, however, that one of the integral characteristics of agriculture is rooted in the sphere of circulation; that is, while consumption of a minimum number of calories of food is essential for human existence, there are limits to increased consumption once basic food needs are met. Therefore, agricultural product prices tend to exhibit volatile shifts in response to changes in demand. Agricultural production therefore tends to be subject to market saturation and stagnation.

Thus to borrow McMichael's (1987) expression, there has been increased interest in "bringing circulation back in." McMichael has done so with regard to the historical sociology of the Southern plantation economy, while Friedmann (1990) has examined the role of consumption patterns in leading to changes in the social and spatial division of labor in agriculture in the post-World War II period.

MAJOR GAPS IN THE SOCIOLOGY OF AGRICULTURE

Gap #1: While there has been growing attention paid to agricultural policy, little progress has been made toward understanding agricultural policy from the vantage point of comprehensive theories of the state. Rural sociologists interested in agriculture have become increasingly concerned with agricultural policy. However, most of this attention, especially in the past two or three years, has been devoted to how to influence policy rather than to how policies are determined. It can, in fact, be argued that the tendency of rural sociologists to eschew the explanation of agricultural policy formation from the vantage point of parsimonious sociological explanations is today the single most important barrier to growth of knowledge in the field.

One of the reasons for the slow progress in understanding state agricultural policy formation has no doubt been that the task is not an easy one. The few rural sociologists who have been interested in approaching state policy formation systematically have found that the task could not be accomplished through a straightforward adaptation of any one of the major prevailing "theories of the state" (instrumentalist and structuralist Marxism, statist or state-centered theory, world-systems theory, or pluralism) to agricultural policy issues.

Agricultural policy issues have not lent themselves well to assessment through extant theories of the state for several reasons. First, these theories have tended to assume that policies are formulated by national states according to forces largely internal to particular national societies; by contrast, as agriculture has become increasingly internationalized, prevailing theories of intrasocietal determinants of public policies have serious limits. Second, prevailing theories of the state have been formulated for understanding the major policy arenas—welfare-state policy, industrial policy, and so on—contested by major social classes and peak associations. By contrast, agriculture in the advanced societies has long been a declining sector, and its political centrality in national politics has steadily declined; hence it has received virtually no attention among prominent theorists of the state. Third, agricultural politics is extraordinarily complex in the range of issues that fall under its rubric and the variety of fora in which policies are determined. Only pluralism has been suitable for accounting for complexity of this sort, but pluralism has remained unattractive for many sociologists because of its neglect of class forces (the advantage of neo-Marxist or "post-Marxist" approaches such as by Block, 1987) and of the state as a sphere of domination (the contribution of neo-Weberian scholarship, e.g., Skocpol, 1979). Finally, the major theories of the state have tended to be focused on issues relating to the "class bias" of state policymaking. Agricultural policy, however, is extremely complex in its class character. Agriculturalists tend to occupy "contradictory class locations" (Mooney, 1983), and agricultural policy may involve unusual class relationships and coalitions (e.g., the historical tendency for farmers and agricultural input firms to favor high food prices, while high food prices are resisted by workers and most fractions of capital).

As a result of these limitations of received theories for understanding agrarian politics, assessing agricultural policy comprehensively will require a long period of sustained, innovative scholarship. Among the handful of efforts in this direction has been a recent paper by Howe and Gilbert (1988), which is a critique of state-centered theories of New Deal agricultural policy. Green (1987b) has made a notable attempt to combine a commodity systems framework (see Chapter 3) with analysis of state policy in the case of flue-cured tobacco. Also noteworthy is Browne's recent (1987) book, which although not largely theoretically driven, is exemplary in its treatment of a wide range of agricultural-political issues and presentation of useful generalizations.

Gap #2: There is a growing trickle of interest in credit, finance capital, and agriculture—topics that deserve far more interest than they have received. Rural sociology has historically largely conceded the areas of finance and credit to economists. This has been no less the case among neo-Marxists than non-Marxist sociologists, despite the considerable emphasis by Marx on finance capital as one of the three major branches of capital along with industrial and merchant-circulation capital. This void has only recently begun to be filled, with the publication of work by Mooney (1986b) and especially by Green (1987a). Green has demonstrated that credit and finance are of sociological interest not only because differential advantages of farmers in credit markets may contribute to social differentiation. He has also demonstrated that finance capital involves important processes of extracting surplus and controlling a wide range of investments relating to agriculture and the rural economy. Green's book, although a pioneering effort, has been limited by the poorly developed research literature. There is a considerable need for expanded efforts, such as by Mooney (1986b), to examine the role of credit institutions and finance capital in understanding the lingering farm crisis.

Gap #3: While there has been some exemplary work on agrarian crises, there is a need to better understand the relationships between the contemporary farm crisis and both the crisis of accumulation in the world economy as a whole and its current restructuring process. There has been growing recognition that the scope of the farm crisis is global (Goodman and Redclift, 1989) and that the U.S. farm crisis cannot be entirely explained by situational factors such as high real interest rates, declining world commodity prices, and so on (though obviously such factors have been important). The farm crisis appears to have been far more deeply rooted in the decade-and-a-half-long cycle of global economic stagnation. Likewise, the character of global and North American agriculture is likely to be shaped by the nature of the institutions—the social structure (or regime) of accumulation (Gordon et al., 1982; Lipietz, 1987)—that emerge within the next decade or so. However, with a very few exceptions, such as the analysis by Kenney et al. (1989) of the Fordist regime of post-World War II agriculture and its contradictions in the late 1970s and 1980s and a more modest attempt by Buttel (1989b), there have been few attempts to view agriculture in these broad terms. This lacuna is no doubt due, in part, to some of the conceptual problems of "regulation theory" and theories of long waves of world economic expansion and contraction (see, for example, Jessop, 1988). But we would argue that these broad parameters of change in national social structures and the world economy are of great significance in understanding the historical, contemporary, and future forces that have affected and will affect North American agriculture.

Gap #4: There is a need to better understand the agriculture-environment nexus, particularly in terms of the socioeconomic significance of the environmental contradictions of agriculture and of how environmental mobilization may affect agricultural structures and policies. As suggested in Chapter 4, the environmental implications of agriculture in North America seemingly is a well-researched area—given, for example, the sustained research that has been done on sociological aspects of soil erosion. Rural sociologists, however, have given little attention to some of the broader environmental issues in agriculture, particularly the implications of environmental contradictions for long-term structural changes or of how environmental mobilization may affect agricultural organization.

Most of the important work on this topic is now being done either by Europeans or about European agricultures. Cox et al. (1986), Cox and Lowe (1984), and Lowe et al. (1986) have done exemplary work on the environment-agriculture nexus in England, as has Vail (1990) on Sweden. Also noteworthy is Redclift's (1987) exploration of the political economy of "sustainable development" in the Third World. Work of this quality and comprehensiveness is urgently needed on North America.

Gap #5: There has been a lack of systematic comparative cross-national research in the sociology of agriculture. Again, as a legacy of the land-grant (and USDA) milieu of research in the sociology of agriculture, there has been little work toward developing a comparative sociology of agriculture. Few such efforts have been made along this line among North American rural sociologists (e.g., Bonanno, 1987a; Friedmann and McMichael, 1989). But, for the most part, sociology of agriculture research is conducted within national boundaries and is comparative only in the sense of interregional comparisons, while the major comparative works on western agricultures remain those written by nonrural sociologists (e.g., Moore, 1966; Skocpol, 1979).

Gap #6: There is a need for more critical ethnographic fieldwork research in the sociology of agriculture. As noted in Chapter 1, fieldwork has long been a major method in rural sociological research. Although this approach fell into disfavor during the social psychological-behaviorist era and continues to be peripheral to the subdiscipline of rural sociology, it has experienced something of a renaissance in research by those trained in anthropology (e.g., Barlett, 1987; Chibnik, 1987; Salamon, 1984). Also, several of the most important studies in the political economy of agriculture (Friedland et al., 1981; Marsden et al., 1986, 1987; Sachs, 1983) have involved fieldwork methodologies. Within the various branches of the new sociology of agriculture this general approach is growing in importance, although at a rather slow rate.

Field research is done in many styles, and consensus among practitioners on important issues is unlikely, but its contributions could come in several different ways. Perhaps the highest priority for the contribution of fieldwork will lie in its application to issues relating to the role of "subjectivity" or "agency" (versus "structure") in sociological explanation (see, for example, Giddens, 1979). For example, we noted in Chapter 3 that the increased emphasis on human agency in the neo-Weberian tradition (e.g., Mooney, 1988) poses some interesting theoretical questions relating to the persistence of family labor farms, the origins and consequences of farmer ideology, and the political mobilization of farmers. Fieldwork will be integral in elaborating this neo-Weberian research agenda and in critically assessing its limitations. In particular, we feel that the work of Gaventa (1980) has a major contribution to make in resolving the "structure-agency" dilemma in modern social and rural sociological theory.

CONCLUSION

In this chapter we have provided some evaluative observations on the tradition of the political economy of agriculture as this body of scholarship enters its second decade. We recognize that others, especially those coming from different theoretical traditions, would no doubt identify a far different set of strengths and weaknesses of the contemporary literature. Nonetheless, we hope that these frank comments will stimulate both critical thinking and needed advances in theory and research.

NOTES

This chapter draws on Buttel (1989c) and Buttel and Goodman (1989).

1. It should be noted, however, that the critique of deductive theories of agrarian development was only implicit in Goodman and Redclift (1982) and only briefly discussed in Goodman et al. (1984). Nonetheless, the more explicit treatment of this issue in Goodman et al. (1987) was clearly prefigured by these earlier treatments.

2. See, however, Thompson's (1981) provocative analysis of the marginal role currently played by the international food regime centered around the Food and Agriculture Organization of the United Nations.

3. See Sanderson (1985) for a provocative set of articles on the "new international division of labor," especially Sanderson's papers that focus on how Central and North American agriculture have been implicated in this restructuring process. See, however, Jenkins' (1984) provocative critique of the "new international division of labor" approach.

6

Rural Sociological Research on Agriculture: A Backward Glance Toward the Future

This overview of the evolution of the sociology of agriculture since the founding of rural sociology shortly after the turn of the century has emphasized more recent work in the "new sociology of agriculture" tradition and has focused on roughly a dozen major topics within this tradition. There have, however, been several important and promising areas of work over the past decade that have not been considered in this review. These have generally been areas with relatively small literatures—at least within North American rural sociology—in which only a small handful of people are currently doing research. Each of these areas can nonetheless be seen to be highly germane to a comprehensive understanding of the social organization and "environment" of agriculture.

Among the more promising and important areas of recent research has been on agriculture and the state, particularly with regard to the "theories of the state" tradition referred to in Chapter 5. The first major contributions to the emerging literature on agriculture and the state were by Mann and Dickinson (1980) and Sinclair (1980). Major recent contributions have been by Fligstein (1986), Skocpol and Finegold (1982), Murray and Post (1983), Havens and Newby (1986), and Kloppenburg and Buttel (1987). But as noted in Chapter 5, the field of the state and agriculture remains undeveloped and is a high-priority area for further work.

Another emergent area of rural sociological research on agriculture pertains to the changing structure of farmland ownership.

Prior to the 1970s farmland ownership patterns had been largely the research domain of agricultural economists. The past few years, however, have witnessed growth of research on this topic stimulated by work such as that by Massey and Catalano (1978) and Newby et al. (1978). Major publications in this area have included Gilbert (1983), Gilbert and Harris (1984), Geisler et al. (1983), and Geisler and Popper (1984). Related to farmland ownership research has been the increased attention to the mobility of farmers into and out of agriculture. Steeves (1979) stimulated much of this work by pointing out that the rates of entry and exit in Canadian agriculture have historically been higher than generally assumed in research based on cross-sectional census data. Ehrensaft et al. (1984) have expanded upon Steeves' research with more recent farm-household-level data from the Canadian agricultural census. Lyson (1982, 1984) and Molnar and Dunkelberger (1981) have focused on the structuring of recruitment into agriculture, while Kloppenburg and Geisler (1985) have reexamined the notion of the "agricultural ladder" with longitudinal farmland ownership data.

Although rural sociologists have long been aware of the increased importance of agribusiness as a component of the socioeconomic "environment" of agriculture, it has been only recently that sociologists have conducted research on the structure and impacts of agribusiness. The earliest papers focusing on agribusiness were those by Martinson and Campbell (1980) and Schulman (1981). Other recent efforts have included Friedmann (1982), Buttel et al. (1984), and Hansen et al. (1986), Newby and Utting (1984), and Sanderson (1985, 1986).

Farmers' movements and agrarian politics have been longstanding concerns of rural sociologists, especially prior to the mid-1950s (e.g., Taylor, 1953) and in the late 1970s and early 1980s (Howe, 1986; Schwartz, 1976). The major themes of recent research have revolved around the impact of farm structural change on agrarian protest and agrarian social movements (see especially Howe, 1986) and around research on the socioeconomic determinants of agrarian political ideology (e.g., Buttel et al., 1982).

A Backward Glance Toward the Future 189

We noted earlier in Chapters 1 and 4 that the earliest research by rural sociologists on technological change was strongly focused on the South (see, for example, Bertrand, 1948, 1950; Pedersen, 1954; Williams, 1939). There has continued to be substantial literature on farm structural and technological change in the South, particularly in relation to the rapid transformation of the sharecropping system since the 1930s (Fligstein, 1986; James, 1986; Mann, 1984), to the status of black farmers (Banks, 1986; Brown and Larson, 1979; Muñoz, 1985), and to the relationships between agriculture and rural well-being (Beaulieu, 1988; Skees and Swanson, 1988). Another major topic on which there has been significant rural sociological research has been the role of organic farming in American agriculture (Buttel and Gillespie, 1988; Dalecki and Bealer, 1984; Harris et al., 1980; Lockeretz and Wernick, 1979).

The dozen major topics in contemporary sociology of agriculture discussed in Chapters 3 and 4, plus nearly that number of more minor areas mentioned at the outset of this chapter, suggest strongly that North American rural sociology has decisively expanded its scope of inquiry over the 50 years since the founding of the Rural Sociological Society. And it must be kept in mind that while the sociology of agriculture currently is one of the larger specialty areas among RSS members, it is but one of perhaps 10 major foci of contemporary North American rural sociology, each of which has a substantial number of important subareas. We think it is fair to say that, to amend slightly our organizing rubric for this book, the history of the Rural Sociological Society has been one of a progressive cumulation of subject-matter foci and theoretical and methodological approaches. North American rural sociology (especially its "sociology of agriculture") was dominated by rural life and rural community studies until the early 1950s, but it is important to recognize that this approach, albeit with major modifications, remains alive and well up to this day (though it is probably more important in Europe than the United States; see, e.g., Bradley and Lowe, 1985). The general social psychological-behaviorist approach, as well as its specific methodological/subject-matter foci (e.g., diffusion-adoption), is also alive and well in 1980s rural sociology. If we add neo-Marxist and neo-Weberian political economy, several variants of an ecological approach, the continued influence of classical human ecology, and longstanding diversity along the continuum of basic and applied research, we can see that latter-day North American rural sociology is characterized by a hyperpluralism of subject-matter foci, theories, methods, and approaches.

As rural sociology begins its second half-century with its plate overflowing with attractive research foci, a diversity of theories and methods, and an increasingly heady sense of its having arrived intellectually and institutionally (within the land-grant system), the future of rural sociology will depend on how rural sociologists, individually and collectively, manage this hyperpluralism. It seems inconceivable at this time of public-sector fiscal austerity that there will be new legions of rural sociologists in expanding rural sociology programs to take up this diversity of research topics and intellectual orientations on a comprehensive basis. The long-term prospect may well be that we will continually be striving to do more with less. If this proves to be the case, will the growing diversity of rural sociology and the sociology of agriculture prove to have been a beneficial or a detrimental trend?

There are obvious advantages to the route that rural sociology and the sociology of agriculture have taken over the past two decades or so. By focusing on an expanded range of topics, rural sociologists are generating a broader knowledge base on the social, political, and economic fabric of rural America. This broadened base of knowledge can become the basis for more comprehensive or holistic theories of agricultural and rural phenomena in the advanced industrial societies and elsewhere. Theoretical and methodological pluralism will ensure that empirical foci are examined from many analytical angles and will no doubt generate productive scholarly debate and dialogue.

On the negative side, however, one must consider some potential problems with this "hundred-flowers" state of contemporary sociology of agriculture and rural sociology. The Rural Sociological Society has predictably followed the same general path as had the American Sociological Association during the 1970s and 1980s—namely, toward devolution toward multiple research and interest groups (comparable to the ASA's nearly 30 "sections"). As attention turns increasingly toward the small research and interest groups and less toward rural sociology (and sociology) as a whole, the outcome can be hyperspecialization and fragmentation in which most rural sociologists work exclusively on their small area of the fabric of rural North America and become decreasingly aware of advances in other specialty areas. We may move increasingly toward a situation in which rural sociology is dominated by a great many small research communities that have little interaction with each other, and in which rural sociologists know a great deal about a very little.

Our purpose in making these comments is not to lament the current state of affairs in rural sociology and the sociology of agriculture. There are, indeed, a good many highly positive aspects to this dramatically increased pluralism. But there are costs to sustaining high levels of empirical, theoretical, and methodological diversity. If we take a matrix of 10 major subject-matter areas (sociology of agriculture, rural population, community, international development, rural women, education and labor markets, environment and natural resources, and so on) and of 5 major theoretical and conceptual approaches (neo-Marxist, neo-Weberian, neo-Durkheimian, ecological, social psychological, community studies), there would be 50 cells—and perhaps only 250 "core" RSS members to fill them. If we add to each major subject-matter area the several distinct foci that tend to exist in each (e.g., the dozen specialty areas we have emphasized in the past dozen or so years in the sociology of agriculture), the arithmetic becomes even more daunting. Since personnel and research resources are limited, the trend toward hyperpluralism cannot continue long without being strained by excessive fragmentation and the lack of interacting research communities.

This mathematical exercise is not intended to be a call to action. Rather, we are suggesting that the 50-year evolution of North

American rural sociology has proceeded down a path that makes continued major changes in the future very likely. Just as the rural/community life studies tradition prior to the Korean War yielded to the social-psychological era of the early 1950s to the early 1970s, and as the social-psychological approach yielded to a diverse "new sociology of agriculture" about a dozen years ago, so too are we likely to see further evolution over the next few decades.

We have little way of predicting the future configuration of rural sociology one or two decades hence. But one intriguing component of how rural sociology will evolve will no doubt concern whether the sociology of agriculture per se will exist 20 or so years into the future. It should be kept in mind that the sociology of agriculture, *tout court,* has only existed for about a dozen years. Its emergence as a distinctive subject-matter area was in large part a reflection of the ongoing specialization within rural sociology. Some (e.g., Friedland, 1982) who are supportive of this trend have gone so far as to argue that rural sociology should be focused entirely on agriculture and ignore subject-matter areas unrelated to agriculture. Others (e.g., Newby, 1980) see the future of rural sociology as hinging on its ability to integrate the agricultural and nonagricultural aspects of rural life into a single comprehensive explanatory apparatus.

Either trajectory—Friedland's notion that rural sociology and the sociology of agriculture should become coterminous, or Newby's suggestion that a mature rural sociology would emphasize the interrelations of agriculture and nonmetropolitan regions and places—is plausible. Each would be a strategy for dealing with the daunting arithmetic of rural sociological specialization and fragmentation. It is not unlikely that RSS' 75th and 100th anniversary monographs will bear far different titles those of its 50th anniversary as a reflection of how rural sociology came to grapple with the advantages and disadvantages of diversity.

But the sociology of agriculture is not an island unto itself, and the same is true for rural sociology as a subdiscipline and sociology as the parent discipline. Each is shaped by the context in which it exists and in turn shapes that context. Thus not unlike the agricultural social relations and systems we study, the future of the sociology of agriculture will be influenced by social structural factors and the actions of its practitioners. While the actions of sociologists of agriculture in response to structural factors is difficult to anticipate, some comments about the emerging structural and institutional context of the sociology of agriculture are appropriate.

As noted earlier, the sociology of agriculture, with some exceptions, has been conducted in the context of the American land-grant university system, and historically the lion's share of research in the sociology of agriculture has been funded intramurally, through "Hatch" or "formula" funds administered by land-grant universities. Therefore, barring dramatic change, the fortunes of the sociology of agriculture can be expected to be related to continuity and change in this funding system. If, for example, the intramural funding system persists—especially with modest institutional scrutiny of the merit [however defined] of proposed research—sociology of agriculture research may continue to be funded in roughly the same way (though at declining real levels) and its research priorities be determined primarily on the basis of researcher interests and preferences. On the other hand, if formula funding declines and land-grant funding practices are shifted to competitive grants, with an emphasis on the development of proprietary technologies and basic biological research, sociology of agriculture research may become decreasingly attractive for intramural research funding. Given the internal politics that would accompany the competition for increasingly scarcer intramural resources, it is unclear how the sociology of agriculture research would fare, especially given its often-critical posture and its tenuous links to improving the economic competitiveness of a particular state or commodity. Also, the home of much sociology of agriculture research, the land-grant system, itself may decline, undermining the institutional base of the field.

Another consideration in contemplating the future of the sociology of agriculture is the institutional and larger political context.

This field, in the form of the "new rural sociology," had its origins in the early 1970s—the twilight years of a period of social unrest and criticism, and a time when the legitimacy of many established institutions and ideologies was undergoing scrutiny by large numbers of people. This critical thinking about the goals of the landgrant and larger "agricultural establishment," especially the neo-Marxian theories employed in much of the early sociology of agriculture research and theorizing, required "space" and tolerance in colleges of agriculture and rural sociology departments. This tolerance did not always (and still does not always) exist. Political tolerance waxes and wanes, and it would be surprising if the level of tolerance that existed in the early 1970s were to persist indefinitely.

Just as agriculture is affected by the technologies employed, and agricultural research by the data and instrumentation currently available, so too is the sociology of agriculture. As has been discussed in Chapter 2, the development, diffusion, and adoption of high-speed computing technology led to many changes in sociology as a whole and in the sociology of agriculture in particular. Currently, microcomputers and associated software are being adopted for use in analyzing quantitative and qualitative data, displaying data in innovative ways, and so on. Electronic retrieval of materials may greatly enhance one's ability to conduct comprehensive historical and comparative studies. With high costs of primary data collection, sociologists of agriculture are increasingly turning to existing secondary or documentary sources. One of the problems for some sociologists of agriculture mentioned in Chapter 3 is that certain kinds of data, such as detailed information about hired labor, are simply not collected. This reflects the politics of data collection, a topic that became more transparent during the years of the Reagan presidency as various cuts in data collection capacities were implemented and as the quantity and quality of public data consequently declined. By the same token, one possible improvement in data availability on the horizon concerns the new system for reporting census data in which precise geographic coordinates for respondents will be included. In general, the future probably holds both improvements and losses in the kinds and quality of data, and the future directions and effectiveness of sociology of agriculture research will be shaped by the kinds of data and data analysis technologies that are available. Another factor influencing the future of the sociology of agriculture is the emergence of theoretical breakthroughs that seek to explain the heretofore unexplained. These kinds of breakthroughs are difficult to predict, but can have effects as profound as the introduction of serious neo-Marxian theorizing into rural sociological thinking that accompanied the rise of the "new rural sociology" movement within the discipline. Even in the absence of major breakthroughs, an important characteristic of the structure of social sciences is the tendency for research to be driven by novelty (and the concomitant deemphasis on replication studies that are relatively common in the natural sciences). A key requirement for a work to be publishable is that it add something new to the existing stock of theories, methodologies, or empirical findings. Thus, "normal science" (Kuhn, 1970) in the social sciences typically involves quite ingenious attempts to find new wrinkles in familiar topics and approaches. The extreme example of this was the case of the field of small-group research in the 1960s, which suffered from a profusion of concepts referring to similar phenomena. The net result is that we can expect the sociology of agriculture to continue to manifest theoretical, methodological, and empirical change, whether this change comes in the form of incremental novelty ("normal science") or by discontinuities ("scientific revolutions") along the lines suggested by Kuhn in his *The Structure of Scientific Revolutions* (1970).

A further reason to expect changes in the sociology of agriculture is that its subject matter is a moving target, i.e., agriculture is to a greater or lesser extent dynamic. Changes in the structure of agriculture, in agricultural production technologies, and in the structure of the agro-food industries lead to new characteristics, opportunities, and problems for the farming population, rural communities, and the environment. Thus this context cannot help but be conducive to the diverse sociology of agriculture community encountering a never-ending source of questions, puzzles, and problems. The details, however, will depend on the social, economic, and political factors that shape agriculture. By their current work, sociologists of agriculture will influence the future of their specialties.

A final unknown in the future of sociological research on agriculture will be the succeeding chapters in the long, often-tangled story of the relations between rural sociology and its parent discipline. Rural sociology, as noted by Newby (1980), has tended to lag behind the parent discipline in embracing new theoretical and methodological approaches. But the course taken by rural sociology is not simply that of sociology lagged by five or so years. Rural sociology also has its own internal dynamics, some of which arguably favor sustained, innovative scholarship and others of which do not. Within the past two decades rural sociology has gone through two full cycles—a closer embracement of the larger discipline from the early 1970s to the early 1980s, and a return to the relative separateness of the 1960s since that time. The extent of the autonomy of rural sociology and the sociology of agriculture from the parent discipline will likely be shaped by the uncertainties over funding noted earlier. Sustained land-grant intramural funding will encourage rural sociological autonomy, while a drying-up of intramural funding will spur the sociology of agriculture to march to different drummers: the emphases and fads of the parent discipline, the shifting priorities of external funding agencies, and so on.

In sum, the dynamic environment of the contemporary sociology of agriculture will continue to make this field an exciting one. Yet its very dynamism may ultimately render the field obsolete, causing this to be both the first and the last monograph on such a topic for purposes of RSS anniversary celebrations.

References

Abd-Ella, Mokhtar M., Eric O. Hoiberg, and Richard D. Warren. 1981. "Adoption behavior in family farm systems: an Iowa study." *Rural Sociology* 46 (Spring):42–61.
Albrecht, Don E., and Steve H. Murdock. 1984. "Toward a human ecological perspective on part-time farming." *Rural Sociology* 49 (Fall):389–411.
Albrecht, Don E., and Steve H. Murdock. 1985. "In defense of ecological analyses of agricultural phenomena: a reply to Swanson and Busch." *Rural Sociology* 50 (Fall):437–456.
Ali, Yousif Ahmed. 1983. "Social changes in thirteen New York rural communities: 1920–1970." Unpublished M.S. thesis, Cornell University.
Allen, R. H., L. S. Cottrell, Jr., W. W. Troxwell, H. L. Herring, and A. D. Edwards. 1937. *Part-Time Farming in the Southeast*. Research Monograph IX. Washington, DC: Division of Social Research, Works Progress Administration.
Anderson, C. Arnold. 1954. "Economic status differentials within Southern agriculture." *Rural Sociology* 19 (March):50–67.
Anderson, W. A. 1954. *Social Change in a Central New York Rural Community*. Agricultural Experiment Station Bulletin 907. Ithaca, NY: Cornell University Agricultural Experiment Station.
Anderson, W. A. 1957. *Bibliography of Researches in Rural Sociology*. Rural Sociology Publication 52. Ithaca, NY: Cornell University, Department of Rural Sociology.
Asch, Berta, and A. R. Mangus. 1937. *Farmers on Relief and Rehabilitation*. Research Monograph VIII. Washington, DC: Division of Social Research, Works Progress Administration.
Ashby, Jacqueline A. 1982. "Technology and ecology: implications for innovation research in peasant agriculture." *Rural Sociology* 47 (Summer):234–250.
Ashby, Jacqueline A., and E. Walter Coward, Jr. 1980. "Putting agriculture back

into the study of farm practice innovation: comment on status, knowledge, and innovation." *Rural Sociology* 45 (Fall):520–523.
Audriac, Ivonne, and Lionel J. Beaulieu. 1986. "Microcomputers in agriculture: a proposed model to study their diffusion/adoption." *Rural Sociology* 51 (Spring):60–77.
Banaji, Jarius. 1980. "Summary of selected parts of Kautsky's *The Agrarian Question.*" Pp. 39–82 in F. H. Buttel and H. Newby (eds.), *The Rural Sociology of the Advanced Societies.* Montclair, NJ: Allanheld, Osmun & Co.
Banks, Vera J. 1986. *Black Farmers and Their Farms.* Rural Development Research Report No. 59. Washington, DC: Economic Research Service, U.S. Department of Agriculture.
Barban, Arnold M., C. H. Sandage, Waltraud M. Kassarjian, and Harold H. Kassarjian. 1970. "A study of Riesman's inner-other directedness among farmers." *Rural Sociology* 35 (June):232–243.
Barlett, Peggy F. 1984. "The dynamics of debt, drought, and default in South Georgia." *American Journal of Agricultural Economics* 66 (December):836–843.
Barlett, Peggy F. 1986a. "Profile of full-time farmworkers in a Georgia county." *Rural Sociology* 51 (Spring):78–96.
Barlett, Peggy F. 1986b. "Part-time farming: saving the farm or saving the life-style?" *Rural Sociology* 51 (Fall):289–313.
Barlett, Peggy F. 1986c. "The 'disappearing middle' and other myths of the changing structure of agriculture." In J. J. Molnar (ed.), *Agricultural Change.* Boulder, CO: Westview Press.
Barlett, Peggy F. 1987. "The crisis in family farming: who will survive?" Pp. 29–57 in M. Chibnik (ed.), *Farm Work and Fieldwork.* Ithaca, NY: Cornell University Press.
Batie, Sandra S. 1983. *Soil Erosion.* Washington, DC: Conservation Foundation.
Baumgartel, Walter H. 1925. *Centralized Management of a Large Corporate Estate Operated by Tenants in the Wheat Belt.* Department Circular 351. Washington, DC: U.S. Department of Agriculture.
Beal, George M., and Joe M. Bohlen. 1957. *The Diffusion Process.* Special Report 18. Ames: Iowa Agricultural Extension Service.
Beal, George M., and Everett M. Rogers. 1960. *The Adoption of Two Farm Practices in a Central Iowa Community.* Special Report 26. Ames: Iowa Agricultural Experiment Station.
Beal, George M, Joe M. Bohlen, and Everett M. Rogers. 1957. "Validity of the concept of stages in the adoption process." *Rural Sociology* 22 (June):166-168.
Beale, Calvin L. 1966. "The Negro in American agriculture." Pp. 161–204 in John P. Davis (ed.), *The American Negro Reference Book.* Englewood Cliffs, NJ: Prentice-Hall.

References

Beale, Calvin L. 1976. "The black American in agriculture." Pp. 284–315 in Mabel M. Smythe (ed.), *The Black American Reference Book*. Englewood Cliffs, NJ: Prentice-Hall.

Beaulieu, Lionel (ed.). 1988. *The Rural South in Crisis*. Boulder, CO: Westview Press.

Belcher, John C. 1954. "The nonresident farmer in the new rural society." *Rural Sociology* 19 (June):121–136.

Belknap, Helen O. 1922. *The Church on the Changing Frontier: A Study of the Homesteader and His Church*. New York: George H. Doran Co.

Bell, Earl H. 1942. *Culture of a Contemporary Rural Community: Sublette, Kansas*. Rural Life Studies 2. Washington, DC: Bureau of Agricultural Economics, U.S. Department of Agriculture.

Berardi, G. M. 1981. "Socio-economic consequences of agricultural mechanization in the United States: needed redirections for mechanization research." *Rural Sociology* 46 (Fall):483–504.

Berardi, Gigi M., and Charles C. Geisler (eds.). 1984. *Social Consequences and Challenges of New Agricultural Technologies*. Boulder, CO: Westview Press.

Berlan, Jean-Pierre. 1990. "Long-term origins of the world agricultural crisis." In W. H. Friedland et al. (eds.), The New Political Economy of Agriculture.

Berlan Darque, Martine. 1988. "The division of labour and decision-making in farming couples: power and negotiation." *Sociologia Ruralis* 28, 4:271–292.

Bernstein, Henry. 1986. "Is there a concept of petty commodity production generic to capitalism?" Paper presented at the 13th European Congress for Rural Sociology, Braga, Portugal, April.

Bertrand, Alvin L. 1948. "The social processes and the mechanization of southern agricultural systems." *Rural Sociology* 13:31–39.

Bertrand, Alvin L. 1950. "Some social implications of the mechanization of southern agriculture." *Southwestern Social Science Quarterly* 31:121.

Bertrand, Alvin L. 1955. *The Many Louisianas: A Study of Rural Social Areas and Cultural Islands*. Bulletin No. 496. Baton Rouge: Louisiana Agricultural Experiment Station.

Bertrand, Alvin L. 1958a. "The family: characteristics and trends." Chapter 14 in A. L. Bertrand (ed.), *Rural Sociology*. New York: McGraw-Hill Book Co.

Bertrand, Alvin L. 1958b. "Agricultural technology and rural social change." Chapter 26 in A. L. Bertrand (ed.), *Rural Sociology*. New York: McGraw-Hill Book Co.

Bertrand, Alvin L. 1967. "Research on part-time farming in the United States." *Sociologia Ruralis* 7, 3:295–306.

Billings, Dwight. 1979. *Planters and the Making of a "New South."* Chapel Hill: University of North Carolina Press.

Blackwell, Gordon W. 1934. "The displaced tenant farm family in North Carolina." *Social Forces* 13 (October):65–73.

Block, Fred. 1987. *Revising State Theory.* Philadelphia: Temple University Press.

Bohlen, Joe M. 1964. "The adoption and diffusion of ideas in agriculture." Pp. 265–287 in J. H. Copp (ed.), *Our Changing Rural Society.* Ames: Iowa State University Press.

Bohlen, Joe M. 1967. "Needed research on adoption models." *Sociologia Ruralis* 7, 2:113–129.

Bokemeier, Janet L., and C. Milton Coughenour. 1980. "Men and women in four types of farm families: work and attitudes." Paper presented at the annual meeting of the Rural Sociological Society, Cornell University, August.

Bokemeier, Janet, and Lorraine Garkovich. 1987. "Assessing the influence of farm women's self-identity on task allocation and decision making." *Rural Sociology* 52 (Spring):13–36.

Bokemeier, Janet L., Carolyn Sachs, and Verna Keith. 1983. "Labor force participation of metropolitan, nonmetropolitan, and farm women: a comparative study." *Rural Sociology* 48 (Winter):515–539.

Bonanno, Alessandro. 1985. "The persistence of small farms in marginal areas of advanced Western societies: the case of Italy." Unpublished Ph.D. dissertation, Department of Sociology, University of Kentucky.

Bonanno, Alessandro. 1987a. *Small Farms.* Boulder, CO: Westview Press.

Bonanno, Alessandro. 1987b. "Decentralization, Informalization, and the State: A Reinterpretation of the Farm Crisis in the U.S." *Mid-American Review of Sociology* 12:15–34.

Booth, David. 1985. "Marxism and development sociology: interpreting the impasse." *World Development* 13:761–787.

Boserup, Ester. 1970. *Women's Role in Economic Development.* New York: St. Martin's Press.

Boyd, John Paul. 1980. "Three orthogonal models of the adoption of agricultural innovation." *Rural Sociology* 45 (Summer):309–324.

Bradley, Tony, and Philip Lowe (eds.). 1985. *Locality and Rurality.* Norwich, U.K.: Geo Books.

Brandner, Lowell, and Bryant Kearl. 1964. "Evaluation for congruence as a factor in adoption rate of innovations." *Rural Sociology* 29 (September):288-303.

Braverman, Harry. 1974. *Labor and Monopoly Capital.* New York: Monthly Review Press.

Brooks, Nora L., Thomas A. Stucker, and Jennifer A. Bailey. 1986. "Income

and well-being of farmers and the farm financial crisis." *Rural Sociology* 51 (Winter):391–405.
Brown, David L., and Jeanne M. O'Leary. 1979. *Labor Force Activity of Women in Metropolitan and Nonmetropolitan America*. Rural Development Research Report No. 15. Washington, DC: Economics, Statistics, and Cooperatives Service, U.S. Department of Agriculture.
Brown, Minnie M., and Olaf F. Larson. 1979. "Successful black farmers: factors in their achievement." *Rural Sociology* 44 (Spring):153–175.
Browne, William P. 1987. *Private Interests, Public Policy, and American Agriculture*. Lawrence: University Press of Kansas.
Brunner, Edmund deS. 1923. *Church Life in the Rural South: A Study of the Opportunity of Protestantism Based upon Data from Seventy Counties*. New York: George H. Doran Co.
Brunner, Edmund deS. 1925. *Surveying Your Community: A Handbook of Method for the Rural Church*. New York: George H. Doran Co.
Brunner, Edmund deS. 1927. *Village Communities*. New York: George H. Doran Co.
Brunner, Edmund deS. 1957. *The Growth of a Science: A Half-Century of Rural Sociological Research in the United States*. New York: Harper & Brothers.
Brunner, Edmund deS., and Mary V. Brunner. 1922. *Irrigation and Religion: A Study of Religious and Social Conditions in Two California Counties*. New York: George H. Doran Co.
Brunner, Edmund deS., and J. H. Kolb. 1933. *Rural Social Trends*. New York: McGraw-Hill Book Co.
Brunner, Edmund deS., and Irving Lorge. 1937. *Rural Trends in Depression Years: A Survey of Village-Centered Agricultural Communities, 1930–1936*. New York: Columbia University Press.
Brunner, Edmund deS., Gwendolyn S. Hughes, and Marjorie Patten. 1927. *American Agricultural Villages*. New York: George H. Doran Co.
Bultena, Gordon, Paul Lasely, and Jack Geller. 1986. "The farm crisis: patterns and impacts of financial distress among Iowa farm families." *Rural Sociology* 51 (Winter):436–438.
Burchinal, Lee G. 1961. "Differences in educational and occupational aspirations of farm, small-town and city boys." *Rural Sociology* 26 (June):107–121.
Burnight, Robert, Walter McKain, Jr., and Paul Putman. 1953. *Regular Hired Workers on Commercial Dairy Farms in Connecticut, April 1950–April 1952*. Storrs: University of Connecticut Agricultural Experiment Station.
Busch, Lawrence. 1978. "On understanding understanding: two views of communication." *Rural Sociology* 43 (Fall):450–473.
Busch, Lawrence (ed.). 1981. *Science and Agricultural Development*. Montclair, NJ: Allanheld, Osmun & Co.

Busch, Lawrence, and William B. Lacy. 1981. "Sources of influence on problem choice in the agricultural sciences: the New Atlantis revisited." Pp. 113–128 in Lawrence Busch (ed.), *Science and Agricultural Development*. Montclair, NJ: Allanheld, Osmun & Co.

Busch, Lawrence, and William B. Lacy. 1983. *Science, Agriculture, and the Politics of Research*. Boulder, CO: Westview Press.

Busch, Lawrence, and Carolyn Sachs. 1981. "The agricultural sciences and the modern world system." Pp. 131–156 in Lawrence Busch (ed.), *Science and Agricultural Development*. Montclair, NJ: Allanheld, Osmun & Co.

Buttel, Frederick H. 1980a. "W(h)ither the family farm? toward a sociological perspective on independent commodity production in U.S. agriculture." *Cornell Journal of Social Relations* 15 (Summer):10–37.

Buttel, Frederick H. 1980b. "Agricultural structure and rural ecology: toward a political economy of rural development." *Sociologia Ruralis* 20, 1/2: 44–62.

Buttel, Frederick H. 1981. "American agriculture and rural America: challenges for progressive politics." Bulletin No. 120. Ithaca, NY: Department of Rural Sociology, Cornell University.

Buttel, Frederick H. 1982a. "The political economy of agriculture in advanced industrial societies: some observations on theory and method." Pp. 27–55 in Scott G. McNall (ed.), *Current Perspectives on Social Theory*, Vol. 3. Greenwich, CT: JAI Press.

Buttel, Frederick H. 1982b. "The political economy of part-time farming." *GeoJournal* 6, 4:293–300.

Buttel, Frederick H. 1982c. "Farm structure and rural development." Pp. 213–235 in William P. Browne and Don F. Hadwiger (eds.), *Rural Policy Problems: Changing Dimensions*. Lexington, Mass.: Lexington Books.

Buttel, Frederick H. 1983a. "Beyond the family farm." Pp. 87–107 in Gene F. Summers (ed.), *Technology and Social Change in Rural Areas*. Boulder, CO: Westview Press.

Buttel, Frederick H. 1983b. "Farm structure and the quality of life in agricultural communities: a review of literature and look toward the future." Pp. 150–173 in *Agricultural Communities: The Interrelationship of Agriculture, Business, Industry and Government in the Rural Economy*. Committee print prepared by the Congressional Research Service, Library of Congress, for the Committee on Agriculture, U.S. House of Representatives, 98th Congress. Washington, D.C.: U.S. Government Printing Office.

Buttel, Frederick H. 1984a. "Socioeconomic equity and environmental quality in North American agriculture: alternative trajectories for future development." In Gordon K. Douglass (ed.), *Agricultural Sustainability in a Changing World Order*. Boulder, CO: Westview Press.

Buttel, Frederick H. 1984b. "Discussion." Pp. 269–275 in Burton C. English et al. (eds.), *Future Agricultural Technology and Resource Conservation*. Ames: Iowa State University Press.

Buttel, Frederick H. 1985a. "The land-grant system: a sociological perspective on value conflicts and ethical issues." *Agriculture and Human Values* 2 (Spring):78–95.

Buttel, Frederick H. 1985b. "Biotechnology and genetic information: implications for rural people and the institutions that serve them." *The Rural Sociologist* 5 (January):68–78.

Buttel, Frederick H. 1986a. "Biotechnology and agricultural research policy: emergent issues." Pp. 312–347 in Kenneth A. Dahlberg (ed.), *New Directions for Agriculture and Agricultural Research: Neglected Dimensions and Emerging Alternatives*. Totowa, NJ: Rowman and Allanheld.

Buttel, Frederick H. 1986b. "Agricultural research and farm structural change: bovine growth hormone and beyond." *Agriculture and Human Values* 3 (Fall):88–98.

Buttel, Frederick H. 1986c. "Biotechnology and the future of rural America." Pp. 234–243 in Joint Economic Committee, *New Dimensions in Rural Policy*. Washington, DC: Joint Economic Committee, U.S. Congress.

Buttel, Frederick H. 1987. "The Crisis and Opportunity of Northeast Agriculture." Pp. 7–35 in *Sunrise Agriculture in the Northeast: Foundations of a Sustainable Agriculture for the Twenty-First Century*. Miscellaneous Publication No. 694. Orono: Maine Agricultural Experiment Station, University of Maine.

Buttel, Frederick H. 1989a. "Are high-technologies epoch-making? the case of biotechnology." *Sociological Forum* 4: (in press).

Buttel, Frederick H. 1989b. "The U.S. farm crisis and the restructuring of American agriculture: domestic and international dimensions." In D. Goodman and M. Redclift (eds.), *The International Farm Crisis*. London: Macmillan (forthcoming).

Buttel, Frederick H. 1989c. "The sociology of agriculture: current conceptual status." *The Rural Sociologist* 9:16–26.

Buttel, Frederick H., and Lawrence Busch. 1988. "The public agricultural research system at the crossroads." *Agricultural History* 62:303–324.

Buttel, Frederick H., and Charles C. Geisler. 1989. "The social impacts of bovine somatotropin: emerging issues." In J. J. Molnar and H. Kinnucan (eds.), *Biotechnology and the New Agricultural Revolution*. Boulder, CO: Westview Press.

Buttel, Frederick H., and Michael E. Gertler. 1982. "Small farm businesses: a typology of farm, operator, and family characteristics with implications for public research and extension policy." *Journal of the Northeastern Agricultural Economics Council* 11 (Spring):35–44.

Buttel, Frederick H., and Gilbert W. Gillespie Jr. 1984. "The sexual division of farm household labor: an exploratory study of the structure of on-farm and off-farm labor allocation among farm men and women." *Rural Sociology* 49 (Summer):183–209.

Buttel, Frederick H., and Gilbert W. Gillespie Jr. 1988. "Preferences for crop production practices among conventional and alternative agriculturalists." *American Journal of Alternative Agriculture* 3 (Winter):11–18.

Buttel, Frederick H., and David Goodman. 1989. "Class, state, technology, and international food regimes: an introduction to recent trends in the sociology and political economy of agriculture." *Sociologia Ruralis* 29, no. 2.

Buttel, Frederick H., and Pierre LaRamee. Forthcoming. "Some observations on the 'disappearing middle' debate." In W. H. Friedland et al. (eds.), *The New Political Economy of Agriculture*.

Buttel, Frederick H., and Oscar W. Larson, III. 1979. "Farm size, structure, and energy intensity: an ecological analysis of U.S. agriculture." *Rural Sociology* 44 (Fall):471–488.

Buttel, Frederick H., and Oscar W. Larson III. 1982. "Political implications of multiple jobholding in U.S. agriculture: an exploratory analysis." *Rural Sociology* 47 (Summer):272–294.

Buttel, Frederick H., and Philip McMichael. 1988. "Sociology and rural history: summary and critique." *Social Science History* 12 (Summer):93–120.

Buttel, Frederick H., and Howard Newby (eds.). 1980. *The Rural Sociology of the Advanced Societies*. Montclair, NJ: Allanheld, Osmun & Co.

Buttel, Frederick H., and Louis Swanson. 1986. "The farm structural and public policy context of soil and water conservation." Pp. 26–39 in S. Lovejoy and T. L. Napier (eds.), *Conserving Soil: Insights from Socioeconomic Research*. Ankeny, IA: Soil Conservation Society of America.

Buttel, Frederick H., Martin Kenney, and Jack Kloppenburg, Jr. 1985. "From green revolution to biorevolution: some observations on the changing technological bases of economic transformation in the Third World." *Economic Development and Cultural Change* 34:31–55.

Buttel, Frederick H., Mark Lancelle, and David R. Lee. 1988. "Farm structure and rural communities in the Northeast." Pp. 181–237 in L. Swanson (ed.), *Agriculture and Community Change in the U.S.* Boulder, CO: Westview Press.

Buttel, Frederick H., J. Tadlock Cowan, Martin Kenney, and Jack Kloppenburg, Jr. 1984. "Biotechnology in agriculture: the political economy of agribusiness reorganization and industry-university relationships." *Research in Rural Sociology and Development* 1:315-343.

Buttel, Frederick H., Gilbert W. Gillespie Jr., Oscar W. Larson III, and Craig K. Harris. 1981. "The social bases of agrarian environmentalism: a

comparative analysis of New York and Michigan farm operators." *Rural Sociology* 46:391–410.
Buttel, Frederick H., Martin Kenney, Jack Kloppenburg, Jr., and Douglas Smith. 1986a. "Industry-university relationships and the land-grant system." *Agricultural Administration* 23:147–181.
Buttel, Frederick H., Oscar W. Larson III, Craig K. Harris, and Sharon Powers. 1982. "Social class and agrarian political ideology: the determinants of political attitudes among full- and part-time farmers." *Social Forces* 61 (September):277-283.
Buttel, Frederick H., Steve H. Murdock, F. Larry Leistritz, and Rita R. Hamm. 1987. "Rural environments." Pp. 107–128 in Ervin H. Zube and Gary T. Moore (eds.), *Advances in Environment, Behavior, and Design*. New York: Plenum.
Buttel, Frederick H., Martin Kenney, Jack Kloppenburg, Jr., Douglas Smith, and J. Tadlock Cowan. 1986b. "Industry/land-grant university relationships in transition." In Lawrence Busch and William B. Lacy (eds.), *The Agricultural Scientific Enterprise*. Boulder, CO: Westview Press.
Campbell, Rex R. 1966. "A suggested paradigm of the individual adoption process." *Rural Sociology* 31 (December):458–466.
Campbell, Mary F., and Rex R. Campbell. 1986. "Sociology of agriculture bibliography, 1975–1985." Columbia, MO: Department of Rural Sociology, University Extension, and the Missouri Agricultural Experiment Station, University of Missouri.
Campbell, Rex R., William D. Heffernan, and Jere Lee Gilles. 1984. "Farm Operator Cycles and Farm Debts: An Accident of Timing." *The Rural Sociologist* 4:404–408.
Cancian, Frank. 1967. "Stratification and risk-taking: a theory tested on agricultural innovation." *American Sociological Review* 32:912–927.
Carlin, Thomas A., and Jon Crecink. 1979. "Small farm definition and public policy." *American Journal of Agricultural Economics* 61:933–939.
Carlson, John E., and Don A. Dillman. 1983. "Influence of kinship arrangements on farmer innovativeness." *Rural Sociology* 48 (Summer):183–200.
Carlson, John E., Don A. Dillman, and William R. Lassey. 1981. *The Farmer and Erosion: Factors Influencing the Use of Control Practices*, Report No. 601. Moscow: Agricultural Experiment Station, University of Idaho.
Carnoy, Martin. 1984. *The State and Political Theory*. Princeton: Princeton University Press.
Castle, Emory M. 1984. "Land use." Pp. 98–110 in Burton C. English et al. (eds.), *Future Agricultural Technology and Resource Conservation*. Ames: Iowa State University Press.
Cavazzani, Ada. 1979. "Part-time farming in advanced industrial societies: role

and characteristics in the United States." Bulletin No. 106. Ithaca, NY: Department of Rural Sociology, Cornell University.
Cavazzani, Ada, and Anthony M. Fuller. 1982. "International perspectives on part-time farming: a review." *GeoJournal* 6, 4:383–389.
Charlton, J. L. 1947. *Social Aspects of Farm Ownership and Tenancy in the Arkansas Ozarks*, Bulletin 471. Fayetteville: Arkansas Agricultural Experiment Station.
Charlton, J. L. 1954. *Social Aspects of Farm Ownership and Tenancy in the Arkansas Coastal Plain*, Bulletin 545. Fayetteville: Arkansas Agricultural Experiment Station.
Chayanov, A. V. 1966. *The Theory of Peasant Economy*. R. E. F. Smith, Daniel Thorner, and Basile Kerblay (eds.). Homewood, IL.: Richard Irwin.
Chibnik, Michael (ed.). 1987. *Farm Work and Fieldwork*. Ithaca, NY: Cornell University Press.
Chicoine, David L. 1987. "Issues and implications of the financial stress in agriculture: the state-local finance dimension." *Agricultural Finance Review* 47:62–71.
Choi, H., and C. Milton Coughenour. 1979. *Socioeconomic aspects of no-tillage agriculture: a case study of farmers in Christian County, Kentucky*. Report RS-63, Department of Sociology, University of Kentucky.
Clark, Edwin H. II, J. A. Haverkamp, and W. Chapman. 1985. *Eroding Soils: The Off-Farm Impacts*. Washington, DC: The Conservation Foundation.
Cochrane, Willard W. 1958. Farm Prices. Minneapolis: University of Minnesota Press.
Cochrane, Willard W. 1979. *The Development of American Agriculture*. Minneapolis: University of Minnesota Press.
Copp, James H. (Task Force Chairman). 1983. *Agricultural Mechanization*, Report No. 96. Ames: Council for Agricultural Science and Technology.
Copp, James H., Maurice L. Sill, and Emory J. Brown. 1958. "The function of information sources in the farm adoption process." *Rural Sociology* 23 (June):146–157.
Coughenour, C. Milton. 1960. "The functioning of farmers' characteristics in relation to contact with media and practice adoption." *Rural Sociology* 25 (September):283–297.
Coughenour, C. Milton. 1965. "The problem of reliability of adoption data in survey research." *Rural Sociology* 30 (June):184–203.
Coughenour, C. Milton. 1984a. "Farmers and farm workers: perspectives on occupational complexity and change." *Research in Rural Sociology and Development* 1:1–35.
Coughenour, C. Milton. 1984b. "Social ecology and agriculture." *Rural Sociology* 49 (Spring):1–22.
Coughenour, C. Milton. 1985. "Institution, environment, management and soil

conservation practice." Paper presented at the annual meeting of the Rural Sociological Society, Virginia Polytechnic Institute and State University, August.

Coughenour, C. Milton, and James A. Christenson. 1983. "Farm structure, social class, and farmers' policy perspectives." Pp. 67–86 in David E. Brewster, Wayne D. Rasmussen, and Garth Youngberg (eds.), *Farms in Transition: Interdisciplinary Perspectives on Farm Structure*. Ames: Iowa State University Press.

Coughenour, C. Milton, and Louis E. Swanson. 1983. "Work statuses and occupations of men and women in farm families and the structure of farms." *Rural Sociology* 48 (Spring):23–43.

Coughenour, C. Milton, and Ronald C. Wimberly. 1982. "Small and part-time farmers." Pp. 347–356 in Don A. Dillman and Daryl J. Hobbs (eds.), *Rural Society in the U.S.: Issues for the 1980s*. Boulder, CO: Westview Press.

Cowhig, James D. 1962. "Early occupational status as related to education and residence." *Rural Sociology* 27 (March):18–27.

Cox, Graham, and Philip Lowe. 1984 "Agricultural corporatism and rural conservation." Pp. 147-166 in T. Bradley and P. Lowe (eds.), *Locality and Rurality*. Norwich, CT: Geo Books.

Cox, Graham, Philip Lowe, and Michael Winter. 1986. "Agriculture and conservation in Britain: a policy community under siege." Pp. 181-215 in G. Cox et al. (eds.), *Agriculture: People and Policies*. London: Allen & Unwin.

Crosson, Pierre R. 1981. *Conservation Tillage and Conventional Tillage: A Comparative Assessment*. Ankeny, Iowa: Soil Conservation Society of America.

Crosson, Pierre R., and Sterling Brubaker. 1982. *Resource and Environmental Effects of U.S. Agriculture*. Washington, DC: Resources for the Future.

Dalecki, Michael G., and Bob Bealer. 1984. "Who is the 'organic' farmer?" *The Rural Sociologist* 4 (January):11–18.

Danbom, David B. 1979. *The Resisted Revolution*. Ames: Iowa State University Press.

Davis, John Emmeus. 1980. "Capitalist agricultural development and the exploitation of the propertied laborer." Pp. 133–153 in Frederick H. Buttel and Howard Newby (eds.), *The Rural Sociology of the Advanced Societies*. Montclair, NJ: Allanheld, Osmun & Co.

Dean, Alfred, Herbert A. Aurbach, and C. Paul Marsh. 1958. "Some factors related to rationality in decision making among farm operators." *Rural Sociology* 23 (June):121–135.

Deininger, Marian, and Douglas Marshall. 1955. "A study of land ownership by ethnic groups from frontier times to the present in a marginal farming area in Minnesota." *Land Economics* 31 (November):351–360.

de Janvry, Alain. 1980. "Social differentiation in agriculture and the ideology of neopopulism." Pp. 155–168 in Frederick H. Buttel and Howard Newby (eds.), *The Rural Sociology of the Advanced Societies*. Montclair, NJ: Allanheld, Osmun & Co.

de Janvry, Alain. 1981. *The Agrarian Question and Reformism in Latin America*. Baltimore: Johns Hopkins University Press.

de Janvry, Alain, and Jean-Jacques Dethier. 1985. *Technological Innovation in Agriculture: The Political Economy of Its Rate and Bias*. Washington, DC: World Bank.

de Janvry, Alain, and E. Phillip LeVeen. 1986. "Historical forces that have shaped world agriculture: a structural perspective." Pp. 83–104 in K. A. Dahlberg (ed.), *New Directions for Agriculture and Agricultural Research*. Totowa, NJ: Rowman and Allanheld.

Djurfeldt, Goren. 1981. "What happened to the agrarian bourgeoisie and rural proletariat under monopoly capitalism?" *Acta Sociologica* 24, 3:167–191.

DuBois, W. E. B. 1898. "The Negroes of Farmville, Virginia: a social study." Pp. 1–38 in *Bulletin of the Department of Labor*, Vol. 3, No. 14. Washington, DC: Government Printing Office.

DuBois, W. E. B. 1901. "The Negro landholders of Georgia." Pp. 647-777 in *Bulletin of the Department of Labor*, Vol. 6, No. 35. Washington, DC: U.S. Government Printing Office.

DuBois, W. E. B. 1904. "The Negro farmer." Pp. 69–98 in U.S. Bureau of the Census, *Negroes in the United States*. Washington, DC: U.S. Government Printing Office.

Ducoff, Louis J. 1945. *Wages of Agricultural Labor in the United States*. Technical Bulletin No. 895. Washington, DC: U.S. Department of Agriculture.

Duncan, James A., and Burton W. Kreitlow. 1954. "Selected cultural characteristics and the acceptance of educational programs and practices." *Rural Sociology* 19 (December):349–357.

Duncan, Otis Durant. 1940. "A sociological approach to farm tenancy research." *Rural Sociology* 5 (September):285–291.

Dunlap, Riley E. 1986. "Environment, ecology and agriculture revisited: ancestor worship and the dangers of disciplinary myopia." *The Rural Sociologist* 6 (July).

Dunlap, Riley E., and William R. Catton, Jr. 1979. "Environmental sociology." *Annual Review of Sociology* 5:243–273.

Dunlap, Riley E., and Kenneth E. Martin. 1983. "Bringing environment into the study of agriculture: observations and suggestions regarding the sociology of agriculture." *Rural Sociology* 48 (Summer):201–218.

Eaton, Allen, and Shelby M. Harrison. 1930. *A Bibliography of Social Surveys: Reports of Fact-Finding Studies Made as a Basis for Social*

Action; Arranged by Subjects and Localities. New York: Russell Sage Foundation.
Edwards, Clark, Matthew G. Smith, and R. Neal Peterson. 1985. "The changing distribution of farms by size: a Markov analysis." *Agricultural Economics Research* 37 (Fall):1–16.
Ehrensaft, Philip, Pierre LaRamee, Ray D. Bollman, and Frederick H. Buttel. 1984. "The microdynamics of farm structural change: the Canadian experience and Canada-U.S.A. comparisons." *American Journal of Agricultural Economics* 66 (December):823–828.
Ervin, C. A., and David E. Ervin. 1982. "Factors affecting the use of soil conservation practices: hypotheses, evidence, and policy implications." *Land Economics* 58 (August):277–292.
Evans, Peter, Dietrich Rueschemeyer, and Theda Skocpol (eds.). 1985. *Bringing the State Back In*. New York: Cambridge University Press.
Fassinger, Polly A., and Harry K. Schwarzweller. 1984. "The work of farm women: a Midwestern study." *Research in Rural Sociology and Development* 1:37–60.
Field, Donald R., and William R. Burch, Jr. 1988. *Rural Sociology and the Environment*. Westport, CT: Greenwood Press.
Field, Donald R., and Darryll R. Johnson. 1986. "Rural communities and natural resources: a classical interest." *The Rural Sociologist* 6 (May):187–196.
Fine, Ben. 1979. "On Marx's theory of agricultural rent." *Economy and Society* 8, 3:41–78.
Fine, Ben. 1980. "On Marx's theory of agricultural rent." *Economy and Society* 9, 3:327–331.
Fliegel, Frederick C. 1956. "A multiple correlation analysis of factors associated with adoption of farm practices." *Rural Sociology* 21 (September/December):284–292.
Fliegel, Frederick C. 1957. "Farm income and the adoption of farm practices." *Rural Sociology* 22 (June):159–162.
Fliegel, Frederick C. 1959. "Aspirations of low-income farmers and their performance and potential for change." *Rural Sociology* 24 (September):205–214.
Fliegel, Frederick C. 1960. "Obstacles to change for the low-income farmer." *Rural Sociology* 25 (September):347–351.
Fliegel, Frederick C. 1962. "Traditionalism in the farm family and technological change." *Rural Sociology* 27 (March):70–76.
Fliegel, Frederick C., and Joseph E. Kivlin. 1966. "Farmers' perception of farm practice attributes." *Rural Sociology* 31 (June):197–206.
Fliegel, Frederick C., and J. C. van Es. 1983. "The diffusion-adoption process in agriculture: changes in technology and changing paradigms." Pp. 13–28 in Gene F. Summers (ed.), *Technology and Social Change in Rural Areas*. Boulder, CO: Westview Press.

Fligstein, Neil. 1986. "The underdevelopment of the South: state and agriculture, 1865-1900." Pp. 60–103 in Archie E. Havens et al. (eds.) *Studies in the Transformation of U.S. Agriculture*. Boulder, CO: Westview Press.
Flinn, William L. 1970. "The influence of community values on innovativeness." *American Journal of Sociology* 75:983–981.
Flora, Cornelia, and Sue Johnson. 1978. "Discarding the distaff: new roles for rural women." Pp. 168-181 in Thomas R. Ford (ed.), *Rural U.S.A.* Ames: Iowa State University Press.
Flora, Cornelia Butler, and Jan L. Flora. 1988. "Public policy, farm size, and community well-being in farming-dependent counties of the plains." Pp. 76–129 in L. Swanson (ed.), *Agriculture and Community Change in the U.S.* Boulder, CO: Westview Press.
Flora, Jan L., and Judith L. Conboy. 1977. "Impact of type of agriculture on class structure, social well-being, and inequities." Paper presented at the annual meeting of the Rural Sociological Society, Madison, Wisconsin, August.
Flora, Jan L., and John M. Stitz. 1985. "Ethnicity, persistence, and capitalization of agriculture in the Great Plains during the settlement period." *Rural Sociology* 50 (Fall):341–360.
Foster, Gary, Richard Hummel, and Robert Whittenbarger. 1987. "Ethnic echos through 100 years of Midwestern agriculture." *Rural Sociology* 52 (Spring):365–378.
Frank, Andre Gunder. 1967. *Capitalism and Underdevelopment in Latin America*. New York: Monthly Review Press.
Friedland, William H. 1980. "Technology in agriculture: labor and the rate of accumulation." Pp. 201–214 in Frederick H. Buttel and Howard Newby (eds.), *The Rural Sociology of the Advanced Societies*. Montclair, NJ: Allanheld, Osmun & Co.
Friedland, William H. 1982. "The end of rural society and the future of rural sociology." *Rural Sociology* 47 (Winter):589–608.
Friedland, William H. 1984a. "Commodity systems analysis: an approach to the sociology of agriculture." *Research in Rural Sociology and Development* 1:221–235.
Friedland, William H. 1984b. "The labor force in U.S. agriculture." Pp. 143–181 in Lawrence Busch and William B. Lacy (eds.), *Food Security in the United States*. Boulder, CO: Westview Press.
Friedland, William H., and Amy Barton. 1975. *Destalking the Wily Tomato: A Case Study in Social Consequences in California Agricultural Research*, Research Monograph No. 15. Davis: Department of Applied Behavioral Sciences, University of California.
Friedland, William H., and Tim Kappel. 1979. *Production or Perish: Changing*

the Inequalities of Agricultural Research Priorities. Santa Cruz: Project on Social Impact Assessment and Values, University of California.
Friedland, William H., Amy Barton, and Robert J. Thomas. 1981. *Manufacturing Green Gold.* New York: Cambridge University Press.
Friedmann, Harriet. 1978a. "World market, state, and family farm: social bases of household production in an era of wage labor." *Comparative Studies in Society and History* 20:545–586.
Friedmann, Harriet. 1978b. "Simple commodity production and wage labour in the American plains." *Journal of Peasant Studies* 6, 1:71–99.
Friedmann, Harriet. 1980. "Household production and the national economy." *Journal of Peasant Studies* 7, 2:158–184.
Friedmann, Harriet. 1981. "The family farm in advanced capitalism: outline of a theory of simple commodity production in agriculture." Paper presented at the annual meeting of the American Sociological Association, Toronto, August.
Friedmann, Harriet. 1982. "The political economy of food: the rise and fall of the postwar international food order." *American Journal of Sociology* 88 (Supplement):S248–286.
Friedmann, Harriet. Forthcoming. "Agro-food industries and export agriculture: the changing international division of labour, 1945–73." In W. H. Friedland et al. (eds.), *The New Political Economy of Agriculture.*
Friedmann, Harriet, and Philip McMichael. 1989. "The world-historical development of agriculture: western agriculture in comparative perspective." *Sociologia Ruralis* 29.
Fry, C. Luther. 1922. *The New and Old Immigrant on the Land: A Study of Americanization and the Rural Church.* New York: George H. Doran Co.
Fuguitt, Glenn V. 1959. "Part-time farming and the push-pull hypothesis." *American Journal of Sociology* 64 (Winter):375–379.
Fuguitt, Glenn V. 1961. "A typology of the part-time farmer." *Rural Sociology* 26 (March):39–48.
Fuguitt, Glenn V. 1965. "Career patterns of part-time farmers and their contact with the Agricultural Extension Service." *Rural Sociology* 30 (March): 49–62.
Fujimoto, Isao, and Emmett Fiske. 1975. "What research gets done at a land-grant college: internal factors at work." Unpublished manuscript, Department of Applied Behavioral Sciences, University of California, Davis.
Fujimoto, Isao, and William Kopper. 1975. "Outside influences on what research gets done at a land-grant school: impact of marketing orders." Paper presented at the annual meeting of the Rural Sociological Society, San Francisco, August.

Fuller, Anthony M. 1984. "Part-time farming: the enigmas and the realities." *Research in Rural Sociology and Development* 1:187–219.
Galeski, Boguslaw. 1972. *Basic Concepts in Rural Sociology*. Manchester, England: University of Manchester Press.
Galpin, Charles Josiah. 1911. "The social agencies in a rural community." Pp. 12–18 in *First Wisconsin Country Life Conference*, Bulletin of the University of Wisconsin, Serial No. 472, General Series No. 308. Madison: College of Agriculture, University of Wisconsin.
Galpin, Charles Josiah. 1938. *My Drift into Rural Sociology*. Baton Rouge: Louisiana State University Press.
Galpin, Charles J., and Emily F. Hoag. 1919. *Farm Tenancy, an Analysis of the Occupancy of 500 Farms*, Research Bulletin 44. Madison: Wisconsin Agricultural Experiment Station.
Garcia-Ramon, Maria Dolors, and Gemma Canoves. 1988. "The role of women on the family farm: the case of Catalonia." *Sociologia Ruralis* 28, 4:263–270.
Garkovich, Lorraine (compiler). "50-year index." 1985. *Rural Sociology* 50, supplement (Winter).
Gartrell, John W., and C. David Gartrell. 1979. "Status, knowledge, and innovation." *Rural Sociology* 44 (Spring):73–94.
Gartrell, John W., and C. David Gartrell. 1980. "Beyond earth, water, weather, and wind." *Rural Sociology* 45 (Fall):524–530.
Gartrell, John W., and E. A. Wilkening. 1973. "Curvilinear and linear models relating status and innovative behavior: a reassessment." *Rural Sociology* 38 (Winter):391–411.
Gasson, Ruth. 1967. "Some economic characteristics of part-time farming in Britain." *Journal of Agricultural Economics* 18, 1:111–120.
Gasson, Ruth. 1983. *Gainful Occupations of Farm Families*. Ashford, Kent: School of Rural Economics, Wye College, University of London.
Gasson, Ruth. 1986. "Part-time farming: strategy for survival?" Paper presented at the 13th European Congress for Rural Sociology, Braga, Portugal, April.
Gasson, Ruth. 1986. "Part time farming—strategy for survival?" *Sociologia Ruralis* 26, 3/4:364–376.
Gasson, Ruth. 1988. "Changing gender roles: a workshop report." *Sociologia Ruralis* 28, 4:300–305.
Gaventa, John. 1980. *Power and Powerlessness*. Urbana: University of Illinois Press.
Geisler, Charles C., and Frank R. Popper (eds.). 1984. *Land Reform, American Style*. Totowa, NJ: Rowman and Allanheld. .
Geisler, Charles C., J. Tadlock Cowan, Michael R. Hattery, and Harvey M. Jacobs. 1984. "Sustained land productivity: equity consequences of alternative agricultural technologies." Pp. 213–236 in Gigi M. Berardi

and Charles C. Geisler (eds.), *The Social Consequences and Challenges of New Agricultural Technologies.* Boulder, CO: Westview Press.
Geisler, Charles C., Nelson L Bills, Jack R. Kloppenburg, Jr., and William F. Waters. 1983. *The Changing Structure of Agricultural Landownership in the United States, 1946 and 1978,* Search: Agriculture, No. 26. Ithaca, NY: Cornell University Agricultural Experiment Station.
Giddens, Anthony. 1971. *Capitalism and Modern Social Theory.* Cambridge, England: Cambridge University Press.
Giddens, Anthony. 1979. *Central Problems in Social Theory.* Berkeley: University of California Press.
Gilbert, Jess. 1982. "Rural theory: the grounding of rural sociology." *Rural Sociology* 47 (Winter):609–633.
Gilbert, Jess. 1983. "Class structure, property ownership, and income determination." Unpublished Ph.D. dissertation, Michigan State University.
Gilbert, Jess, and Raymond Akor. 1986. "Dairying in California and Wisconsin." *Wisconsin Academy Review* 33 (December):56–59.
Gilbert, Jess, and Raymond Akor. 1988. "Increasing structural divergence in U.S. dairying: California and Wisconsin since 1950." *Rural Sociology* 53 (Spring):56–72.
Gilbert, Jess, and Craig K. Harris. 1984. "Changes in type, tenure, and concentration of U.S. farmland owners." *Research in Rural Sociology and Development* 1:135–160.
Gilles, Jere. 1980. "Farm size, farm structure, energy and climate: an alternate ecological analysis of United States agriculture." *Rural Sociology* 45 (Summer):332–339.
Gilles, Jere Lee, and Michael Dalecki. 1988. "Rural well-being and agricultural change in two farming regions." *Rural Sociology* 53 (Spring):40–55.
Gillespie, Gilbert W. Jr., and Frederick H. Buttel. 1989. "Farmer ambivalence toward agricultural research: an empirical assessment." *Rural Sociology* 54:(in press).
Gillette, John M. 1913. *Constructive Rural Sociology.* New York: Sturgis & Walton.
Gillette, John M. 1946. "Farm enlargement in North Dakota: Reasons and causes." *Rural Sociology* 11:253–269.
Ginder, Roger G., Kenneth E. Stone, and Daniel Otto. 1985. "Impact of the farm crisis on agribusiness firms and rural communities." *American Journal of Agricultural Economics* 65, 5:1184–1190.
Gladwin, Christina H. 1985. "Changes in women's roles on the farm: a response to the intensification or capitalization of agriculture?" Paper presented at the Center for Rural Women, Pennsylvania State University, March.
Gladwin, Christina H., and Robert Zabawa. 1984. "Survival strategies of small, part-time Florida farmers: a response to structural change." Paper pre-

sented at the 42nd Professional Agricultural Workers Conference, Tuskegee Institute, December.
Goe, W. Richard. 1986. "U.S. agriculture in an information society: rural sociology research issues." *The Rural Sociologist* 6 (March):96–101.
Goldschmidt, Walter. 1978a. *As You Sow*. New York: Harcourt, Brace & Co., 1947; reprinted: Montclair, NJ: Allanheld, Osmun & Co.
Goldschmidt, Walter. 1978b. "Large-scale farming and the rural social structure." *Rural Sociology* 43 (Fall):362–366.
Goodman, David, and Michael Redclift. 1982. *From Peasant to Proletarian*. New York: St. Martin's Press.
Goodman, David, and Michael Redclift. 1985. "Capitalism, petty commodity production, and the farm enterprise." *Sociologia Ruralis* 15, 3/4: 231–247.
Goodman, David, and Michael Redclift (eds.). 1989. *The International Farm Crisis*. London: Macmillan.
Goodman, David, Bernardo Sorj, and John Wilkinson. 1984. "Agro-industry, state policy and rural social structures: recent analyses of proletarianization in Brazilian agriculture." In B. Munslow and H. Finch (eds.), *Proletarianization in the Third World*. London: Croom Helm.
Goodman, David, Bernardo Sorj, and John Wilkinson. 1987. *From Farming to Biotechnology: A Theory of Agro-Industrial Development*. Oxford: Basil Blackwell.
Gordon, David M., Richard Edwards, and Michael Reich. 1982. *Segmented Work, Divided Workers*. New York: Cambridge University Press.
Gordon, W. R. 1942. *Satellite Acres: A Study of 1,100 Households in Rural Rhode Island with Income from Combinations of Non-Agricultural Employment and Agricultural Production*. Bulletin 282. Kingston: Agricultural Experiment Station of the Rhode Island State College.
Goss, Kevin F. 1979a. "Consequences of diffusion of innovations." *Rural Sociology* 44 (Winter):754–772.
Goss, Kevin F. 1979b. Review of *As You Sow*, by Walter Goldschmidt, *Rural Sociology* 44 (Winter):802–806.
Goss, Kevin F., Richard D. Rodefeld, and Frederick H. Buttel. 1980. "The political economy of class structure in U.S. agriculture: a theoretical outline." Pp. 83–132 in Frederick H. Buttel and Howard Newby (eds.), *The Rural Sociology of the Advanced Societies*. Montclair, NJ: Allanheld, Osmun & Co.
Gouldner, Alvin. 1970. *The Coming Crisis of Western Sociology*. New York: Avon.
Graham, Katherine Helga. 1986. "A description of the transition experiences of 28 New York State farm families forced from their farms: 1982–1985." Unpublished M.S. thesis, Cornell University.
Grasmick, Harold G., and Mary K. Grasmick. 1978. "The effect of farm family

background on the value orientations of urban residents: a study of cultural lag." *Rural Sociology* 43 (Fall):367–385.
Green, Gary P. 1984. "Credit and agriculture: some consequences of the centralization of the banking system." *Rural Sociology* 49 (Winter):568–579.
Green, Gary. 1985. "Large-scale farming and the quality of life in rural communities: further specification of the Goldschmidt hypothesis." *Rural Sociology* 50 (Summer):260–272.
Green, Gary P. 1987a. *Finance Capital and Uneven Development*. Boulder, CO: Westview Press.
Green, Gary P. 1987b. "The political economy of flue-cured tobacco production." *Rural Sociology* 52 (Summer):221–241.
Green, Gary, and William D. Heffernan. 1984. "Economic dualism in agriculture." *Southern Rural Sociology* 2:1–10.
Gregory, Cecil L. 1958. *Rural Social Areas in Missouri*, Bulletin 665. Columbia, MO: Missouri Agricultural Experiment Station.
Griffin, Keith. 1974. *The Political Economy of Agrarian Change*. Cambridge, Mass.: Harvard University Press.
Grigsby, S. Earl, and Harold Hoffsommer. 1941. *Cotton Plantation Laborers: A Socio-economic Study of Laborers on Cotton Plantations in Concordia Parish, Louisiana*. Bulletin 328. Baton Rouge: Louisiana State University and Agricultural and Mechanical College Agricultural Experiment Stations.
Gross, Neil C., and Marvin J. Taves. 1952. "Characteristics associated with acceptance of recommended farm practices." *Rural Sociology* 17 (December):321–327.
Hadwiger, Don F. 1982. *The Politics of Agricultural Research*. Lincoln: University of Nebraska Press.
Hagood, Margaret Jarman, and Eleanor H. Bernert. 1945. "Component indexes as a basis for stratification in sampling." *Journal of the American Statistical Association* 40 (September):330–341.
Haller, A. O. 1957. "The influence of planning to enter farming on plans to attend college." *Rural Sociology* 22 (June):137–141.
Haller, A. O. 1958. "Research problems on the occupational achievement levels of farm-reared people." *Rural Sociology* 23 (December):355–362.
Haller, A. O. 1960. "The occupational achievement process of farm-reared youth in urban-industrial society." *Rural Sociology* 25 (September):321–333.
Haller, Archibald O., and William H. Sewell. 1967. "Occupational choices of Wisconsin farm boys." *Rural Sociology* 32 (March):37–55.
Haller, A. O., and Carole Ellis Wolff. 1962. "Personality orientations of farm, village, and urban boys." *Rural Sociology* 27 (September):275–293.
Haney, Wava G. 1982. "Women." Pp. 124–135 in Don A. Dillman

and Daryl J. Hobbs (eds.), *Rural Society in the U.S.* Boulder, CO: Westview Press.

Haney, Wava G., and Jane B. Knowles (eds.). 1988. *Women and Farming.* Boulder, CO: Westview Press.

Hansen, Michel, Lawrence Busch, Jeffrey Burkhardt, William B. Lacy, and Laura R. Lacy. 1986. "Plant breeding and biotechnology." *BioScience* 36 (January):29–39.

Harper, Emily B., Frederick C. Fliegel, and J. C. van Es. 1980. "Growing number of small farms in the north central states." *Rural Sociology* 45 (Winter):608–620.

Harris, Craig K., and Jess Gilbert. 1982. "Large-scale farming, rural income, and Goldschmidt's agrarian thesis." *Rural Sociology* 47 (Fall):449–458.

Harris, Craig K., Sharon Powers, and Frederick H. Buttel. 1980. "Myth and reality in organic farming." (Rural Sociological Society) *Newsline* 8, 4:33–43.

Harrison, David. 1988. *Sociology of Modernization and Development.* London: Unwin Hyman.

Havens, A. Eugene. 1965. "Increasing the effectiveness of predicting innovativeness." *Rural Sociology* 30 (June):150–166.

Havens, A. Eugene. 1972. "Methodological issues in the study of development." *Sociologia Ruralis* 12, 3/4:252–272.

Havens, A. Eugene, and William L. Flinn. 1975. "Green revolution technology and community development: the limits of action programs." *Economic Development and Cultural Change* 23 (April):469–481.

Havens, A. Eugene, and Howard Newby. 1986. "Agriculture and the state: an analytical approach." Pp. 287–304 in A. Eugene Havens et al., (eds.) *Studies in the Transformation of U.S. Agriculture.* Boulder, CO: Westview Press.

Havens, A. Eugene, with Gregory Hooks, Patrick H. Mooney, and Max J. Pfeffer (eds.). 1986. *Studies in the Transformation of U.S. Agriculture.* Boulder, CO: Westview Press.

Hawley, Amos H. 1950. *Human Ecology.* New York: Ronald Press.

Hayes, M. N., and A. L. Olmstead. 1984. "Farm size and community quality: "Arvin and Dinuba revisited." *American Journal of Agricultural Economics* 66 (November):430–436.

Heady, Earl O. 1984. "The setting for agricultural production and resource use in the future." Pp. 8–30 in Burton C. English et al. (eds.), *Future Agricultural Technology and Resource Conservation.* Ames: Iowa State University Press.

Heaton, Tim B., and David L. Brown. 1982. "Farm structure and energy intensity: another look." *Rural Sociology* 47 (Spring):17–31.

Hedley, Max J. 1981. "Relations of production of the 'family farm'." *Journal of Peasant Studies* 9, 1:71–85.

Heffernan, William D. 1972. "Sociological dimensions of agricultural structures in the United States." *Sociologia Ruralis* 12, 3/4:481–499.

Heffernan, William D. 1982. "Structure of agriculture and quality of life in rural communities." Pp. 337–346 in Don A. Dillman and Daryl J. Hobbs (eds.), *Rural Society in the U.S.: Issues for the 1980s*. Boulder, CO: Westview Press.

Heffernan, William D. 1984. "Constraints in the U.S. poultry industry." *Research in Rural Sociology and Development* 1:237–260.

Heffernan, William D., and Gary P. Green. 1986. "Farm size and soil loss: prospects for a sustainable agriculture." *Rural Sociology* 51 (Spring):31–42.

Heffernan, William D., and Judith Bortner Heffernan. 1986. "Impact of the Farm Crisis on Rural Families and Communities." *The Rural Sociologist* 6, 3:160–170.

Heffernan, William D., and Paul Lasley. 1978. "Agricultural structure and interaction in the local community: a case study." *Rural Sociology* 43 (Fall):348–361.

Heffernan, William D., Gary Green, R. Paul Lasley, and Michael F. Nolan. 1981. "Part-time farming and the rural community." *Rural Sociology* 46 (Summer):245–262.

Heffernan, William D., Gary Green, Paul Lasley, and Michael F. Nolan. 1982. "Small farms: a heterogeneous category." *The Rural Sociologist* 2 (March):62–71.

Hetland, Per. 1986. "Pluriactivity as a strategy for employment in rural Norway." *Sociologia Ruralis* 26, 3/4:385–395.

Hickey, Jo Ann S., and Anthony Andrew Hickey. 1987. "Black farmers in Virginia, 1930–1978: an analysis of the social organization of agriculture." *Rural Sociology* 52 (Spring):75–88.

Hightower, Jim. 1973. *Hard Tomatoes, Hard Times*. Cambridge, MA: Schenkman.

Hoffer, Charles M. 1942. *Acceptance of Approved Farming Practices Among Farmers of Dutch Descent*, Special Bulletin No. 316. East Lansing: Michigan Agricultural Experiment Station.

Hoffer, Charles M., and Dale Stangland. 1958. "Farmers' attitudes and values in relation to adoption of approved practices in corn growing." *Rural Sociology* 23 (June):112–120.

Hoffsommer, Harold. 1935. "The AAA and the cropper." *Social Forces* 13 (May):494–502.

Hoffsommer, Harold. 1940. *The Sugar Cane Farm: A Social Study of Labor and Tenancy*, Bulletin 320. Baton Rouge: Louisiana State University and Agricultural and Mechanical College Agricultural Experiment Stations.

Hoffsommer, Harold (ed.). 1950. *The Social and Economic Significance of Land*

Tenure in the Southwestern States: A Report of the Regional Land Tenure Research Project. Chapel Hill: University of North Carolina Press.

Holley, William C., Ellen Winston, and T. J. Woofter, Jr. 1940. *The Plantation South, 1934–1937*. Research Monograph XXII. Washington, DC: Division of Research, Work Projects Administration.

Hooks, Gregory. 1986. "Critical rural sociology of yesterday and today." Pp. 1–25 in A. Eugene Havens et al. (eds.), *Studies in the Transformation of U.S. Agriculture*. Boulder CO: Westview Press.

Hooks, Gregory M., Ted L. Napier, and Michael V. Carter. 1983. "Correlates of adoption behaviors: the case of farm technologies." *Rural Sociology* 48 (Summer):308–323.

Howe, Carolyn. 1986. "Farmers' movements and the changing structure of agriculture." Pp. 104–149 in A. Eugene Havens et al. (eds.), *Studies in the Transformation of U.S. Agriculture*. Boulder, CO: Westview Press.

Howe, Carolyn, and Jess Gilbert. 1988. "'State centered' and 'class struggle' theories of the state: the case of New Deal agricultural policies." Paper presented at the annual meeting of the American Sociological Association, Atlanta, August.

Hussain, Arthur, and Keith Tribe. 1981a. *Marxism and the Agrarian Question, Vol. 1: German Social Democracy and the Peasantry, 1890–1907*. London: Macmillan Publishing Co.

Hussain, Arthur, and Keith Tribe. 1981b. *Marxism and the Agrarian Question, Vol. 2: Russian Marxism and the Peasantry, 1861–1930*. London: Macmillan Publishing Co.

James, David R. 1986. "Local state structure and the transformation of Southern agriculture." Pp. 150–178 in A. Eugene Havens et al. (eds.), *Studies in the Transformation of U.S. Agriculture*. Boulder, CO: Westview Press.

Jenkins, Ryss. 1984. "Divisions over the international division of labour." *Capital and Class* 22:28–57.

Jessop, Bob. 1988. "Regulation theory, post Fordism and the state: more than a reply to Werner Bonefield." *Capital and Class* 34:147–168.

John, M. E. 1938. *Part-time Farming in Six Industrial Areas in Pennsylvania*. Bulletin 361. State College: Pennsylvania Agricultural Experiment Station.

Johnson, Charles S., and associates. 1941. *Statistical Atlas of Southern Counties: Listing and Analysis of Socio-economic Indices of 1104 Southern Counties*. Chapel Hill: University of North Carolina Press.

Johnson, Charles S., Edwin R. Embree, and W. W. Alexander. 1935. *The Collapse of Cotton Tenancy: Summary of Field Studies & Statistical Surveys 1933–35*. Chapel Hill: University of North Carolina Press.

Jones, Calvin, and Rachel Rosenfeld. 1981. *American Farm Women: Findings*

from a National Survey, National Opinion Research Center Report 130. Chicago: National Opinion Research Center.
Joyce, Lynda, and Samuel Leadley. 1977. *An Assessment of Research Needs of Women in the Rural United States: Literature Review and Annotated Bibliography,* Bulletin 127. University Park: Department of Agricultural Economics and Rural Sociology, Pennsylvania State University.
Kada, Ryohei. 1980. *Part-Time Family Farming.* Tokyo: Center for Academic Publications-Japan.
Kalbacher, Judith Z. 1985. *A Profile of Female Farmers in America,* Rural Development Research Report No. 45. Washington, DC: Economic Research Service, U.S. Department of Agriculture.
Kenney, Martin F. 1986. *Biotechnology: The University-Industrial Complex.* New Haven: Yale University Press.
Kenney, Martin F., and Frederick H. Buttel. 1985. "Biotechnology: prospects and dilemmas for Third World development." *Development and Change* 16:61–91.
Kenney, Martin F., and Jack Kloppenburg, Jr. 1983. "The American agricultural research system: an obsolete structure?" *Agricultural Administration* 14:1–10.
Kenney, Martin F., J. Tadlock Cowan, and Frederick H. Buttel. 1982. *Genetic Engineering and Agriculture: Exploring the Impacts of Biotechnology on Industrial Structure, University-Industry Relationships, and the Social Organization of U.S. Agriculture,* Bulletin No. 123. Ithaca, NY: Department of Rural Sociology, Cornell University.
Kenney, Martin, Linda M. Lobao, James Curry, and Richard Goe. 1989. "Midwestern agriculture in U.S. Fordism: from the New Deal to economic restructuring." *Sociologia Ruralis* 29, no. 2: 131–48.
Kirkpatrick, E. L. 1938. *Analysis of 70,000 Rural Rehabilitation Families,* Social Research Report No. IX. Washington, DC: Farm Security Administration and Bureau of Agricultural Economics cooperating, U.S. Department of Agriculture.
Kivlin, Joseph E., and Frederick C. Fliegel. 1967. "Differential perceptions of innovations and rate of adoption." *Rural Sociology* 32 (March):78–91.
Kivlin, Joseph E., and Frederick C. Fliegel. 1968. "Orientations to agriculture: a factor analysis of farmers' perceptions of new practices." *Rural Sociology* 33 (June):127–140.
Klonglan, Gerald E., and E. Walter Coward, Jr. 1970. "The concept of symbolic adoption: a suggested interpretation." *Rural Sociology* 35 (March):77–83.
Klonglan, Gerald E., George M. Beal, Joe M. Bohlen, and E. Walter Coward, Jr. 1971. "Conceptualizing and measuring the diffusion of innovations." *Sociologia Ruralis* 11:36–48.
Kloppenburg, Jack, Jr. 1984. "The social impacts of biogenetic technology in

agriculture: past and future." Pp. 291–321 in Gigi M. Berardi and Charles C. Geisler (eds.), *The Social Consequences and Challenges of New Agricultural Technologies*. Boulder, CO: Westview Press.

Kloppenburg, Jack, Jr. 1988a. *First the Seed*. New York: Cambridge University Press.

Kloppenburg, Jack, Jr. (ed.). 1988b. *Seeds and Sovereignty*. Durham, NC: Duke University Press.

Kloppenburg, Jack, Jr., and Frederick H. Buttel. 1987. "Two blades of grass: the contradictions of agricultural research as state intervention." *Research in Political Sociology* 3:111–135.

Kloppenburg, Jack, Jr., and Charles C. Geisler. 1985. "The agricultural ladder: agrarian ideology and the changing structure of U.S. agriculture." *Journal of Rural Studies* 1, 1:59–72.

Kloppenburg, Jack, Jr., and Daniel Lee Kleinman. 1987. "Seed wars: common heritage, private property, and political strategy." *Socialist Review* 95 (September/October):7–41.

Kloppenburg, Jack, Jr., and Daniel Lee Kleinman. 1988. "Plant genetic resources: the common bowl." Pp. 1–15 in J. Kloppenburg, Jr. (ed.), *Seeds and Sovereignty*. Durham, NC: Duke University Press.

Kolb, J. H., and Edmund deS. Brunner. 1933. "Rural life." Pp. 497–552 in *Report of the President's Research Committee on Social Trends: Recent Social Trends in the United States*. New York: McGraw Hill Book Co.

Kollmorgen, Walter M. 1940. *The German-Swiss in Franklin County, Tennessee: A Study of the Significance of Cultural Considerations in Farming Enterprises*. Washington, DC: Bureau of Agricultural Economics, U.S. Department of Agriculture.

Kollmorgen, Walter M. 1942. *Culture of a Contemporary Rural Community: The Old Order Amish of Lancaster County, Pennsylvania*, Rural Life Studies 4. Washington, DC: Bureau of Agricultural Economics, U.S. Department of Agriculture.

Koppel, Bruce. 1985. "Themes on genes: comments on biotechnology, agricultural research, and rural sociology." *The Rural Sociologist* 5 (March):79–88.

Korsching, Peter. 1984. "Farm structural characteristics and proximity of purchase location of goods and services." *Research in Rural Sociology and Development* 1:261–287.

Korsching, Peter, and Peter J. Nowak. 1983. "Flexibility in conservation policy." Pp. 149–159 in David E. Brewster, Wayne D. Rasmussen, and Garth Youngberg, *Farms in Transition*. Ames: Iowa State University Press.

Kraenzel, Carl F. 1955. *The Great Plains in Transition*. Norman: University of Oklahoma Press.

Krasner, Stephen D. (ed.). 1983. *International Regimes*. Ithaca: Cornell University Press.

Krasner, Stephen D. 1986. *Structural Conflict: The Third World Against Global Liberalism.* Berkeley: University of California Press.

Kuhn, Thomas. 1970. *The Structure of Scientific Revolutions.* Chicago: University of Chicago Press.

Kuvlesky, William P., and Robert C. Bealer. 1967. "The relevance of adolescents' occupational aspirations for subsequent job attainment." *Rural Sociology* 32 (September):290–301.

Lackey, A. S., and O. F. Larson. 1959. "Turnover and changing characteristics of the farm operator population." *Canadian Journal of Agricultural Economics* 7:70–85.

Lacy, William B., and Lawrence Busch. 1989. "The changing division of labor between the university and industry: the case of biotechnology." Pp. 21–50 in J. J. Molnar and H. Kinnucan (eds.), *Biotechnology and the New Agricultural Revolution.* Boulder, CO: Westview Press.

Lancelle, Mark, and Richard D. Rodefeld. 1980. "The influence of social origins on the ability to attain ownership of large farms." *Rural Sociology* 45 (Fall):381–395.

Landis, Benson Y. 1922. *Rural Church Life in the Middle West: As Illustrated by Clay County, Iowa, and Jennings County, Indiana, with Comparative Data from Studies of Thirty-Five Middle Western Counties.* New York: George H. Doran Co.

LaRose, Bruce L. 1973. "Arvin and Dinuba revisited: a new look at community structure and the effects of scale of farm operations." In *The Role of Giant Corporations in the American and World Economies, Part 3: Corporate Secrecy: Agribusiness.* Hearings before the Subcommittee on Monopoly, Select Committee on Small Business, U.S. Senate, 92nd Congress. Washington, DC: U.S. Government Printing Office.

Larson, Olaf F. 1950. *Ten Years of Rural Rehabilitation in the United States.* Washington, DC: Bureau of Agricultural Economics, U.S. Department of Agriculture, 1947. Reprinted, Bombay, India: Indian Society of Agricultural Economics.

Larson, Olaf F. 1968. "Migratory agricultural workers in the Eastern Seaboard states." Pp. 442–458 in *A Report by the President's National Advisory Commission on Rural Poverty: Rural Poverty in the United States.* Washington, DC: U.S. Government Printing Office.

Larson, Olaf F. 1981. "Agriculture and the community." Pp. 147–193 in Amos H. Hawley and Sara Mills Mazie (eds.), *Nonmetropolitan America in Transition.* Chapel Hill: University of North Carolina Press.

Larson, Olaf F., and Thomas B. Jones. 1976. "The unpublished data from Roosevelt's Commission on Country Life." *Agricultural History* 50 (October):583–599.

Larson, Olaf F., and Emmit F. Sharp. 1960. *Migratory Farm Workers in the*

Atlantic Coast Stream: I. Changes in New York, 1953 and 1957, Bulletin 948. Ithaca, NY: Cornell Agricultural Experiment Station.

Larson, Oscar W. III, and Frederick H. Buttel. 1980. "Farm size, farm structure, climate, and energy: a reconsideration." *Rural Sociology* 45 (Summer):340–348.

Lehmann, David. 1986. "Two paths of agrarian capitalism, or a critique of Chayanovian Marxism." *Comparative Studies in Society and History* 28:601–627.

Lenin, V. I. 1974. *The Development of Capitalism in Russia*. Moscow: Progress Publishers.

Leonard, Olen, and C. P. Loomis. 1941. *Culture of a Contemporary Rural Community: El Cerrito, New Mexico*, Rural Life Studies 1. Washington, DC: Bureau of Agricultural Economics, U.S. Department of Agriculture.

LeVeen, E. Phillip. 1978. "The prospects for small-scale farming in an industrial society: a critical appraisal of Small Is Beautiful." Pp. 106–125 in Richard C. Dorf and Yvonne L. Hunter (eds.), *Appropriate Visions*. San Francisco: Boyd and Fraser.

LeVeen, E. Phillip. 1979. "Enforcing the reclamation act and rural development in California." *Rural Sociology* 44 (Winter):667–690.

Lianos, Theodore P. 1984. "Concentration and centralization of capital in agriculture." *Studies in Political Economy* 13:99–116.

Lionberger, Herbert F. 1948. *Low-income Farmers in Missouri: Situation and Characteristics of 459 Farm Operators in Four Social Area B Counties*, Research Bulletin 413. Columbia: Missouri Agricultural Experiment Station.

Lionberger, Herbert F. 1960. *Adoption of New Ideas and Practices*. Ames: Iowa State University Press.

Lionberger, Herbert F., and Joe D. Francis. 1969. "Views held of innovator and influence referents as sources of farm information in a Missouri community." *Rural Sociology* 34 (June):197–211.

Lipietz, Alain. 1987. *Mirages and Miracles*. London: Verso.

Lipset, Seymour Martin. 1955. "Social mobility and urbanization." *Rural Sociology* 20 (September-December):220–228.

Lipton, Michael, with Richard Longhurst. 1985. *Modern Varieties, International Agricultural Research and the Poor*. Washington, DC: World Bank.

Lively, C. E. 1928. "Type of agriculture as a conditioning factor in community organization." *Publications of the American Sociological Society* 23:35–50.

Lively, C. E., and R. B. Almack. 1938. *A Method of Determining Rural Social Subareas with Application to Ohio, Part I: Text and Maps*. Department of Rural Economics Mimeograph Bulletin No. 106. Columbus: Ohio

State Agricultural Experiment Station and Farm Security Administration, Region III, cooperating.
Lively, C. E., and C. L. Gregory. 1939. *Rural Social Areas in Missouri*, Research Bulletin 305. Columbia: Missouri Agricultural Experiment Station.
Lively, C. E., and C. L. Gregory. 1948. *Rural Social Areas in Missouri*, Research Bulletin 414. Columbia: Missouri Agricultural Experiment Station.
Lockeretz, William, and Sarah Wernick. 1979. "Commercial organic farming in the corn belt in comparison to conventional practices." *Rural Sociology* 44 (Winter):773–790.
Long, Norman. 1984. "Introduction." Pp. 1–29 in Norman Long (ed.), *Family and Work in Rural Societies: Perspectives on Non-wage Labour*. London: Tavistock.
Long, Norman, and Jan Douwe van der Ploeg. 1988. "New challenges in the sociology of rural development." *Sociologia Ruralis* 28 1:30–41.
Loomis, Charles P., and J. Allan Beegle. 1957. *Rural Sociology*. Englewood Cliffs, NJ: Prentice-Hall.
Lowe, Philip, Graham Cox, M. MacEwan, Tim O'Riordan, and Michael Winter. 1986. *Countryside Conflicts: The Politics of Farming, Forestry, and Conservation*. London: Gower.
Lyson, Thomas A. 1979. "Going to college: an emerging rung on the agricultural ladder." *Rural Sociology* 44 (Winter):773–790.
Lyson, Thomas A. 1982. "Stability and change in farming plans: results from a longitudinal study of young adults." *Rural Sociology* 47 (Fall):544–556.
Lyson, Thomas A. 1984. "Pathways into production agriculture: the structuring of farm recruitment in the United States." *Research in Rural Sociology and Development* 1:79–103.
Lyson, Thomas A. 1986. "Who cares about the farmer? Apathy and the current farm crisis." *Rural Sociology* 51 (Winter):490–502.
MacCannell, Dean. 1988. "Industrial agriculture and rural community degradation." Pp. 15–75 in L. Swanson (ed.), *Agriculture and Community Change in the U.S.* Boulder, CO: Westview Press.
MacCannell, Dean, and Edward Dolber-Smith. 1986. "Report on the structure of agriculture and impacts of new technologies on rural communities in Arizona, California, Florida, and Texas." Background Paper 2 in *Technology, Public Policy, and the Changing Structure of American Agriculture*. Washington, DC:U.S. Congress, Office of Technology Assessment. (Vol. 2.)
MacLeish, Kenneth, and Kimball Young. 1942. *Culture of a Contemporary Rural Community: Landaff, New Hampshire*, Rural Life Studies 3. Washington, DC: Bureau of Agricultural Economics, U.S. Department of Agriculture.
Mage, J. A. 1982. "The geography of part-time farming—a new vista for agricultural geographers." *GeoJournal* 6, 4:301–311.

Majka, Linda C., and Theo J. Majka. 1982. *Farm Workers, Agribusiness, and the State*. Philadelphia: Temple University Press.

Mandel, Ernest. 1978. *Marxist Economic Theory*. New York: Monthly Review Press.

Mangus, A. R. 1940. *Rural Regions of the United States*. Washington, DC: Division of Research, Work Projects Administration.

Mann, Susan A. 1984. "Sharecropping in the cotton South: a case of uneven development in agriculture." *Rural Sociology* 49 (Fall):412–429.

Mann, Susan A. 1987. "The rise of wage labour in the cotton south: a global analysis." *Journal of Peasant Studies* 14:226–242.

Mann, Susan A. 1989. *Capitalism and Agriculture*. Chapel Hill: University of North Carolina Press.

Mann, Susan A., and James M. Dickinson. 1978. "Obstacles to the development of a capitalist agriculture." *Journal of Peasant Studies* 5, 4:466–481.

Mann, Susan A., and James M. Dickinson. 1980. "State and agriculture in two eras of American capitalism." Pp. 283–325 in Frederick H. Buttel and Howard Newby (eds.), *The Rural Sociology of the Advanced Societies*. Montclair, NJ: Allanheld, Osmun & Co.

Mann, Susan A., and James M. Dickinson. 1986. "One furrow forward, two furrows back: a Marx-Weber synthesis for rural sociology?" Paper presented at the annual meeting of the Southern Sociological Society, New Orleans, April.

Mann, Susan A., and James M. Dickinson. 1987a. "One furrow forward, two furrows back: a Marx-Weber synthesis for rural sociology?" *Rural Sociology* 52 (Summer):264–285.

Mann, Susan A., and James M. Dickinson. 1987b. "Collectivizing our thoughts: a reply to Patrick Mooney." *Rural Sociology* 52 (Summer):296–303.

Manny, T. B. 1929. *Problems in Cooperation and Experiences of Farmers in Marketing Potatoes*. Circular No. 87. Washington, DC: U.S. Department of Agriculture.

Manny, T. B. 1931. *Farmers' Experiences and Opinions as Factors Influencing Their Cotton-marketing Methods*. Circular No. 144. Washington, DC: U.S. Department of Agriculture.

Manny, T. B. 1932. *What Ohio Farmers Think of Farmer-owned Business Organizations in That State*. Circular No. 240. Washington, DC: U.S. Department of Agriculture.

Marsden, Terry K., Sara J. Whatmore, and Richard J. C. Munton. 1987. "Uneven development and the restructuring process in British agriculture: a preliminary exploration." *Journal of Rural Studies* 3:297–308.

Marsden, Terry K., Richard J. Munton, Sarah J. Whatmore, and Jo K. Little. 1986. "Towards a political economy of capitalist agriculture: a British perspective." *International Journal of Urban and Regional Research* 4:498–521.

Marsh, C. Paul, and A. Lee Coleman. 1954. "The relation of neighborhood of residence to adoption of recommended farm practices." *Rural Sociology* 19 (December):385–389.

Marsh, C. Paul, and A. Lee Coleman. 1955. "The relation of farmer characteristics to the adoption of recommended farm practices." *Rural Sociology* 20 (September-December):289–296.

Martinson, Oscar B., and Gerald R. Campbell. 1980. "Betwixt and between: farmers and the marketing of agricultural inputs and outputs." Pp. 215–253 in Frederick H. Buttel and Howard Newby (eds.), *The Rural Sociology of the Advanced Societies*. Montclair, NJ: Allanheld, Osmun & Co.

Martinson, Oscar B., Eugene A. Wilkening, and Richard D. Rodefeld. 1976. "Feelings of powerlessness and social isolation among 'large-scale' farm personnel." *Rural Sociology* 41 (Winter):452–472.

Mason, Robert. 1964. "The use of information sources in the process of adoption." *Rural Sociology* 29 (March):40–52.

Massey, Doreen. 1984. *Spatial Divisions of Labor*. London: Methuen.

Massey, Doreen, and Alejandrina Catalano. 1978. *Capital and Land*. London: Arnold.

Mather, W. G., T. H. Townsend, and Dwight Sanderson. 1934. *A Study of Rural Community Development in Waterville, New York*, Bulletin 608. Ithaca, NY: Cornell University Agricultural Experiment Station.

McIntosh, Wm. Alex, and Mary Zey-Ferrell. 1986. "Lending officers' decisions to recommend innovative agricultural technology." *Rural Sociology* 51 (Winter):471–489.

McKain, W. C., Jr., and H. O. Dahlke. 1946. *Turnover of Farm Owners and Operators, Vale and Owhyee Irrigation Projects*. Washington, DC: Bureau of Agricultural Economics, U.S. Department of Agriculture.

McMichael, Philip. 1984. *Settlers and the Agrarian Question*. New York: Cambridge University Press.

McMichael, Philip. 1987. "Bringing circulation back into agricultural political economy: analyzing the Antebellum plantation in its world economy context." *Rural Sociology* 52 (Summer):242–263.

McMillan, Robert T. 1943. "The relationship of selected social background factors to farm tenure status." *Southwestern Social Science Quarterly* 23 (March):320–330.

McMillan, Robert T., and Otis D. Duncan. 1945. *Social Factors of Farm Ownership in Oklahoma*. Bulletin No. B-289. Stillwater: Oklahoma Agricultural Experiment Station.

McMillan, Robert T., and Marylee Mason. 1945. "Social background and farm ownership." *Rural Sociology* 10 (December):414–416.

Merton, Robert K. 1957. *Social Theory and Social Structure*. New York: Free Press.

Merton, Robert K. 1973. *Sociology of Science*. Chicago: University of Chicago Press.
Metzler, William H. 1955. *Migratory Farm Workers in the Atlantic Coast Stream — Study in the Belle Glade Area of Florida*. Circular No. 966. Washington, DC: U.S. Department of Agriculture.
Micklin, Michael, and Harvey M. Choldin. 1984. *Sociological Human Ecology*. Boulder, CO: Westview Press.
Mills, C. Wright. 1959. *The Sociological Imagination*. New York: Oxford University Press.
Moe, Edward O., and Carl C. Taylor. 1942. *Culture of a Contemporary Rural Community: Irwin, Iowa*. Rural Life Studies 5. Washington, DC: Bureau of Agricultural Economics, U.S. Department of Agriculture.
Molnar, Joseph J. (ed.). 1986. *Agricultural Change*. Boulder, CO: Westview Press.
Molnar, Joseph J., and John E. Dunkelberger. 1981. "The expectation to farm: an interaction of background and experience." *Rural Sociology* 46 (Spring):62–84.
Molnar, Joseph J., and Henry Kinnican (eds.). 1989. *Biotechnology and the New Agricultural Revolution*. Boulder, CO: Westview Press.
Molnar, Joseph J., and Henry Kinnucan. 1985. "Biotechnology and the small farm: implications of an emerging trend." Pp. 3–13 in T. T. Williams (ed.), *Strategy for the Survival of Small Farmers*. Tuskegee, AL: Human Resources Development Center, Tuskegee Institute.
Molnar, Joseph J., Henry Kinnucan, and Upton Hatch. 1985. "Anticipating the impacts of biotechnology on agriculture: a review and synthesis." Paper presented at the annual meeting of the American Chemical Society, Symposium on Applications of Biotechnology to Agricultural Chemistry, Chicago.
Mooney, Patrick H. 1982. "Labor time, production time and capitalist development in agriculture: a reconsideration of the Mann-Dickinson thesis." *Sociologia Ruralis* 22, 3/4:279–292.
Mooney, Patrick H. 1983. "Toward a class analysis of midwestern agriculture." *Rural Sociology* 48:563–584.
Mooney, Patrick H. 1985. "The transformation of class relations in Wisconsin agriculture, 1945–1982." Unpublished Ph.D. dissertation, University of Wisconsin.
Mooney, Patrick H. 1986a. "Class relations and class structure in the Midwest." Pp. 206–251 in A. Eugene Havens et al. (eds.), *Studies in the Transformation of U.S. Agriculture*. Boulder, CO: Westview Press.
Mooney, Patrick H. 1986b. "The political economy of credit in American agriculture." *Rural Sociology* 51 (Winter):449–470.
Mooney, Patrick H. 1987a. "Desperately seeking: one dimensional Mann and Dickinson." *Rural Sociology* 52 (Summer):286–295.

Mooney, Patrick H. 1987b. "Sociology and the Farm Crisis." *Mid-American Review of Sociology* 12:3–14.
Mooney, Patrick H. 1988. *My Own Boss.* Boulder, CO: Westview Press.
Moore, Barrington. 1966. *Social Origins of Dictatorship and Democracy.* Boston: Beacon.
Morrison, Denton E. 1964. "Achievement motivation of farm operators: a measurement study." *Rural Sociology* 29 (December):367–384.
Morrison, Denton E., Krishna Kumar, Everett M. Rogers, and Frederick C. Fliegel. 1976. "Stratification and risk-taking: a further negative replication of Cancian's theory." *American Sociological Review* 41 (October):912–919.
Morse, H. N. 1922. *The Country Church in Industrial Zones.* New York: George H. Doran Co.
Morse, H. N. 1924. *The Social Survey in Town and Country Areas.* New York: George H. Doran Co.
Morse, H. N., and Edmund deS. Brunner. 1923. *The Town and Country Church in the United States.* New York: George H. Doran Co.
Mottura, Giovanni, and Enrico Pugliese. 1980. "Capitalism in agriculture and capitalistic agriculture: the Italian case." Pp. 171–199 in F. H. Buttel and H. Newby (eds.), *The Rural Sociology of the Advanced Societies.* Montclair, NJ: Allanheld, Osmun & Co.
Mouzelis, Nicos. 1976. "Capitalism and the development of agriculture." *Journal of Peasant Studies* 3:483–492.
Muñoz, Robert D. 1984. "Socioeconomic characteristics of small family farms in Mississippi and Tennessee." *The Rural Sociologist* 4 (January): 2–10.
Muñoz, Robert D. 1985. "Characteristics of black farmers in the sand-clay hills of Mississippi and Tennessee." *The Rural Sociologist* 5 (September):322–330.
Murdock, Steve H. Don E. Albrecht, Rita R. Hamm, F. Larry Leistritz, and Arlen G. Leholm. 1986. "The farm crisis in the Great Plains: implications for theory and policy development." *Rural Sociology* 51 (Winter):406–435.
Murray, Martin, and C. Post. 1983. "The 'agrarian question,' class struggle and the capitalist state in the U.S. and South Africa." *Insurgent Sociologist* 11, 4:37–56.
Murray, Robin. 1977. "Value and theory of rent, part 1." *Capital and Class* 3:100–122.
Murray, Robin. 1978. "Value and theory of rent, part 2." *Capital and Class* 4:11–33.
Nakano, Isshin. 1972. "Agricultural policies and the capitalist development of agriculture in the United States." *Kyoto University Economic Review* 42, 1–2:61–92.
Napier, Ted L., and D. Lynn Forster. 1982. "Farmer attitudes and behav-

ior associated with soil conservation control." Pp. 137–150 in Harold G. Halcrow, Earl O. Heady, and Melvin L. Cotner (eds.), *Soil Conservation Policies, Institutions, and Incentives*. Ankeny, Iowa: Soil Conservation Society of America.

Napier, Ted L., C. Thraen, A. Gore, and W. Gore. 1984. "Factors affecting the adoption of conventional and conservation practices in Ohio." *Journal of Soil and Water Conservation* 39:205–208.

Neal, Ernest E., and Lewis W. Jones. 1950. "The place of the Negro farmer in the changing economy of the cotton South." *Rural Sociology* 15 (March):30–41.

Nelson, Lowry. 1925. *A Social Survey of Escalante, Utah*. Brigham Young University Studies No. 1. Provo, Utah: Brigham Young University.

Nelson, Lowry. 1928. *The Utah Farm Village of Ephraim*, Brigham Young University Studies No. 2. Provo, Utah: Brigham Young University.

Nelson, Lowry. 1933. *Some Social and Economic Features of American Fork, Utah*, Brigham Young University Studies No. 4. Provo, Utah: Brigham Young University.

Nelson, Lowry. 1952. *The Mormon Village*. Salt Lake City: University of Utah Press.

Nelson, Lowry. 1966. "On George Edgar Vincent: rural social scientist." *Rural Sociology* 31 (December):478–482.

Nelson, Lowry. 1969. *Rural Sociology*. Minneapolis: University of Minnesota Press.

Newby, Howard. 1977. *The Deferential Worker*. London: Allen Lane.

Newby, Howard. 1978. "The rural sociology of advanced capitalist societies." Pp. 3–30 in H. Newby (ed.), *International Perspectives in Rural Sociology*. Chichester, England: Wiley.

Newby, Howard. 1980. "Rural sociology—a trend report." *Current Sociology* 28, 1:1–141.

Newby, Howard. 1983a. "The sociology of agriculture: toward a new rural sociology." *Annual Review of Sociology* 9:67–81.

Newby, Howard. 1983b. "European social theory and the agrarian question: towards a sociology of agriculture." Pp. 109–123 in Gene F. Summers (ed.), *Technology and Social Change in Rural Areas*. Boulder, CO: Westview Press.

Newby, Howard, Colin Bell, David Rose, and Peter Saunders. 1978. *Property, Paternalism, and Power*. London, Hutchinson.

Newby, Howard, and Frederick H. Buttel. 1980. "Toward a critical rural sociology." Pp. 1–35 in Frederick H. Buttel and Howard Newby (eds.), *The Rural Sociology of the Advanced Societies*. Montclair, NJ: Allanheld, Osmun & Co.

Newby, Howard, and Peter Utting. 1984. "Agribusiness in the United Kingdom: social and political implications." Pp. 265–289 in G. M. Berardi and C.

References

C. Geisler (eds.), *The Social Consequences and Challenges of New Agricultural Technology*. Boulder, CO: Westview Press.

Norris, P. E., and Sandra S. Batie. 1985. "Factors influencing the adoption of soil conservation practices: a Virginia case study." Paper presented at the annual meeting of the Rural Sociological Society, Virginia Polytechnic Institute and State University, August.

Nowak, Peter J. 1983a. "Adoption and diffusion of soil and water conservation practices." *The Rural Sociologist* 3 (March):83–91.

Nowak, Peter J. 1983b. "Strategies for increasing the adoption of conservation strategies." *The Rural Sociologist* 3 (July):243–246.

Nowak, Peter J. 1984. "Adoption and diffusion of soil and water conservation practices." Pp. 214–237 in Burton C. English et al. (eds.), *Future Agricultural Technology and Resource Conservation*. Ames: Iowa State University Press.

Nowak, Peter J. 1985. "The adoption of agricultural conservation technologies." Paper presented at the annual meeting of the Rural Sociological Society, Virginia Polytechnic Institute and State University, August.

Nowak, Peter J. 1987. "The adoption of agricultural conservation technologies: economic and diffusion explanations." *Rural Sociology* 52 (Summer):208–220.

Nowak, Peter J., and Peter F. Korsching. 1983. "Social and institutional factors affecting the adoption and maintenance of agricultural BMPs." Pp. 349–373 in Frank W. Schaller and George W. Bailey (eds.), *Agricultural Management and Water Quality*. Ames: Iowa State University Press.

Nuckton, Carole Frank, Refugio I. Rochin, and Douglas Gwynn. 1982. "Farm size and rural community welfare: an interdisciplinary approach." *Rural Sociology* 47 (Spring):32–46.

Odum, Howard W. 1936. *Southern Regions of the United States*. Chapel Hill: The University of North Carolina Press.

Odum, Howard W., and Harry E. Moore. 1938. *American Regionalism: A Cultural-Historical Approach to National Integration*. New York: Henry Holt and Company.

Office of Technology Assessment. 1986. *Technology, Public Policy, and the Changing Structure of American Agriculture*. Washington, DC: Office of Technology Assessment.

Olshan, Marc A. 1979. *The Old Order Amish in New York State*. Bulletin No. 94. Ithaca, NY: Department of Rural Sociology, Cornell University.

Pampel, Fred, Jr., and J. C. van Es. 1977. "Environmental quality and issues of adoption research." *Rural Sociology* 42 (Spring):57–71.

Parsons, Talcott. 1937. *The Structure of Social Action*. Glencoe, IL: Free Press.

Parsons, Talcott. *The Social System*. Glencoe, IL: Free Press. 1951.

Patten, Marjorie. 1922. *The Country Church in Colonial Counties: As Illus-*

trated by Addison County, Vt., Tompkins County, N.Y., and Warren County, N.Y. New York: George H. Doran Co.

Pearse, Andrew. 1980. *Seeds of Plenty, Seeds of Want.* New York: Oxford University Press.

Pedersen, Harald A. 1951. "Cultural differences in the acceptance of recommended practices." *Rural Sociology* 16 (March):37–49.

Pedersen, Harald A. 1952. "Attitudes relating to mechanization and farm labor changes in the Yazoo-Mississippi Delta." *Land Economics* 48, 4:353–361.

Pedersen, Harald A. 1954. "Mechanized agriculture and the farm laborer." *Rural Sociology* 19 (June):143–151.

Pedersen, Harald A., and Arthur F. Raper. 1954. *The Cotton Plantation in Transition*, Bulletin 508. State College: Mississippi Agricultural Experiment Station.

Perelman, Michael. 1977. *Farming for Profit in a Hungry World.* Montclair, NJ: Allanheld, Osmun & Co.

Perry, Astor, Gene A. Sullivan, Robert J. Dolan, and C. Paul Marsh. 1967. "The adoption process: S curve or J curve?" *Rural Sociology* 32 (June):220–222.

Perry, Charles S. 1982. "The rationalization of U.S. farm labor: trends between 1956 and 1979." *Rural Sociology* 47 (Winter):670–691.

Pfeffer, Max John. 1983. "Social origins of three systems of farm production in the United States." *Rural Sociology* 48 (Winter):540–562.

Photiadis, John D. 1962. "Motivation, contacts, and technological change." *Rural Sociology* 27 (September):316–326.

Pimentel, David, et al. 1976. "Land degradation: effects on food and energy resources." *Science* 194 (8 October):149–155.

Ploch, Louis A. 1960. *Social and Family Characteristics of Maine Contract Broiler Growers*, Bulletin No. 569. Orono: Maine Agricultural Experiment Station.

Portes, Alejandro, Archibald O. Haller, and William H. Sewell. 1968. "Professional-executive vs. farming as unique occupational choices." *Rural Sociology* 33 (June):153–159.

Powell, Lanny C., and Curtis C. Roseman. 1972. "An investigation of the subprocesses of diffusion." *Rural Sociology* 37 (June):221–227.

Presser, H. A. 1969. "Measuring innovativeness rather than adoption." *Rural Sociology* 34 (December):510–527.

Ramsey, Charles E., Robert A. Polson, and George E. Spencer. 1959. "Values and the adoption of practices." *Rural Sociology* 24 (March):35–47.

Randolph, S. Randi, and Carolyn Sachs. 1981. "The establishment of applied sciences: medicine and agriculture compared." Pp. 83–111 in Lawrence Busch (ed.), *Science and Agricultural Development.* Montclair, NJ: Allanheld, Osmun & Co.

Rankin, J. O. 1923a. *Nebraska Farm Homes: A Comparison of Some Living Conditions of Owners, Part-Owners, and Tenants.* Bulletin 191. Lincoln: Nebraska Agricultural Experiment Station.
Rankin, J. O. 1923b. *Nebraska Farm Tenancy—Some Community Phases.* Bulletin 196. Lincoln: Nebraska Agricultural Experiment Station.
Rankin, J. O. 1924. *Landlords of Nebraska Farms.* Bulletin 202. Lincoln: Nebraska Agricultural Experiment Station.
Rankin, J. O. 1926. *Steps to Nebraska Farm Ownership*, Bulletin 210. Lincoln: Nebraska Agricultural Experiment Station.
Raper, Arthur F. 1971. *Preface to Peasantry: A Tale of Two Black Belt Counties.* Chapel Hill: University of North Carolina Press, 1936. Reprinted, New York: Arno Press & *The New York Times.*
Raper, Arthur F. 1943. *Tenants of the Almighty.* New York: Macmillan Publishing Co.
Raper, Arthur F. 1946. "The role of agricultural technology in Southern social change." *Sociological Focus* 25:21–30.
Raper, Arthur F., and Carl C. Taylor. 1949. "Rural culture." Pp. 329-343 in Carl C. Taylor and others, *Rural Life in the United States.* New York: Alfred A. Knopf.
Rathge, Richard W., F. Larry Leistritz, and Gary A. Goreham. 1988. "Farmers displaced in economically depressed times." *Rural Sociology* 53 (Fall):346–356.
Redclift, Michael. 1986. "Survival strategies in rural Europe: continuity and change." *Sociologia Ruralis* 26, 3/4:218–227.
Redclift, Michael. 1987. *Sustainable Development.* London: Methuen.
Reif, Linda Lobao. 1987. "Farm structure, industry structure, and socioeconomic conditions in the United States." *Rural Sociology* 52 (Winter):462–482.
Reimer, Bill. 1986. "Women as farm labor." *Rural Sociology* 51 (Summer):143–155.
Research and Information System for the Non-Aligned and Other Developing Countries (RIS). 1988. *Biotechnology Revolution and the Third World.* New Dehli: RIS.
Reuss, Carl, Paul Landis, and Richard Wakefield. 1938. *Migratory Farm Labor and the Hop Industry on the Pacific Coast, with Special Application to Problems of the Yakima Valley, Washington.* Bulletin No. 363. Pullman: Washington State Agricultural Experiment Station.
Richardson, Joseph L., and Olaf F. Larson. 1976. "Small community trends: a 50-year perspective on social-economic change in 13 New York communities." *Rural Sociology* 41 (Spring):45–59.
Riley, Marvin P., and Darryll R. Johnson. 1970. *South Dakota's Hutterite Colonies: 1874–1969.* Bulletin 565. Brookings: South Dakota State Agricultural Experiment Station.

Riley, Marvin P., and James R. Stewart. 1966. *The Hutterites: South Dakota's Communal Farmers.* Bulletin 530. Brookings: South Dakota State Agricultural Experiment Station.

Rodefeld, Richard D. 1974. "The changing organizational and occupational structure of farming and the implications for farm work force individuals, families, and communities." Unpublished Ph.D. dissertation, University of Wisconsin.

Rodefeld, Richard D. 1978. "Trends in U.S. farm organizational structure and type." Pp. 158–177 in Richard D. Rodefeld et al. (eds.), *Change in Rural America.* St. Louis: C. V. Mosby, Co.

Rodefeld, Richard D. 1980. "Farm structural characteristics: recent trends, causes, implications, and research needs—excerpts." Part III in Luther Tweeten et al. (eds.), *Structure of Agriculture and Information Needs Regarding Small Farms.* Washington, DC: National Rural Center.

Rodefeld, Richard D., Jan Flora, Donald Voth, Isao Fujimoto, and Jim Converse (eds.). 1978. *Change in Rural America: Causes, Consequences and Alternatives.* St. Louis: C. V. Mosby Co.

Rogers, Everett M. 1957. "Personality correlates of the adoption of technological practices." *Rural Sociology* 22 (September):267–268.

Rogers, Everett M. 1958a. "Categorizing the adopters of agricultural practices." *Rural Sociology* 23 (December):345–354.

Rogers, Everett M. 1958b. "A conceptual variable analysis of technological change." *Rural Sociology* 23 (June):136–145.

Rogers, Everett M. 1962. *Diffusion of Innovations.* New York: Free Press.

Rogers, Everett M., (ed.). 1976. "Communications and development: critical perspectives." special issue of *Communication Research* 3, 2.

Rogers, Everett M., and L. Edna Rogers. 1961. "A methodological analysis of adoption scales." *Rural Sociology* 26 (December):325–336.

Rogers, Everett M. with Floyd F. Shoemaker. 1971. *Communication of Innovations.* 2nd ed. New York: Free Press.

Rohwer, Robert A. 1950. *Family Factors in Tenure Experience.* Research Bulletin 375. Ames: Iowa State Agricultural Experiment Station.

Rosenfeld, Rachel. 1985. *U.S. Farm Women.* Chapel Hill: University of North Carolina Press.

Ross, Peggy J. 1985. "A commentary on research on American farm women." *Agriculture and Human Values* 2 (Winter):19–30.

Rushing, William A. 1970. "Class differences in goal orientations and aspirations: rural patterns." *Rural Sociology* 35 (September):377–395.

Ruttan, Vernon W. 1982. *Agricultural Research Policy.* Minneapolis: University of Minnesota Press.

Ryan, Bryce, and Neal C. Gross. 1943. "The diffusion of hybrid seed corn in two Iowa communities." *Rural Sociology* 8 (March):15–24.

Sachs, Carolyn E. 1983. *The Invisible Farmers*. Totowa, NJ: Rowman and Allanheld.
Salamon, Sonya. 1980. "Ethnic differences in farm family land transfers." *Rural Sociology* 45 (Summer):290–308.
Salamon, Sonya. 1984. "Ethnic origin as explanation for local land ownership patterns." *Research in Rural Sociology and Development* 1:161–186.
Salamon, Sonya. 1985. "Ethnic communities and the structure of agriculture." *Rural Sociology* 50 (Fall):323–340.
Salamon, Sonya, and Karen Davis-Brown. 1986. "Middle-range farmers persisting through the agricultural crisis." *Rural Sociology* 51 (Winter):503–512.
Salamon, Sonya, and Shirley O'Reilly. 1979. "Family land and developmental cycles among Illinois farmers." *Rural Sociology* 45 (Summer):290–308.
Salant, Priscilla. 1983. *Farm Women: Contribution to Farm and Family*. Agricultural Economics Research Report No. 140. Washington, DC: Economic Research Service, U.S. Department of Agriculture.
Samson, A'Delbert. 1958. *Church Groups in Four Agricultural Settings in Montana*. Bulletin 538. Bozeman: Montana Agricultural Experiment Station.
Sanderson, Steven E. (ed.). 1985. *The Americas in the New International Division of Labor*. New York: Holmes & Meier.
Sanderson, Steven E. 1986. "The emergence of the 'world steer': internationalization and foreign domination in Latin American cattle production." Pp. 123–148 in F. L. Tullis and W. L. Hollist (eds.), *Food, the State, and International Political Economy*. Lincoln: University of Nebraska Press.
Sasson, Albert. 1988. *Biotechnologies and Development*. Paris: UNESCO.
Schroeder, Emily Harper, Frederick C. Fliegel, and J. C. van Es. 1983. "The effects of nonfarm background on orientation to farming among small-scale farmers." *Rural Sociology* 48 (Fall):349–366.
Schroeder, Emily Harper, Frederick C. Fliegel, and J. C. van Es. 1985. "Measurement of the lifestyle dimensions of farming for small-scale farmers." *Rural Sociology* 50 (Fall):305–322.
Schuler, E. A. 1938. *Social Status and Farm Tenure—Attitudes and Social Conditions of Corn Belt and Cotton Belt Farmers*. Social Research Report No. IV. Washington, DC: Farm Security Administration and Bureau of Agricultural Economics cooperating, U.S. Department of Agriculture.
Schulman, Michael D. 1981. "Ownership and control in agribusiness corporations." *Rural Sociology* 46 (Winter):652–668.
Schulman, Michael D., and Regina Luginbuhl. 1985. *The Small Farmer in North Carolina: Attitudes and Beliefs Toward Agriculture*, International Programs Paper Series 4. Raleigh: North Carolina State University.
Schulman, Michael D., Patricia Garrett, and Regina Luginbuhl. 1985. "Dimen-

sions of the internal stratification of smallholders: insights from North Carolina Piedmont counties." *Rural Sociology* 50 (Summer):249–259.
Schwartz, Michael. 1976. *Radical Protest and Social Structure.* New York: Academic Press.
Simpson, Ida Harper, John Wilson, and Kristina Young. 1988. "The sexual division of farm household labor: a replication and extension." *Rural Sociology* 53 (Summer):145–165.
Sims, Newell Leroy. 1912. *A Hoosier Village.* Columbia University Studies in History, Economics and Public Law, Vol. 46, No. 4, Whole Number 117. New York: Columbia University.
Sinclair, Peter R. 1980. "Agricultural policy and the decline of commercial family farming." Pp. 327–349 in Frederick H. Buttel and Howard Newby (eds.), *The Rural Sociology of the Advanced Societies.* Montclair, NJ: Allanheld, Osmun & Co.
Singer, Edward G., Gary P. Green, and Jere L. Gilles. 1983. "The Mann-Dickinson thesis: reject or revise?" *Sociologia Ruralis* 23:267–287.
Sivini, G. 1976. "Some remarks on the development of capitalism and specific forms of part-time farming in Europe." In Anthony M. Fuller and Julius A. Mage (eds.), *Part-Time Farming.* Guelph, Ont.: University of Guelph.
Skees, Jerry R., and Louis E. Swanson. 1988. "Farm structure and rural well-being in the South." Pp. 238–321 in L. E. Swanson (ed.), *Agriculture and Community Change in the U.S.* Boulder, CO: Westview Press.
Skocpol, Theda. 1979. *States and Social Revolutions.* New York: Cambridge University Press.
Skocpol, Theda, and Kenneth Finegold. 1982. "State capacity and economic intervention in the early New Deal." *Political Science Quarterly* 97, 2:255–278.
Skrabanek, R. L. 1954. "Commercial farming in the United States." *Rural Sociology* 19 (June):136–142.
Slocum, Walter L. 1942. *The Influence of Tenure Status upon Rural Life in Eastern South Dakota,* Circular 39. Brookings: South Dakota State Agricultural Experiment Station.
Slocum, Walter L. 1967. "The influence of reference group values on educational aspirations of rural high school students." *Rural Sociology* 32 (September):269–277.
Small Farm Viability Project. 1977. *The Family Farm in California.* Sacramento: Small Farm Viability Project.
Smith, John P. 1987. "The social and ecological correlates of bankruptcy during the fiscal crisis, 1970-1987." *Mid-American Review of Sociology* 12:35–54.
Smith, Leslie Whitener, and Robert Coltrane. 1981. *Hired Farmworkers.* Rural

Development Research Report No. 32. Washington, DC: Economic Research Service, U.S. Department of Agriculture.
Smith, Mervin G., and Carlton F. Christian (eds.). 1961. *Adjustments in Agriculture*. Ames: Iowa State University Press.
Smith, T. Lynn. 1957. "Rural sociology in the United States and Canada—a trend report." *Current Sociology* 6, 1:5–18.
Smith, T. Lynn. 1974. "Sociocultural changes in 12 midwestern communities, 1930-1970." *Social Science* 49 (Autumn):195–207.
Smith, T. Lynn, and Paul E. Zopf, Jr. 1970. *Principles of Inductive Rural-Urban Sociology*. Philadelphia: Davis.
Sonka, Steven T., and Earl O. Heady. 1974. "Farm size, rural community income, and consumer welfare." *American Journal of Agricultural Economics* 56:534–542.
Sorokin, Pitirim A. 1927. *Social Mobility*. New York: Harper.
Sorokin, Pitirim A., and Carle C. Zimmerman. 1929. *Principles of Rural-Urban Sociology*. New York: Henry Holt.
Steeves, Allan D. 1972. "Proletarianization and class identification." *Rural Sociology* 37 (March):5–26.
Steeves, Allan D. 1979. "Mobility into and out of Canadian agriculture." *Rural Sociology* 44 (Fall):566–583.
Stinchcombe, Arthur. 1961. "Agricultural enterprise and rural class relations." *American Journal of Sociology* 67 (September):165–176.
Stockdale, Jerry D. 1977. "Technology and change in U.S. agriculture: model or warning?" *Sociologia Ruralis* 17:43–58.
Stone, Kenneth E. 1987. "Impact of the farm financial crisis on the retail and service sectors of rural communities." *Agricultural Finance Review* 47:40–47.
Stratigaki, Maria. 1988. "Agricultural modernization and gender division of labor." *Sociologia Ruralis* 28, 4:248–262.
Straus, Murray A. 1958. *Matching Farms and Families in the Columbia Basin Project*. Bulletin 588. Pullman: Washington Agricultural Experiment Station.
Straus, Murray A. 1956. "Personal characteristics and functional needs in the choice of farming as an occupation." *Rural Sociology* 21 (September-December):257–266.
Straus, Murray A. 1962. "Work roles and financial responsibility in the socialization of farm, fringe, and town boys." *Rural Sociology* 27 (September):257–274.
Straus, Murray A. 1964. "Societal needs and personal characteristics in the choice of farm, blue collar, and white collar occupations by farmers' sons." Rural Sociology 29 (December):408–425.
Straus, Murray A., and Barnard D. Parrish. 1956. *The Columbia Basin Settler:*

A Study of Social and Economic Resources in New Land Settlement. Bulletin 566. Pullman: Washington Agricultural Experiment Station.
Straus, Murray A., and Cecilia E. Sudia. 1965. "Entrepreneurial orientation of farm, working class, and middle class boys." *Rural Sociology* 30 (September):291–298.
Subcommittee for the Study of Diffusion of Farm Practices, North Central Rural Sociology Committee. 1955. *How Farm People Accept New Ideas.* Special Report 15. Ames: Iowa Agricultural Extension Service.
Subcommittee of the Rural Sociological Society. 1952. *Sociological Research on Diffusion and Adoption of Farm Practices.* Bulletin RS-2. Lexington: Kentucky Agricultural Experiment Station.
Swanson, Louis E. 1982. "Farm and trade center transition in an industrial society: Pennsylvania, 1930–1960." Unpublished Ph.D. dissertation, Pennsylvania State University.
Swanson, Louis E. (ed.). 1988. *Agriculture and Community Change in the U.S.* Boulder, CO: Westview Press.
Swanson, Louis E., and Lawrence Busch. 1985. "A part-time farming model reconsidered: a comment on a POET model." *Rural Sociology* 50 (Fall):427–436.
Swanson, Louis E., S. Camboni, and T. L. Napier. 1985. "Barriers to the adoption of soil conservation practices at the farm level." Paper presented at the symposium on Soil and Water Conservation: Implications of Social and Economic Research for Policy Development and Program Implementation, Zion, Illinois, June.
Sweet, James A. 1972. "The employment of rural farm wives." *Rural Sociology* 37 (December):553–577.
Taylor, Carl C. 1948. "Dr. Galpin at Washington." *Rural Sociology* 13 (June):145–155.
Taylor, Carl C. 1953. *The Farmers' Movement, 1620–1920.* New York: American Book Co.
Taylor, Carl C., and C. C. Zimmerman. 1922. *Economic and Social Conditions of North Carolina Farmers: Based on a Survey of 1000 North Carolina Farmers in Three Typical Counties of the State.* Raleigh: North Carolina State College of Agriculture.
Taylor, Carl C., Louis J. Ducoff, and Margaret Jarman Hagood. 1948. *Trends in the Tenure Status of Farm Workers in the United States Since 1880.* Washington, DC: Bureau of Agricultural Economics, U.S. Department of Agriculture.
Taylor, Carl C., Arthur F. Raper, Douglas Ensminger, Margaret Jarman Hagood, T. Wilson Longmore, Walter C. McKain, Jr., Louis J. Ducoff, and Edgar A. Schuler. 1949. *Rural Life in the United States.* New York: Alfred A. Knopf.
Taylor, David L., and William L. Miller. 1978. "The adoption process and

environmental innovations: a case study of a government project." *Rural Sociology* 43 (Winter):634–648.
Taylor, Grady W. 1962. "An analysis of certain social and psychological factors differentiating successful from unsuccessful farm families." *Rural Sociology* 27 (September):303–315.
Thomas, Robert J. 1981a. "The social organization of industrial agriculture." *Insurgent Sociologist* 10 (Winter):5–20.
Thomas, Robert J. 1981b. "Citizenship, work organization, and earnings." Paper presented at the annual meeting of the Rural Sociological Society, University of Guelph, August.
Thomas, Robert J. 1985. *Citizenship, Gender, and Work: Social Organization of Industrial Agriculture*. Berkeley: University of California Press.
Thomas-Lycklama a Niejholt, G. 1980. *On the Road for Work*. Boston: Martinus Nijhoff Publishing Co.
Thompson, S. B. 1981. "International organizations and the improbability of a global food regime." Pp. 191–206 in D. N. Balaam and M. J. Carey (eds.), *Food Politics*. London: Croom Helm.
Thorner, Alice. 1982. "Semi-feudalism or capitalism? Contemporary debate on classes and modes of production in India." *Economic and Political Weekly* 17 (4 December, 11 December, and 18 December):1961–1968, 1993–1999, 2061–2066.
Tigges, Leann M., and Rachel A. Rosenfeld. 1987. "Independent farming: correlates and consequences for women and men." *Rural Sociology* 52 (Fall):345–364.
Tweeten, Luther, and Wallace Huffman. 1980. "Structural change." Part I in Luther Tweeten et al. (eds.), *Structure of Agriculture and Information Needs Regarding Small Farms*. Washington, DC: National Rural Center.
U.S. Congress, Senate. 1944. *Report to the Country Life Commission*. Senate Document 705, 60th Congress, 2nd session, 1909. Published by Sturgis & Walton, 1911; reprinted, Chapel Hill: University of North Carolina Press.
U.S. Department of Agriculture. 1979. *Structure Issues of American Agriculture*. Washington, DC: Economics, Statistics, and Cooperatives Service, U.S. Department of Agriculture.
U.S. Department of Agriculture. 1981. *A Time to Choose*. Washington, DC: U.S. Department of Agriculture.
U.S. Department of Agriculture. 1958. Agricultural Research Service, *Federal Grant Research at the State Agricultural Experiment Stations: Projects on Rural Life Studies, Part 20*. Washington, DC: U.S. Department of Agriculture.
Vail, David. 1982. "Exploring the rural political economy of the United States: family farms in the web of community." *Antipode* 14, 3:26–38.
Vail, David. Forthcoming. "Reforming Sweden's non-sustainable agricultural

policy: contrasts with the USA and the European Economic Community." In W. H. Friedland et al. (eds.), *The New Political Economy of Agriculture.*.

Valkonen, Tapani. 1970. "On the theory of diffusion of innovations." *Sociologia Ruralis* 10, 2:162–179.

Vance, Rupert B. 1929. *Human Factors in Cotton Culture: A Study in the Social Geography of the American South.* Chapel Hill: The University of North Carolina Press.

Vance, Rupert B. 1935. *Human Geography of the South: A Study in Regional Resources and Human Adequacy.* Chapel Hill: The University of North Carolina Press.

van den Ban, Anne Willem. 1960. "Locality group differences in the adoption of new farm practices." *Rural Sociology* 25 (September):308–320.

Vandergeest, Peter. 1988. "Commercialization and commoditization: a dialogue between perspectives." *Sociologia Ruralis* 28, 1:7–29.

van Es, J. C. 1983. "The adoption/diffusion tradition applied to resource conservation: inappropriate use of existing knowledge." *The Rural Sociologist* 3 (March):76–82.

van Es, J. C. 1984. "Dilemmas in the soil and water conservation of farmers." Pp. 238–253 in Burton C. English et al. (eds.), *Future Agricultural Technology and Resource Conservation.* Ames: Iowa State University Press.

van Es, John C., David L. Chicoine, and Mark A. Flotow. 1988. "Agricultural technologies, farm structure, and rural communities in the Corn Belt: policies and implications." Pp. 130–180 in L. E. Swanson (ed.), *Agriculture and Community Change in the U.S.* Boulder, CO: Westview Press.

van Es, J. C., and P. Notier. 1985. "No-till farming: research and policy environment in the development and adoption of an innovation." Paper presented at the annual meeting of the Rural Sociological Society, Virginia Polytechnic Institute and State University, August.

van Es, J. C., and Theodore Tsoukalas. 1987. "Kinship arrangements and innovativeness: a comparison of Palouse and prairie findings." *Rural Sociology* 52 (Spring):389–397.

von Tungeln, George H. 1918. *A Rural Social Survey of Orange Township, Blackhawk County, Iowa.* Bulletin No. 184. Ames: Iowa Agricultural Experiment Station.

von Tungeln, George H. 1920. *A Rural Social Survey of Lone Tree Township, Clay County, Iowa.* Bulletin No. 193. Ames: Iowa Agricultural Experiment Station.

von Tungeln, George H., and Harry L. Eells. 1924. *Rural Social Survey of Hudson, Orange and Jesup Consolidated School Districts, Blackhawk*

and Buchanan Counties, Iowa. Bulletin No. 224. Ames: Iowa Agricultural Experiment Station.
von Tungeln, George H., E. L. Kirkpatrick, C. R. Hoffer, and J. F. Thaden. 1923. *The Social Aspects of Rural Life and Farm Tenantry, Cedar County, Iowa.* Bulletin No. 217. Ames: Iowa Agricultural Experiment Station.
Voth, Donald E., W. A. Halbrook, D. D. Chapman, and R. Renfro. 1983. "Characterization study of small farms in western Arkansas: Logan and Yell Counties." Fayetteville: Department of Agricultural Economics and Rural Sociology, University of Arkansas.
Walker, Richard A. 1985. "Technological determination and determinism: industrial growth and location." Pp. 226–264 in M. Castells (ed.), *High Technology, Space, and Society.* Beverly Hills, CA: Sage.
Wallerstein, Immanuel. 1974. *The Modern World System.* New York: Academic Press.
Wayland, Sloan R. 1951. *Social Patterns of Farming.* New York: Columbia University Seminar on Rural Life, Columbia University.
Wenger, Morton G., and Pem Davidson Buck. 1988. "Farms, families, and super-exploitation: an integrative reappraisal." *Rural Sociology* 53 (Winter):460–472.
Whatmore, Sarah. 1988. "From women's roles to gender relations." *Sociologia Ruralis* 28, 4:239–247.
Whatmore, Sarah, Richard Munton, Terry Marsden, and Jo Little. 1987b. "Interpreting a relational typology of farm businesses in southern England." *Sociologia Ruralis* 27, 2/3:103–122.
Whatmore, Sarah J., Richard J. C. Munton, Terry K. Marsden, and Jo K. Little. 1987a. "Towards a typology of farm businesses in contemporary British agriculture." *Sociologia Ruralis* 27:21–37.
Wilkening, Eugene A. 1949. "A sociopsychological study of the adoption of improved farming practices." *Rural Sociology* 14 (March):68–69.
Wilkening, Eugene A. 1950. "A sociopsychological approach to the study of the acceptance of innovations in farming." *Rural Sociology* 15 (December):352–364.
Wilkening, Eugene A. 1952. "Informal leaders and innovators in farm practices." *Rural Sociology* 17 (September):272–275.
Wilkening, Eugene A. 1954. "Change in farm technology as related to familism, family decision-making, and family integration." *American Sociological Review* 19 (February):29–37.
Wilkening, Eugene A. 1958. "An introductory note on the social aspects of practice adoption." *Rural Sociology* 23 (June):97–102.
Wilkening, Eugene A. 1981a. *Farm Husbands and Wives in Wisconsin.* Research Report R3147. Madison: Agricultural Experiment Station, University of Wisconsin.
Wilkening, Eugene A. 1981b. "Farm families and family farming." Pp. 27–37

in Raymond T. Coward and William M. Smith, Jr. (eds.), *The Family in Rural Society*. Boulder, CO: Westview Press.

Wilkening, Eugene A., and Nancy Ahrens. 1979. "Involvement of wives in farm tasks as related to characteristics of the farm, the family, and work off the farm." Paper presented at the annual meeting of the Rural Sociological Society, Burlington, Vermont, August.

Wilkening, Eugene A., and Bugoslaw Galeski (eds.). 1987. *Family Farming in Europe and America*. Boulder, CO: Westview Press.

Williams, Anne S., and A. C. Bjergo. 1982. *Strategies for Successful Small Scale Farming: A Profile of 43 Montana Farm Families*. Bozeman: Montana Agricultural Experiment Station.

Williams, B. O. 1939. "The impact of mechanization of agriculture on the farm population of the South." *Rural Sociology* 4 (September):300–311.

Williams, James M. 1906. *An American Town: A Sociological Study*. Privately printed Ph.D. dissertation, Columbia University.

Williams, James M. 1925. *Our Rural Heritage*. New York: Alfred A. Knopf.

Williams, James M. 1926. *The Expansion of Rural Life*. New York: Alfred A. Knopf.

Wilson, Warren H. 1907. *Quaker Hill*. Privately printed Ph.D. dissertation, Columbia University.

Wilson, Warren H. 1923. *The Evolution of the Country Community*. 2nd ed. Boston: Pilgrim Press, 1912.

Wimberley, Ronald C. 1983. "The emergence of part-time farming as a social form of agriculture." *Research in the Sociology of Work* 2:325–356.

Wimberley, Ronald C. 1987. "Dimensions of U.S. agristructure: 1969-1982." *Rural Sociology* 52 (Winter):445–461.

Woofter, Thomas Jackson. 1930. "Summary and recommendations on the study of the economic status of the Negro." Mimeographed, University of North Carolina, Chapel Hill.

Woofter, Thomas Jackson. 1936. *Landlord and Tenant on the Cotton Plantation*. Research Monograph V. Washington, DC: Division of Social Research, Works Progress Administration.

Wright, Erik Olin. 1978. *Class, Crisis, and the State*. London: New Left Books.

Wynne, Walter. 1943. *Culture of a Contemporary Rural Community: Harmony, Georgia*. Rural Life Studies 6. Washington, DC: Bureau of Agricultural Economics, U.S. Department of Agriculture.

Young, Ruth. 1959. "Observations on adoption studies reported in June, 1958, issue." *Rural Sociology* 24 (September):272–274.

Zey-Farrell, Mary, and William Alex McIntosh. 1987. "Agricultural lending policies of commercial banks: consequences of bank dominance and dependency." *Rural Sociology* 52 (Summer):187–207.

Zimmerman, Carle C., and John D. Black. 1926. *The Marketing Attitudes of Minnesota Farmers*. Technical Bulletin 45. University Farm, St. Paul: University of Minnesota Agricultural Experiment Station in cooperation with U.S. Department of Agriculture, Division of Farm Population and Rural Life.

Name Index

Abd-Ella, Mokhtar M., 50
Ahrens, Nancy, 116–17
Akor, Raymond, 100–101
Albrecht, Don E., 153, 167–69
Alexander, W. W., 37
Ali, Yousif Ahmed, 22
Allen, R. H., 40
Almack, R. B., 28
Anderson, C. Arnold, 40
Anderson, W. A., 1, 7, 61
Asch, Berta, 39
Ashby, Jacqueline A., 164
Audriac, Ivonne, 63
Aurbach, Herbert A., 52, 64

Bailey, Jennifer A., 189
Bailey, Liberty Hyde, 9
Baker, O. E., 18
Banaji, Jarius, 79, 83, 84
Banks, Vera J.,
Barban, Arnold M., 66
Barlett, Peggy F., 95, 104, 105, 109, 113, 185
Barton, Amy, 77, 80, 84–85, 98– 100, 103, 104, 130, 132–33, 136, 185
Batie, Sandra S., 156, 159, 160, 161, 162
Baumgartel, Walter H., 36
Beal, George M., 47, 57, 58
Beale, Calvin L., 32
Bealer, Robert C., 71, 189
Beaulieu, Lionel J., 63, 189
Beegle, J. Allan, 74
Belcher, John C., 40
Belknap, Helen O., 15
Bell, Colin, 104, 188
Bell, Earl H., 23
Berardi, Gigi M., 128, 133–34
Berlan Darque, Martine, 125
Berlan, Jean-Pierre, 152, 180
Bernert, Eleanor H., 25
Bernstein, Henry, 93
Bertrand, Alvin L., 28, 61, 106, 107, 115, 128, 189
Billings, Dwight, 179
Bills, Nelson L., 133, 188
Bjergo, A. C., 110

Name Index

Black, John D., 41
Blackwell, Gordon W., 40
Block, Fred, 182
Bohlen, Joe M., 47, 57, 58
Bokemeier, Janet L., 117, 120
Bollman, Ray D., 109, 188
Bonanno, Alessandro, 85–86, 108, 113, 114, 115, 152, 153, 185
Booth, David, 172
Boserup, Ester, 120
Bourdieu, Pierre, 92
Boyd, John Paul, 59
Bradley, Tony, 189
Brandner, Lowell, 54
Branson, E. C., 11
Braverman, Harry, 106
Brooks, Nora L., 153
Brown, David L., 117, 165
Brown, Emory J., 56
Brown, Minnie M., 189
Browne, William P., 183
Brubaker, Sterling, 156
Brunner, Edmund deS., 1, 9, 14, 15, 16, 17, 19, 20, 21, 36
Brunner, Mary V., 15
Buck, Pem Davidson, 86–87, 113
Bultena, Gordon, 153
Burch, William R., Jr., 167
Burchinal, Lee G., 68
Burkhardt, Jeffrey, 142, 188
Burnight, Robert, 40, 41
Busch, Lawrence, 75, 136–40, 142, 143, 144, 168, 169, 177, 188
Buttel, Frederick H., 77, 79, 80, 94, 102, 108, 109, 110, 111, 113, 114, 122, 134, 135, 139, 140–41, 144, 147, 148, 150, 151, 152, 153, 155, 157, 158, 160, 162, 163, 164–65, 178, 179, 184, 187, 188, 189

Camboni, S., 157
Campbell, Gerald R., 188
Campbell, Rex R., 58, 153
Cancian, Frank, 51, 52
Carlin, Thomas A., 112
Carlson, John E., 50, 157, 158, 159, 161
Carnoy, Martin, 142
Carter, Michael V., 53
Castle, Emory M., 163
Catalano, Alejandrina, 188
Catton, William R., Jr., 166
Cavazzani, Ada, 108, 113, 114, 115
Chapman, D. D., 110
Chapman, W., 156–62
Charlton, J. L., 38
Chayanov, A. V., 80, 172
Chibnik, Michael, 95, 185
Chicoine, David L., 148, 150, 155
Choi, H., 158, 161
Choldin, Harvey M., 167
Christenson, James A., 111, 113
Christian, Carlton F., 2
Clark, Edwin H., II, 156, 162
Cochrane, Willard W., 108, 129–30
Coleman, A. Lee, 50, 54
Coltrane, Robert, 102
Conboy, Judith L., 147
Converse, Jim, 146
Copp, James H., 56, 134
Cottrell, L. S., Jr., 40
Coughenour, C. Milton, 47, 50, 56, 60, 107, 110, 111, 113, 117, 121–22, 157, 158, 159, 160, 161, 164, 165–66
Cowan, J. Tadlock, 140–41, 158, 188
Coward, E. Walter, Jr., 58, 164
Cowhig, James D., 68
Cox, Graham, 184
Crecink, Jon, 112

Name Index

Crosson, Pierre R., 156, 162
Curry, James, 143, 178, 180, 184

Dahlke, H. O., 31
Dalecki, Michael G., 149, 150, 189
Danbom, David B., 11
Davis, John Emmeus, 80
Davis-Brown, Karen, 94, 109–10, 153
Dean, Alfred, 52, 64
Deininger, Marian, 39
de Janvry, Alain, 80, 83–84, 85, 93, 115, 177
Dethier, Jean-Jacques, 177
Dickinson, James M., 77, 78, 79, 80-81, 82, 89, 93, 94, 187
Dillman, Don A., 50, 157, 158, 159, 161
Djurfeldt, Goren, 79
Dolan, Robert J., 51, 53, 57–58
Dolber-Smith, 148
DuBois, W. E. B., 2–3
Ducoff, Louis J., 27, 39, 40
Duncan, James A., 54
Duncan, Otis Durant, 38
Dunkelberger, John E., 71–72, 188
Dunlap, Riley E., 77, 164, 165, 166–67, 169

Eaton, Allen, 11, 13
Edwards, A. D., 40
Edwards, Clark, 110
Edwards, Richard, 184
Eells, Harry L., 14
Ehrensaft, Philip, 109, 188
Embree, Edwin R., 37
Ensminger, Douglas, 27
Ervin, C. A., 161
Ervin, David E., 161
Evans, Peter, 142

Fassinger, Polly A., 118, 121
Field, Donald R., 166, 167
Fine, Ben, 93
Finegold, Kenneth, 187
Fiske, Emmett, 135–36
Fliegel, Frederick C., 46, 47, 50, 51, 53, 63, 65, 107, 111, 113, 125
Fligstein, Neil, 187, 189
Flinn, William, 54, 75
Flora, Cornelia, 116, 148
Flora, Jan L., 95, 146, 147, 148
Flotow, Mark A., 148, 150
Forster, D. Lynn, 159
Foster, Gary, 95
Francis, Joe D., 54–55
Frank, Andre Gunder, 75, 86
Friedland, William H., 77, 80, 84–85, 98–100, 102, 103, 104, 130, 132–33, 136, 174, 179, 185, 192
Friedmann, Harriet, 77, 78, 79–80, 81–82, 92, 93, 94, 176, 177, 181, 185, 188
Fry, C. Luther, 15
Fuguitt, Glenn V., 112–13
Fujimoto, Isao, 135–36, 146, 147
Fuller, Anthony M., 107, 113, 114–15

Galeski, Boguslaw, 78
Galpin, Charles J., 11, 16, 34–36
Garkovich, Lorraine, 120
Garrett, Patricia, 111
Gartrell, C. David, 164
Gartrell, John W., 51, 164
Gasson, Ruth, 107–8, 125
Gaventa, John, 186
Gee, Wilson, 11
Geisler, Charles C., 133, 134, 144, 158, 188
Geller, Jack, 153

Gertler, Michael E., 111
Giddens, Anthony, 44, 94, 185
Gilbert, Jess, 73, 100–101, 148, 179, 180, 182, 188
Gilles, Jere Lee, 93, 149, 150, 153, 165
Gillespie, Gilbert W. Jr., 122, 143, 160, 189
Gillette, John M., 18, 41
Ginder, Roger G., 155
Gladwin, Christina H., 110, 120–21
Goe, W. Richard, 139, 143, 178, 180, 184
Goldschmidt, Walter, 29, 76, 145–47, 148
Goodman, David, 92, 93, 141, 152, 173 n.1, 174, 178, 180, 183
Gordon, David M., 184
Gordon, W. R., 40
Gore, A., 157
Gore, W., 157
Goss, Kevin F., 61–62, 63, 75, 80, 94, 131–32, 146, 150
Gouldner, Alvin, 72, 74
Graham, Katherine Helga, 154
Grasmick, Harold G., 66
Grasmick, Mary K., 66
Green, Gary, 83, 93, 108, 111, 113, 149, 159, 182, 183
Gregory, Cecil L., 28, 29
Griffin, Keith, 75
Grigsby, S. Earl, 41
Gross, Neil C., 47, 50
Gwynn, Douglas, 151

Hadwiger, Don F., 135, 136, 177
Hagood, Margaret Jarman, 25, 27, 39
Halbrook, W. A., 110
Haller, Archibald O., 67–68, 71
Hamm, Rita R., 153, 155

Haney, Wava Gillespie, 116–17, 124, 178
Hansen, Michel, 142, 143, 188
Harper, Emily B., 107. *See also* Schroeder, Emily Harper
Harris, Craig K., 111, 148, 160, 188
Harrison, David, 64
Harrison, Shelby M., 11, 13
Hatch, Upton, 139
Hattery, Michael R., 158
Havens, A. Eugene, 54, 75, 76, 77, 187
Haverkamp, J. A., 156, 162
Hawley, Amos H., 43
Hayes, M. N., 146
Heady, Earl O., 147, 162
Heaton, Tim B., 165
Hedley, Max J., 93
Heffernan, Judith Bortner, 153–54
Heffernan, William D., 76–77, 96–97, 108, 111, 113, 146, 147, 148, 149, 153–54, 159
Herring, H. L., 40
Hickey, Anthony Andrew, 110
Hickey, Jo Ann S., 110
Hightower, Jim, 76, 107, 135, 177
Hoag, Emily F., 34
Hoffer, C. R., 35
Hoffer, Charles M., 47, 52
Hoffsommer, Harold, 38, 40, 41
Hoiberg, Eric O., 50
Holley, William C., 31
Hooks, Gregory M., 53, 73, 76, 77
Hoover, President Herbert, 19
Howe, Carolyn, 179, 180, 182, 188
Huffman, Wallace, 108
Hughes, Gwendolyn S., 17, 18
Hummel, Richard, 95
Hussain, Arthur, 84, 93

Jacobs, Harvey M., 158

Name Index

James, David R., 189
Jenkins, Ryss, 177 n.3
Jessop, Bob, 184
John, M. E., 40
Johnson, Charles S., 28, 37
Johnson, Darryll R., 33, 166, 167
Johnson, Sue, 116
Jones, Calvin, 117
Jones, Lewis W., 32
Jones, Thomas B., 9, 10
Joyce, Lynda, 116

Kada, Ryohei, 113
Kalbacher, Judith Z., 118–19
Kappel, Tim, 136
Kassarjian, Harold H., 66
Kassarjian, Waltraud M., 66
Kearl, Bryant, 54
Keith, Verna, 117
Kenney, Martin, 139, 140–41, 142, 143, 144, 178, 180, 184, 188
Kinnucan, Henry, 134, 139, 143, 144
Kirkpatrick, E. L., 35, 39
Kivlin, Joseph E., 53
Kleinman, Daniel Lee, 143
Klonglan, Gerald E., 58
Kloppenburg, Jack, Jr., 133, 134, 139, 140–41, 142, 143–44, 178, 179, 187, 188
Knowles, Jane B., 124, 178
Kolb, J. H., 19, 20
Kollmorgen, Walter M., 24, 33
Koppel, Bruce, 139, 144
Kopper, William, 135–36
Korsching, Peter, 148, 150, 156, 160, 161
Kraenzel, Carl F., 32
Krasner, Stephen D., 176
Kreitlow, Burton W., 54
Kuhn, Thomas, 195

Kumar, Krishna, 51
Kuvlesky, William P., 71

Lackey, A. S., 41
Lacy, Laura R., 142, 143, 188
Lacy, William B., 136–40, 142, 143, 144, 177, 188
Lancelle, Mark, 72, 148
Landis, Benson Y., 15
Landis, Paul, 41
LaRamee, Pierre, 109, 110, 188
LaRose, Bruce L., 29, 147
Larson, Olaf F., 9, 10, 22, 26, 40, 41, 46, 125, 145, 148, 149, 189
Larson, Oscar W., III, 111, 114, 160, 164–65, 188
Lasley, R. Paul, 76, 111, 113, 153
Lassey, William R., 157, 158, 159, 161
Leadley, Samuel, 116
Lee, David R., 148
Lehmann, David, 173
Leholm, Arlen G., 153
Leistritz, F. Larry, 153, 155
Lenin, V. I., 79, 83, 84, 115
Leonard, Olen, 24
LeVeen, E. Phillip, 29, 84, 130, 146
Lianos, Theodore P., 93
Lionberger, Herbert F., 39–40, 47, 48, 54–55
Lipietz, Alain, 178, 184
Lipset, Seymour Martin, 67
Lipton, Michael, 75
Little, Jo K., 91–92, 173, 174, 185
Lively, C. E., 22–23, 28
Lobao, Linda M., 143, 178, 180, 184. *See also* Reif, Linda Lobao
Lockeretz, William, 189
Long, Norman, 92, 116
Longhurst, Richard, 75
Longmore, T. Wilson, 27

Loomis, Charles P., 24, 74
Lorge, Irving, 21
Lowe, Philip, 184, 189
Luginbuhl, Regina, 111
Lyson, Thomas A., 71, 154, 188

MacCannell, Dean, 148
MacEwan, M., 184
MacLeish, Kenneth, 24
Mage, J. A., 113
Majka, Linda C., 98, 104
Majka, Theo J., 98, 104
Mandel, Ernest, 79
Mangus, A. R., 24, 28–29, 39
Mann, Susan A., 77, 78, 79, 80–81, 82, 89, 93, 94, 176, 179, 180, 189
Manny, T. B., 41
Marsden, Terry K., 91–92, 173, 174, 185
Marsh, C. Paul, 50, 51, 52, 53, 54, 57–58, 64
Marshall, Douglas, 39
Martin, Kenneth E., 77, 164, 165, 166, 169
Martinson, Oscar B., 188
Mason, Marylee, 38
Mason, Robert, 56–57
Massey, Doreen, 175, 176, 188
Mather, W. G., 7
McIntosh, William Alex, 83, 152
McKain, Walter C., Jr., 27, 31, 41
McMichael, Philip, 82–83, 93, 176, 177, 179, 181, 185
McMillan, Robert T., 38
Merton, Robert K., 44, 45, 72, 73, 74, 137
Metzler, William H., 40
Micklin, Michael, 167
Miller, William L., 61
Mills, C. Wright, 44, 72, 74

Moe, Edward O., 24
Molnar, Joseph J., 71–72, 134, 139, 143, 144, 188
Mooney, Patrick H., 77, 80, 87–90, 93, 94, 152, 182, 183, 185–86
Moore, Barrington, 179, 185
Moore, Harry E., 24
Morrison, Denton E., 51, 65
Morse, H. N., 12, 14, 15
Mottura, Giovanni, 85
Mouzelis, Nicos, 173
Muñoz, Robert D., 111, 189
Munton, Richard J. C., 91–92, 173, 174, 185
Murdock, Steve H., 153, 155, 167–69
Murray, Martin, 187
Murray, Robin, 93

Nakano, Isshin, 79
Napier, Ted L., 53, 157, 159
Neal, Ernest E., 32
Nelson, Lowry, 4, 11, 12, 33, 36
Newby, Howard, 77, 78–79, 80, 84, 102, 104, 105, 172, 175, 187, 188, 192, 196
Nolan, Michael F., 111, 113
Norris, P. E., 159, 160
Notier, P., 158, 159
Nowak, Peter J., 62–63, 156, 157, 158, 159, 160, 161
Nuckton, Carole Frank, 151

Odum, Howard W., 24
Office of Technology Assessment, 148
O'Leary, Jeanne M., 117
Olmstead, A. L., 146
Olshan, Marc A., 33
O'Reilly, Shirley, 94
O'Riordan, Tim, 184

Name Index

Otto, Daniel, 155

Pampel, Fred, Jr., 61, 62, 130–31, 157
Parrish, Barnard D., 32
Parsons, Talcott, 43, 44, 72, 73
Patten, Marjorie, 15, 17, 18
Pearse, Andrew, 75
Pedersen, Harald A., 31, 54, 61, 128, 189
Perelman, Michael, 102
Perry, Astor, 51, 53, 57–58
Perry, Charles S., 102, 104, 105–6
Peterson, R. Neal, 110
Pfeffer, Max John, 77, 80, 90–91, 94, 176
Photiadis, John D., 50
Pimentel, David, 162
Ploch, Louis A., 96
Polson, Robert A., 53
Popper, Frank R., 188
Portes, Alejandro, 68
Post, C., 187
Powell, Lanny C., 58
Powers, Sharon, 111, 188
Presser, H. A., 60
Pugliese, Enrico, 85
Putman, Paul, 41

Ramsey, Charles E., 53
Randolph, S. Randi, 137
Rankin, J. O., 35
Raper, Arthur F., 24, 25, 27, 31, 37, 40, 128
Reagan, Ronald, 194
Redclift, Michael, 92, 93, 152, 173, 173 n.1, 180, 183, 184–85
Reich, Michael, 184
Reif, Linda Lobao, 149, 150–51. *See also* Lobao, Linda M.
Reimer, Bill, 116

Renfro, R., 110
Research and Information System for the Non-Aligned and Other Developing Countries (RIS), 144
Reuss, Carl, 41
Richardson, Joseph L., 22, 46
Riley, Marvin P., 33
Rochin, Refugio I., 151
Rockefeller, John D., Jr., 15
Rodefeld, Richard D., 72, 75, 76–77, 80, 94, 96-97, 108, 146, 148
Rogers, Everett M., 47, 48, 49, 51, 52, 57, 59–60, 131
Rogers, L. Edna, 59–60
Rohwer, Robert A., 39
Roosevelt, President Theodore, 9
Rose, David, 104, 188
Roseman, Curtis C., 58
Rosenfeld, Rachel A., 117, 119
Ross, Peggy J., 116
Rueschemeyer, Dietrich, 142
Rushing, William A., 66
Ruttan, Vernon W., 136
Ryan, Bryce, 47

Sachs, Carolyn E., 113, 116, 117, 118, 122–24, 137, 178, 185
Salamon, Sonya, 94–95, 109–10, 153, 185
Salant, Priscilla, 117–18
Samson, A'Delbert, 31
Sandage, C. H., 66
Sanderson, Dwight, 7
Sanderson, Steven E., 176–77, 177 n.3, 188
Sasson, Albert, 144
Saunders, Peter, 104, 188
Schroeder, Emily Harper, 107, 111, 113, 125. *See also* Harper, Emily B.
Schuler, Edgar A., 27, 37

Name Index

Schulman, Michael D., 111, 188
Schwartz, Michael, 188
Schwarzweller, Harry K., 118, 121
Sewell, William H., 68
Sharp, Emmit F., 41
Shoemaker, Floyd F., 49
Sill, Maurice L., 56
Simpson, Ida Harper, 122
Sims, Newell Leroy, 8–9
Sinclair, Peter R., 187
Singer, Edward G., 93
Sivini, G., 108, 113
Skees, Jerry R., 148, 189
Skocpol, Theda, 142, 179, 182, 185, 187
Skrabanek, R. L., 40
Slocum, Walter L., 38, 71
Small Farm Viability Project, 147
Smith, Douglas, 140–41
Smith, John P., 153
Smith, Leslie Whitener, 102
Smith, Matthew G., 110
Smith, Mervin G., 2
Smith, T. Lynn, 1, 22, 46, 125
Sonka, Steven T., 147
Sorj, Bernardo, 141, 173, 173 n.1, 175, 177–78
Sorokin, Pitirim A., 43, 67
Spencer, George E., 53
Stangland, Dale, 52
Steeves, Allan D., 78, 188
Stewart, James R., 33
Stinchcombe, Arthur, 76, 96
Stitz, John M., 95
Stockdale, Jerry D., 75, 132, 134
Stone, Kenneth E., 155
Stratigaki, Mari, 120
Straus, Murray A., 32, 67, 68–70, 71
Stucker, Thomas A., 153
Subcommittee for the Study of Diffusion of Farm Practices, North Central Rural Sociology Committee, 50, 57
Subcommittee of the Rural Sociological Society, 50
Sudia, Cecilia E., 70
Sullivan, Gene A., 51, 53, 57–58
Swanson, Louis E., 121–22, 148, 150, 157, 158, 163, 168, 169, 175, 189
Sweet, James A., 117

Taves, Marvin J., 50
Taylor, Carl C., 21, 24, 25, 26, 27, 35, 36, 39, 188
Taylor, David L., 61
Taylor, Grady W., 65–66
Thaden, J. F., 35
Thomas, Robert J., 77, 80, 84–85, 98–100, 103–4, 130, 132–33, 136, 185
Thomas-Lycklama a Niejholt, G., 103, 104
Thompson, S. B., 177 n.2
Thorner, Alice, 79
Thraen, C., 157
Tigges, Leann M., 119
Townsend, T. H., 7
Tribe, Keith, 84, 93
Troxwell, W. W., 40
Tsoukalas, Theodore, 158
Tweeten, Luther, 108

U.S. Department of Agriculture, 107, 109
Utting, Peter, 188

Vail, David, 151, 184
Valkonen, Tapani, 59
Vance, Rupert B., 31
van den Ban, Anne Willem, 54

Name Index

Vandergeest, Peter, 92
van der Ploeg, Jan Douwe, 92
van Es, John C., 46, 53, 61, 62, 107, 111, 113, 125, 130, 148, 150, 157, 158, 159
Vogt, Paul L., 13
von Tungeln, George H., 13, 14, 35
Voth, Donald E., 110, 146

Wakefield, Richard, 41
Walker, Richard A., 176
Wallerstein, Immanuel, 137, 179
Warren, Richard D., 50
Waters, William F., 133, 188
Wayland, Sloan R., 30–31
Wenger, Morton G., 86–87, 113
Wernick, Sarah, 189
Whatmore, Sarah J., 91–92, 125, 173, 174, 185
Whitener, Leslie. *See* Smith, Leslie Whitener
Whittenbarger, Robert, 95
Wilkening, Eugene A., 47, 51, 52, 54, 55–56, 57, 115, 116–17, 119–20
Wilkinson, John, 141, 173, 174, 177–78

Williams, Anne S., 110
Williams, B. O., 128, 189
Williams, James M., 4–7
Wilson, John, 122
Wilson, Warren H., 4, 7–8, 12, 13, 15, 18
Wimberley, Ronald C., 107, 110, 148, 150
Winston, Ellen, 31
Winter, Michael, 184
Wolff, Carole Ellis, 68
Woofter, T. J., Jr., 31
Woofter, Thomas Jackson, 31, 32
Wright, Erik Olin, 87
Wynne, Walter, 24

Young, Kimball, 24
Young, Kristina, 122
Young, Ruth, 45, 72

Zabawa, Robert, 110
Zey-Farrell, Mary, 83, 152
Zimmerman, Carle C., 36, 41, 43
Zopf, Paul E., Jr., 46

Subject Index

Achievement, educational and occupational, among farm-reared people, 67–72. *See also* Farm background.
Achievement orientations, 64–66
Adaptation, 167–69
Adoption of farm practices: adoption and innovativeness scales, 59–60; age and, 50; bulletin reading and, 50; characteristics of adoptors, 49–52, 158; contact with Extension and, 50; correlates of adopting reduced-tillage practices, 158, 159–62; cumulative percentage adoption curve, 48, 51, 53, 57–58; differences between commercial and environmental innovations, 61–63, 130–31, 157; differences in use of information sources according to stage in adoption process, 56–57; differences in use of information sources by farm operator socioeconomic status, 55–56; differential perceptions of attributes of innovations, 53–54, 55; ecological (environmental) factors in, 164; education level and, 50; ethnic, religious, and community effects on, 54; farmers as actors in, 44, 47 (*see also* Political-economic analyses, farmers as actors in capitalist political economy); farm operator socioeconomic status, 49–50; farm size and, 50, 158; group influences on process of, 54–55; informal leadership types and effects on, 54–55; information sources and, 55–57; methodological aspects of research on, 44, 59–60; net worth and, 50; personal and social characteristics of adoptors, 48; personality characteristics and, 52–53; as a process, 47, 57–59, 64; reasons for adopting reduced-tillage practices, 158; risk taking and, 51–

52; social participation and, 50; social psychological profiles of adoptors, 51; social psychology of, 52–54; stages in, 51, 57–59; types of adoptors, 48; value and attitudinal orientations, 52–53, 63–66. See also Diffusion and adoption of agricultural innovations

Agribusiness: structural reorganization in the biotechnology era, 140–41; structure of, and effects on agriculture, 188

Agricultural adaptations in Great Plains, 32; dry-land cotton farmers, 32; dry-land farmers, 32; irrigation farmers, 32; stockmen, 32

Agricultural Adjustment Administration, 40

Agricultural ladder, 14, 35, 39, 188

Agricultural science: biotechnology, 139–45; biotechnology, intellectual property rights, and genetic resources, 142, 143; industry-university relationships and the changing division of labor between private and public research, 140, 177–78; methodological aspects of sociological research on, 144–45; politics of, 136, 137, 138, 139, 140, 177, 194; social structure and social construction of science, 137; sociology of, 135–45; sources of influence on, 136–39

Agricultural scientists, 135–45

An American Town: A Sociological Study (James M. Williams), 4

Appropriationism, 141, 178

Aspirations: antecedents of, to enter farming, 68–70; educational aspirations and, to enter farming, 68–69, 71–72; educational and occupational, among farm-reared people, 67–72; social origins and, to enter farming, 71–72; social psychological characteristics and, to enter farming, 70. See also Farm background

As You Sow (Walter Goldschmidt), 29, 76, 145–46

Bibliography of Research in Rural Sociology (W. A. Anderson), 1

Biotechnology, 134–35; applications and consequences of, 141, 177–78; revolutionary, 178. See also Technological change in agriculture

Blacks in agriculture, studies of, 3, 32, 36, 40–41, 110, 189

Broiler industry, 96–97

California Agricultural Experiment Station, 135–36

Capital (Karl Marx), 79

Capital accumulation in agriculture. See Industrial agriculture; political-economic analyses

Capitalist development in agriculture, 80–94 95–125; categories of farm types according to degree of subsumption, 91. See also Hired workers in agriculture; Industrial agriculture; Political-economic analyses; Small farms and part-time farming; Women in agriculture

Capitalist transformation of agriculture, barriers to, 80–85. See also Hired workers in agriculture; In-

Subject Index

dustrial agriculture; Political-economic analyses; Small farms and part-time farming; Women in agriculture
Census of Agriculture, U.S., 3, 25, 30, 102, 105, 111, 116, 118, 148, 149, 150, 194–95
Circulation, 82–83, 180–81
City centers, as agriculture relates to, 6, 144, 174, 176
The Collapse of Cotton Tenancy (Charles S. Johnson et al.), 37
Columbia University, Council for Research in the Social Sciences, 21
Columbia University, Seminar for Rural Life, 30
The Coming Crisis of Western Sociology (Alvin Gouldner), 74
Commission on Country Life *Report*, 9–11
Commodity complexes, international, 177
Commodity organizations, 136
Commodity systems analysis, 100–101, 132–33, 174–75; limits to generalization of, 175–76
Community conflict, and type of farming enterprises, 12–13
Community social participation: and adoption of farm practices, 50; differences between hired workers and farm proprietors, 97; effects of vertical integration of production on, 97; tenure status and, 34
Community studies, and agriculture, 140; agricultural villages, 16–22, 19–22; *As You Sow*, 29–30, 147–48; "Blanktown" (Waterville, New York), 4–7; correlation analysis of agriculture and community variables in, 19; *A Hoosier Village*, 8–9; Mormon farm-village communities, 33; *Quaker Hill*, 7–8; "Rural Life Studies" and stability-instability, 23
Conservation, 155–63. *See also* Environmental effects of U.S. agriculture
Contradictory class locations, 87, 88, 89, 182
Cornell University, 7, 10
Corporate farms, 97, 147, 150, 165; in the Red River Valley, 36. *See also* Industrial agriculture; Political-economic analyses
Cotton plantation system of Antebellum South, transformation of, 82–83, 90–91
Counties, tiers of, in agriculture, 20–21
Country churches, and agriculture, 13
County level agricultural classification: agricultural complexity in Southern counties, 28; Bureau of Agricultural Economics' type of farming areas, 25; source of farm income in Southern counties, 28
Credit: the 1980s farm crisis and, 90, 183; organizational structure change in agriculture and, 82–83, 90, 183
Crisis, farm. *See* Depression, Great; Farm crisis of the 1980s; Political-economic analyses
Critiques, theoretical: classical deductive theories of agrarian structure, 172–74; diffusion and

adoption of agricultural innovations paradigm, 45, 58–59, 61–63, 75–76, 130–32, 136, 157–58, 161–63; "Disappearing middle" hypothesis, 109–10; ecological variables as explanations of organizational structure of agriculture, 163–69; farmers as actors (agents), 89; Goldschmidt (hypo)thesis, 149–51; Neo-Marxist approaches to capitalist development, 92; Parsonian functionalism, 74; theories of the state for understanding agricultural policy formation, 181–82
Crop areas: as control variable, 18; and farmer cooperatives, 20; and farm tenancy trends, 18; and population density, 18; and size of community area, 18
Cycles of expansion and contraction, 174

Definition of agriculture, broadening, 174–75
Depression, Great, agricultural adjustments in 140 communities, 21. *See also* State, role in farm credit system and farm financial crisis
Development, capitalist, in agriculture. *See* Hired workers in agriculture; Industrial agriculture; Political-economic analyses; Small farms and part-time farming; Women in agriculture
Die Agrarfrage (Karl Kautsky), 79, 83, 84
Differentiation of family farms, 76, 87–89, 108–10, 112–13. *See*

also Hired workers in agriculture; Industrial agriculture; Political-economic analyses; Small farms and part-time farming
Diffusion and adoption of agricultural innovations, 45–72; classical diffusion model, 47–49, 57, 62–63, 130–32; critiques of paradigm, 45, 58–59, 61–63, 75–76, 130–32, 136, 157–58, 161–63
"Disappearing middle" hypothesis, 95, 108–10
Division of labor in farm households. *See* Women in agriculture
"Domestic ideology," 124
Domestic relations of production, 86
Dualistic development in agriculture thesis, 108–10, 150. *See also* Differentiation of family farms

Ecology, effects of agricultural technology on, 132
Economic development and type of farming enterprises, 18
Embourgeoisiement, 113–14
Energy use in U.S. agriculture, 164–65
Entrepreneurial orientations, 64–66, 70
Environment, agriculture and, 155–69, 184–85. *See also* Adoption of farm practices, differences between commercial and environmental effects of U.S. agriculture; Environmental innovations; New environmental debates
Environmental effects of U.S. agriculture, 155–63; conceptual is-

Subject Index

sues in research on, 156–58; correlates of adoption of soil conservation practices, 160–62; costs and consequences of soil erosion, 156; environmental attitudes and beliefs and adoption of soil conservation practices, 159; policy issues relating to soil erosion, 156–57, 162–63; questionable efficacy of voluntary conservation programs, 162–63; reduced-tillage practices, 156–58
Environmental movements and agriculture, 184
Erosion, soil, 155–63. *See also* Environmental effects of U.S. agriculture
Ethnic background and type of farming enterprises, 12–13, 54, 94–95
Ethnographic approaches to research, 185–86
Evolution of the Country Community (Warren H. Wilson), 18
The Expansion of Rural Life: The Social Psychology of Rural Life (James M. Williams), 6
Exploitation, 86–87, 87–89, 183

Farm background: and educational aspirations, 67–69; and occupational mobility, 67, 71; and self-conception of youth, 68
Farm classification, ideal types, individual level, 30–31
Farm crisis of the 1980s, 90, 151–55, 180; causes of, 151–52, 180, 183; characteristics of farms with financial stress, 153; effects on farm households, 153–54; effects on rural communities, 154–55; public reactions to, 154; restructuring of the world economy, link with, 183–84
Farm enlargement, reasons for, 41
Farmer behavior and type of farming enterprises, 5–6
Farmer organizations: commodity groups and influence on agricultural research, 136; and type of farming enterprises, 7, 16
Farmer psychology and type of farming enterprises, 6–7, 23
Farm Foundation, 38
Farm land ownership research, 187–88
Farm occupancy history, 34–42
Farm operators: as actors, 44, 47, 87–93, 94, 95; economic and status aspects, 40; impact of Agricultural Adjustment Administration acreage reduction programs, 40; part-time, 40; nonresident, 40; permanent, temporary, and new compared, 40; receiving relief on rural rehabilitation loans, 39–40; USDA's Unified Farm Program, 40; women, 118–19
Farms. *See* Corporate farms; Farm types; Part-time farming; Small farms
Farm types: according to control over land, capital, labor, and management, 97; according to degree of subsumption, 91
Ferment, social and intellectual, affecting rural sociology around 1970, 74–76
Financial stress, 153
Fiske University, 28

"Fordism," 178, 184

Gender. *See* Women in agriculture
General Education Board, 38
Goldschmidt (hypo)thesis, 29–30, 146–49; critiques of, 149–51; methodological approaches to study of, 145–51 passim
The Growth of a Science: A Half-Century of Rural Sociological Research in the United States (Edmund deS Brunner), 1
Grundrisse (Karl Marx), 79

Hard Tomatoes, Hard Times (Jim Hightower), 135, 177
Hired workers in agriculture, 35, 39, 40–41, 98–99, 101–6; characteristics and ideology, 102, 104–6
Hired workers in agriculture, on cotton and sugar cane plantations, 41; full-time, on family-proprietor farms, 104–5; labor force important in development of organizational structure of agriculture, 90–91; migrant workers, 41, 103–4; technological change and displacement of, 102, 103, 104–6, 130, 133
A Hoosier Village: A Sociological Study with Special Reference to Social Causation (Newell L. Sims), 4, 8–9
Human Factors in Cotton Culture (Rupert B. Vance), 31
Human Geography of the South (Rupert B. Vance), 31

Ideology, agrarian political, 188–89
Independent farmer, 119

Industrial agriculture, 95–101, 132–33
"Informalization" of work, 86
Innovativeness. *See* Adoption of farm practices, adoption and innovativeness scales
Innovators' rents, 129
Institute for Social and Religious Research, 15, 16, 19–20, 22
Interchurch World Movement, 14; Town and Country Life Department, 14
International development research, as a source of challenge to rural sociological orthodoxy, 75
Invisibility of women in agriculture, 122–24

Labor, hired. *See* Hired workers in agriculture; Migrant workers
Labor process, 80, 99. *See also* Hired workers in agriculture; Industrial agriculture; Political-economic analyses; Small farms and part-time farming; Women in agriculture
Landlords, farm, 35–36, 87
Legitimacy, crisis of, in agriculture, 90
Legitimation function: role of part-time farming in, 113; of the state, 86
Lenin, V.I., 77, 79, 84, 87, 171, 172
Lettuce production, need for cheap and disciplined wage labor in, 98–99

Mann-Dickinson thesis, 80–81, 89, 93, 169

Subject Index

Manufacturing Green Gold (William Freidland et al.), 84
Marketing: attitudes toward farmer–owned business organizations, 41; cooperative organizations, 41; cotton marketing, 41; key focus in commodity systems analysis, 100; potato marketing, 41
Marxist Economic Theory (Ernest Mandel), 79
Mechanization, 128–135. *See also* Technological change in agriculture
Migrant workers, 41, 103–4
Mobility, in and out of agriculture, 188
Moravian Country Life Commission, 13
Mormons and agriculture, 33

National Committee on Standardization of Research in Country Life, 34
New environmental debates, 163–69
New sociology of agriculture, 73–186; initial development of alternatives to extant theories for, 76–78; methodological approaches, 178–79, 189–92, 194; social and technological context of, and the future, 192–96; theoretical diversity and common threads characterizing, 76–77, 189–92; theoretical trends in, 171–81, 189–92. *See also* Political-economic analyses

Organic farming, 189
Organizational structure of agriculture: as affected by regional and commodity variations, 90–91, 100–101; as affected by subcultural variations, 90–91, 109–10; in broiler industry in the U.S., 96–97; ecological variables as explanations of, 163–69; effects on rural communities, 145–51, 189; effects of technological change on, 128–29, 143, 177–78; environmental movements and, 184; farm size and energy use, 164–65; historical trends in research, 1–2, 42, 73–80, 80–125 passim, 127–32, 132–45 passim, 145–47, 147–55 passim; regional variation as a limit to monolithic conceptions of, 175–76
Our Rural Heritage: The Social Psychology of Rural Development (James M. Williams), 6

Part-time farming, 106–15; as agricultural adjustment mechanism, 112; definition of, 112–13; as ecological adaptation to changing agricultural conditions, 167–69; farm size and, 107–8; and political orientations, 113–14; role in larger political economy, 113. *See also* Proletarianization
Patriarchy, 123–24
Penetration of capitalist relations of production into agriculture. *See* Hired workers in agriculture; Industrial agriculture; Political-economic analyses; Small farms and part–time farming
Petty commodity production, 87–8, 93. *See also* Simple commodity production

Plant breeding: affects of biotechnological developments on, 141–42, 178; affects of intellectual property policies on, 142
Plant Variety Protection Act of 1970, 140
Policy: effects on agricultural technology and organizational structure change in agriculture, 128, 129, 179–80; formation of, 181–83; issues relating to soil erosion, 156–57, 162–63
Political-economic analyses, 78–94; barriers to capitalist transformation of agriculture, 80–85; exploitation of farm households, 86–87, 87–89, 183; farmers as actors in capitalist political economy, 87–93, 94–95 (*see also* Adoption of farm practices, farmers as actors in); households of small farms as reserve industrial labor force, 85–87; incorporation of noncapitalist agricultural production forms into the capitalist political economy, 85–87; issue of the persistence of the family farm, 79–80; nonidentity between production time and labor time, 80–81
Politics, agricultural (agrarian), 182, 188
Politics and the new sociology of agriculture, 193–94, 195
Preface to Peasantry (Arthur F. Raper), 37
Presbyterian Church, Department of Church and Country Life, 12
President's Research Committee on Social Trends, 19–20

Production contracts, 96
Production relations, capitalistic. *See* Hired workers in agriculture; Industrial agriculture; Political-economic analyses; Small farms and part-time farming; Women in agriculture
Proletarianization, 80, 82, 83, 87, 88, 114. *See also* Differentiation of family farms; Hired workers in agriculture; Industrial agriculture; Political-economic analyses; Small farms and part-time farming
Protestant churches, 31; and type of farming enterprise, 31
Public agricultural research, 135–43, 177–78. *See also* Agricultural science

Quaker Hill: A Sociological Study (Warren H. Wilson), 4, 7
Quaker tradition and type of farming enterprise, 8

Rationality, formal and substantive, 89
Reduced-tillage practices, 157–58
Regime of accumulation, 174
Regimes, international food and agricultural, 176–77
Regional analysis of commodity systems, comparative, 100–101
Regions, rural: delineation and type of farming, 28–29; uniqueness in agricultural development and change, 82–83, 84–85, 90–92, 95, 98–101, 123–25; variation in effects of organizational structure of agriculture on rural communities by, 148–49, 151

Subject Index

Research, comparative and cross-national, need for, 185
Resettlement Administration, 37, 40
Resource management, 155–63
Rural Life in the United States (Carl C. Taylor et al.), 27
Rural social structures, conceptions of, 175

Science, Agriculture, and the Politics of Research (Lawrence Busch and William Lacy), 137–38
Science and Agricultural Development (Lawrence Busch), 137
"Seed-chemical packages," 142
Sexual division of labor. *See* Women in agriculture
Simple commodity production, 81. *See also* Petty commodity production
Simple reproduction, 82
Small farms, 106–15; characteristics of household members, 109; definition of, 107, 111–12; increasing from dualistic pattern of concentration and differentiation, 108–10; multiple survival strategies, 110; poverty and, 107; role of off-farm work, 107, 109; sociopolitical attitudes, 111, 113–14; stability and persistance, 107, 108, 109, 115; stratification in, 110–11
Social class and type of farming enterprises 5, 7
Social environment of agriculture, 127–55
Social impact assessment of agricultural technologies, 128–35; *ex ante*, 132, 133–35, 139, 144
Socialization of farm youth, 68–71
Social survey movement and agriculture, 11–16
Sociological Imagination, The (C. Wright Mills), 72
Sociology of Science (Robert K. Merton), 137
Soil erosion, 155–63. *See also* Environmental effects of U.S. agriculture
Spatial organization of production, 176
Specialization of production, 96–97
State: public agricultural research and government commodity programs as contradictory intervention, 142; quasi-, character of international commodity complexes, 177; role in agriculture, 86, 180, 181–83; role in facilitating a cheap and disciplined migrant labor supply, 104; role in farm credit system and farm financial crisis, 90. *See also* Policy
Structuralism, 80, 114. *See also* Theory, structure vs. agency debates
Structure of agriculture. *See* Organizational structure of agriculture
Subculture and organizational structure of agriculture, 94–95
Subjectivism. *See* Political-economic analyses, farmers as actors in capitalist political economy
Substitutionism, 141, 178

Surveying Your Community (Edmund deS Brunner), 15
Sustainable development, 184–85

Technological change and agriculture, 128–35, 189; ecological effects, 132, 143; issues about ecological (environmental) variables affecting, 165–66; social consequences, 128, 130, 131, 133. *See also* Organizational structure of agriculture
Tenancy and type of farming enterprise, 13
Tenure status, 34–39; church membership and, 13, 16; community social participation and, 34; comparative characteristics and, 36; conservation practices and, 38–39, 160–61; in Cotton Belt, 37; kinship and, 14; large-farm, small-farm communities and, 29; Mormons and, 33; retirement from farming and, 35; social aspects of, 35–36; social correlates of in Corn Belt and Cotton Belt, 37; studies of in Southwest, 38–39
Theory: application of human ecology, to explain organizational structure of agriculture, 167–69; Chicago-style human ecological, 43; disjucture of, with research in rural sociology, 73–74; issues about the importance of ecological variables, 163–69; Marx-Weber synthesis, 89–90, 93; Marxian and Weberian influence on the new sociology of agriculture, 77, 78–80; "of the middle range," 44, 72, 73; modernization, 64; Neo-Marxist (and Neo-Weberian) explanations of the dynamics of U.S. agriculture, 78–94, 171–78, 178–81; social psychological and behavioristic, 43–72; of the state and agriculture, 181–83, 187; state of, in rural sociology in the 1950s, 1960s and early 1970s, 73–74; structure vs. agency debates, 94, 114–15, 185–86 (*see also* Political-economic analyses, farmers as actors in capitalist political economy; Theory, Marx-Weber synthesis); trends in the sociology of agriculture, 2, 92–93, 171–81; underpinning early sociological research, 43. *See also* Adoption of farm practices; Diffusion and adoption of agricultural innovations, classical diffusion model;
Treadmill of technology, 129–30
Type of agricultural system: cotton plantations, 31; irrigation, 31–32, 33; large-farm and small-farm communities compared, 29, 145–51; sugar cane farms, 41
Type of farming areas: county stratification for BAE (Bureau of Agricultural Economics), USDA study, 25–26; cultural reconnaisance studies in BAE study, 26–67; hypotheses for BAE study, 24–25; sociological study by BAE, 24–28
Type of farming enterprises: community effects of, 5–8, 12, 23, 145–51; comparison of grain and dairy areas, 22–23. *See also* Community conflict; Economic

development; Ethnic background; Farmer behavior; Farmer psychology; Farmer's organizations; Social class; Tenancy

U.S. Department of Labor, 3
USDA (U.S. Department of Agriculture): Agricultural Research Service, 1; Bureau of Agricultural Economics, 37–38, 39; Division of Farm Management and Costs, 25; Division of Farm Population and Rural Life, 21, 41; Division of Farm Population and Rural Welfare, 23–24; Farm Life Studies, 11, 16; Farm Security Administration, 39–40

Values and beliefs and agriculture: German-Swiss, 33; Hutterites, 33; Mormon communities, 33; Old-Order Amish, 33
Values of farmers, 63–66; goals, 63–66
Vertical integration of production, 96–97; effects of, on community social participation, 97

Voluntarism, 114. *See also* Theory, structure vs. agency debates

Women in agriculture: changes in the role of, and the sexual division of labor in U.S. farm households, 119–20, 122–24; farm characteristics and women's role, 118, 120–22; mutual interrelations of men's and women's on-farm and off-farm work as influenced by farm size and technology, 121–22; role of, in the U.S. 115–25; roles for women and self concept, 120; studies of participation in farm work, off-farm employment, and household activities, 116–19
Work(s) Progress Administration, Division of Social Research, Rural Research Unit, 21, 28, 39
World market, 176
"World steer," 176–77

Yankee (entrepreneurial) farmers, 95, 109
Yeoman farmers, 94–95, 109

ABOUT THE AUTHORS

FREDERICK H. BUTTEL is Professor of Rural Psychology, a member of the Program on Science, Technology, and Society, and Chairman of the Biology and Society Major at Cornell University. He is currently President-Elect of the Rural Sociological Society and recently served as Chairman of the Section on Environment and Technology of the American Sociological Association. He has previously coauthored or coedited *The Rural Sociology of Advanced Societies* (1980), *Environment, Energy, and Society* (1982), *Los movimientos ecologistas* (1983), and *Labor and the Environment* (1984).

OLAF F. LARSON is Professor of Rural Sociology Emeritus, Cornell University, was Head of the Department of Rural Sociology, 1957–66, and Director, Northeast Regional Center for Rural Development, 1972–75. He received the Rural Sociological Society's Distinguished Rural Sociologist Award in 1985. Larson is the author of *Ten Years of Rural Rehabilitation in the United States* (1947, 1951) and has made contributions to more than twenty books and is also the author of numerous professional journal articles including "Sociological Aspects of the Low-Income Farm Problem" (1955).

GILBERT W. GILLESPIE JR. is Research Associate in the Department of Rural Sociology at Cornell University. His research includes the sociology of agriculture, alternative agriculture, and the environment. He has been the coeditor of *Environment, Technology, and Society*, the newsletter section of the Section on Environment and Technology of the American Sociological Association.

**Recent Titles in
Contributions in Sociology**

Multiculturalism and Intergroup Relations
James S. Frideres, editor

Homelessness in the United States: State Surveys, Volume I
Jamshid A. Momeni, editor

Explorations in the Understanding of Landscape: A Cultural Geography
William Norton

Postmodern Social Analysis and Criticism
John W. Murphy

Suburbia Re-examined
Barbara M. Kelly, editor

Impossible Organizations: Self-Management and Organizational Reproduction
Yohanan Stryjan

Religious Politics in Global and Comparative Perspective
William H. Swatos, Jr., editor

Invisible Victims: White Males and the Crisis of Affirmative Action
Frederick R. Lynch

Theories of Ethnicity: A Critical Appraisal
Richard H. Thompson

Population and Community in Rural America
Lorraine Garkovich

Divided We Stand: Class Structure in Israel from 1948 to the 1980s
Amir Ben-Porat

A Fragile Movement: The Struggle for Neighborhood Stabilization
Juliet Saltman